John Donne, Undone

THOMAS DOCHERTY

John Donne, Undone

Methuen
London and New York

First published in 1986 by
Methuen & Co. Ltd
11 New Fetter Lane, London EC4P 4EE

Published in the USA by
Methuen & Co.
in association with Methuen, Inc.
29 West 35th Street, New York NY 10001

Typeset by AKM Associates (UK) Ltd,
Ajmal House, Hayes Road, Southall, Greater London
Printed and bound in Great Britain

British Library Cataloguing in Publication Data
Docherty, Thomas
    John Donne, undone.
    1. Donne, John —— Criticism and
    interpretation
    I. Title
    821'.3   PR2248

    ISBN 0-416-92040-3

Library of Congress Cataloging in Publication Data
Docherty, Thomas.
    John Donne, undone.

    Bibliography: p.
    Includes index.
    1. Donne, John, 1572–1631 —— Criticism and
interpretation.   I. Title
PR2248.D63   1986   821'.3   86–16381
ISBN 0-416-92040-3
ISBN 0-416-00592-6 (pbk.)

For Bridie May Sullivan

Contents

Acknowledgements

The author and the publishers would like to thank the following for permission to reproduce copyright material:

Richard Scott Simon Ltd. and Viking Penguin Inc. for an extract from the poem 'And ut Pictura Poesis is her name' from *Household Days* by John Ashbery published by Penguin Books.

An extract from 'Burnt Norton' in *Four Quarters* by T. S. Eliot. Copyright 1943 by T. S. Eliot, renewed 1971 by Esme Valerie Eliot is reproduced by permission of Faber and Faber Ltd. and Harcourt Brace Jovanovich Inc.

Jonathan Cape Ltd., Anthony Sheil Associates Ltd., and Little, Brown and Company for an extract from *The Magus* by John Fowles. Copyright © 1965, 1977 by J. R. Fowles Ltd.

Oxford University Press for 'When I summon my sighs to call for you' reprinted from Petrarch: *Selections from the Canzionere* tr. by Mark Musa (1985), © Mark Musa 1985.

Laurence Pollinger Ltd. and New Directions Publishing Corporation for the poem 'I have eaten the plums that were in the icebox' by William Carlos Williams from *Collected Earlier Poems*, copyright 1938 by New Directions.

Extracts from the Authorised King James version of the Bible, which is Crown Copyright in the UK, and reproduced by permission of Eyre and Spottiswoode (Publishers) Ltd., Her Majesty's Printers, London.

A note on the text

References to Donne's poems throughout are to Herbert J.C. Grierson (ed.), *Donne: Poetical Works*, Oxford, Oxford University Press, 1929, reprinted 1979, referred to in the notes as 'Donne'. I have occasionally silently emended this text by collating it with other editions, especially Helen Gardner, *John Donne: The Elegies and Songs and Sonnets*, Oxford, Oxford University Press, 1965, and A.J. Smith's modern-spelling edition, *Donne: Complete English Poems*, Harmondsworth, Penguin Books, 1971.

Humdrum testaments were scattered around. His head
Locked into mine. We were a seesaw. Something
Ought to be written about how this affects
You when you write poetry:
The extreme austerity of an almost empty mind
Colliding with the lush, Rousseau-like foliage of its desire to
        communicate
Something between breaths, if only for the sake
Of others and their desire to understand you and desert you
For other centers of communication, so that understanding
May begin, and in doing so be undone.

    John Ashbery, 'And *Ut Pictura Poesis* Is Her Name'

Introduction: Undoing Donne

Much of what passes for contemporary criticism of Donne contrives to ignore the historical culture which informed his writings, and the ideology which conditioned the act of writing or 'authority' itself. Readers have been content with crude and often reductionist biographical correspondences between poems and persons or events; and 'criticism' has been presented as the rehearsal of older evaluations of 'the dramatic voice', 'witty invention', 'originality', 'masculine persuasive force' in 'strong lines', the 'libertine' versus the 'divine' or Jack versus the Doctor. Scant attention has been paid to the problematic of Donne as a *writer*, writing in the specific historical moment of the later European Renaissance.

In challenging this with a more theoretical and critical reading, and drawing extensively on post-structuralist theory, this book proposes three main culturally significant and historically problematical areas which bear on Donne's writings: the scientific discourse, which troubles secular historicity itself; the socio-cultural, in which woman raises certain defences in this male poet; and the aesthetic, in which mimetic writing itself becomes fraught with difficulty.

An interstitial chapter repudiates entirely the modernist construction of Donne as poet of ethical, cultural and political Individualism in the light of the evidence produced from a consideration of his relation to these three areas.

Attention then turns to the modes of 'therapy' available to Donne in the face of his 'problems and paradoxes': the fact of historical change or secular mutability is replaced in the poems by a call to ritual prayer, but a prayer which turns out to be always ineffective and requiring repetition; woman further complicates any such theological impetus in the writing, making a religious escape from the vagaries of human history and from the materiality of the body appear to be madness; and mimetic adequacy as an aesthetic concept is transposed to the level of faith and fidelity, but a faith which is seen to require some kind of 'infidelity' or betrayal as its central constituent. The reading proposed, then, strives to evade being the final word on Donne, for his 'therapies', rather than curing his relation to the cultural and historical problematics which inform him as a writer, simply complicate those issues further. In opening up or undoing the texts, the argument here requires a *re*-reading of Donne to replace the reading of Donne, not to mention the various 'readings' we already have in our own cultural moment.

Crime and criticism

When John Donne was imprisoned in 1602, a promising secular career took a rather catastrophic turn. Donne, MP for Brackley, had committed a crime against both common and canon law when he contracted marriage, in secrecy, to the 16-year-old Ann More while she was in the care of his employer, Thomas Egerton. The actual imprisonment was occasioned by the revelation of this secret to Ann More's father, George More, Lieutenant of the Tower of London. Dismissed from Egerton's service, and imprisoned with his friend and fellow law-student Christopher Brooke, Donne realised that his reputation was in some danger, if not already in ruins. Far from making a name for himself, the bold step of marriage at this time had him 'undone'; it was just prior to his imprisonment that he signed a letter to his wife with both their names and with the result of their nominal collocation: 'John Donne, Ann Donne, undone'.

Since that time Donne's *literary* reputation has had a complex history. The simplistic notion that the poems enjoyed a brief spell of popularity followed by critical neglect until their 'rediscovery' in our own century has been adequately controverted by the evidence adduced by A.J. Smith in *John Donne: The Critical Heritage.*[1] Smith's documentary evidence closes with the reception of Donne in the late 1880s, just as his reputation is taking one of its frequent upswings, and just as his reputation for the contemporary period is being established. Between 1872, when A.B. Grosart published a major edition of Donne's poems, and 1912, when Grierson supplied a more reliable text, Donne's centrality in what was becoming known as English literature was fixed; and when T.S. Eliot reviewed Grierson's volume of *Metaphysical Lyrics and Poems of the Seventeenth Century*, the critical championing of Donne for our times was more or less complete.[2] It is important to note, then, that the 'Donne' who has been the ostensible object of the most widely known or 'standard' twentieth-century critiques is just as 'old' (or indeed as 'new') as English literature itself, which was establishing itself as an academic discipline only at the turn of the century;[3] and that Donne's acceding to the 'monarchy of wit', though heralded by Carew in 1633, is intimately linked with a self-consciously 'modernist' aesthetic and movement in poetry: the 'Donne' that we read is a post-Eliotic Donne.

What Eliot seems to have admired in Donne is a materiality of thought, a poetry which passes itself off as a *pure* medium or enactment or materialization of the poet's thought. The quotations from Eliot's essay are familiar enough, but their significance is not sufficiently considered. He wrote that what we find in Donne, as in Chapman, is 'a direct sensuous apprehension of thought, or a recreation of thought into feeling', that 'A thought to Donne was an experience; it modified his sensibility', and that Donne, like Racine, looked into more than the pseudo-Romantic heart: 'One must look into the cerebral cortex, the nervous system, and the digestive tracts'.[4] It is almost as if Eliot saw Donne's poetry as being the perfect medium, the purest medium, not of the personality of Donne the individual, but rather of the experience of poetry itself, as if Donne's mind and language were 'a more finely perfected medium in which special, or very varied, feelings are at liberty to enter into new combinations'.[5] Donne's sensibility, in short, was not yet 'dissociated': he lived prior to Milton and the English Revolution.

Subsequent criticism of Donne has followed on from this, admiring the 'presence' of Donne; but it has usually redirected attention to the personality of Donne the individual, not as medium or vehicle of poetry, which is supposedly revealed or heard in its 'directness' or 'strident speaking voice' and so on. But what is of major interest here is this notion of purity in poetry and its mediation. In stressing the purity or instantaneity of Donne's medium, Eliot inaugurated the critical process of restitution of Donne's body, starting not from the cerebral cortex, but from the voice; and perhaps following Grierson instead, the 'student of

Donne's character' has read that character not from a material body but through a hypothetical, though supposedly really present, voice:

> Just because he is so conscious of himself we are aware of him – the man speaking – in a manner and to a degree hardly to be paralleled in our reading of lyric poetry. Every line is resonant with his voice; every line seems to bear the stamp of his peculiar personality. And this impression is not something which we fancy or invent for ourselves. It is deliberately forced upon us ... His personality, or the idea that he contrives to give us of it, is a necessary part of his instrument as a writer.[6]

J.E.V. Crofts here is fairly typical of most twentieth-century criticism in sensing or being fascinated by a real presence of the poet. This presentation of Donne, a self-presentation, is supposedly made possible by the purity of his medium, by the perfect correspondence between that medium and the poetry, a poetry defined as the 'concentration . . . of a very great number of experiences', 'most heterogeneous ideas . . . yoked by violence together',[7] a poetry, in short, identified as the interweaving of disparate experience into one specific formal unity identifiable as the poet. The purity of the medium, of the poem, guarantees, according to this, transparent access to the poet himself. The self-presentation of Donne, then, for most current criticism, is facilitated by the *immediacy* of the medium, which also gives the reader the like poetic experience as the poet had, a 'direct *sensuous* apprehension of thought' (stress added).

In this way, then, this poetry is validated in the course of English literature as a means of countering the effects of the English Revolution, that intellectualizing 'dissociation of sensibility' which has, according to Eliot, marred the poetic consciousness of everyone since Milton and Dryden. The poetry of Donne thus becomes a means of *therapy* for the modernist poet or reader, suffering from our split consciousnesses and in need of restitution, wholeness and pure individuality. The immediacy and unity of Donne's poetry, then, are construed as a therapeutic device which works to maintain the unity, singularity, even individuality (non-dividedness), not only of Donne but also of the present reader. There are, then, fairly clear ideological reasons for such an understanding of Donne, as poet of the Individualist voice, an inviolable voice announcing, among other things, the values of English Literature in a strident, clear and 'fascinating' medium or voice.

But Donne's poetry is also difficult, as it dislocates language into meaning: obscurity of the medium, rather than its clarity, seems to be perhaps more applicable as a means of describing the language of Donne's poetry. This obscurity or secrecy, together with the impurity or contamination or indecorousness of the medium, its *transgressive* stance, is crucially determining of the shape of the poetry, making it appear to be related to other modes of trans-gression, crimes and criminality, which require secrecy or covering up, obscuring from public view. Donne's crime and its relation to secrecy are important for a properly theoretical understanding of his poems. 'Criticism', 'crime' and 'secrecy' are linked by more than mere etymology.[8] Hermeneutics, all the way from Biblical exegesis through Schleiermacher to Frankfurt School Critical Theory, subscribes to a notion that texts are more or less obscurantist, and that they subtend 'secret' meanings which can be deciphered and revealed by the elect, by reason or by theory. The critic becomes an epistemological sleuth, following 'clues' and disclosing layer upon layer of falsifying or mystifying palimpsest in order to run to some ground its 'true' text, or to discover its secret *topos* or informing matrix.[9] Criticism such as this is considered to be demystifying, an act of revelation which lays bare a real or true text beneath the euphemistic or indirect words on the page. In Donne's own historical case, it was precisely the revelation of a secret which constituted him as a criminal: criminality here seems to be coterminous with criticism, with the critical enlightenment, bringing to light or revelation of a secret text, the marriage contract.

This fairly traditional hermeneutic, then, not only places great faith in the detective-critic's abilities to discover and recognize truth, but also assumes that the criticism thus produced is not itself mystifying in turn, that it is a more perfect or purer or more transparent medium than the poetry which was its ostensible quarry. But criticism, while perhaps offering some enlightenment or knowledge about poetry, produces, in its own writing or transcription, its own 'secrets' or linguistic obscurities. The language of criticism is not somehow more pure, perfect, transparent or 'innocent' a medium than that of poetry; it can, to modify de Man's position, produce not only insight but also blindness, obscurity or mystification in turn.[10] That is to say that criticism, while perhaps laying bare some levels of the textual palimpsest, also adds to its textual layers or configurations, and thus actually covers some of that text which is its ostensible object, rendering it secret, obscuring it from view.

Donne too was a critic of sorts: his critical reading and reasoning, which fully inform his writing, embraced the fields of philosophy, astronomy, law, medicine, sexology and theology. The poetry is not only multi-layered, like a palimpsest, but also surrounded by these other texts of which Donne was an enthusiastically eclectic reader. But independent critical thought, a thought which would mark its thinker as being of independent mind, is a likely outcome of such critical reading. It is, however, curiously close to unorthodox or even oppositional thought, and was no less dangerous at this historical moment than the independent action (of contracting a secret marriage) which led to Donne's imprisonment, or than the equally independent action (of secretly harbouring a priest) which had led to the imprisonment and subsequent death of his younger brother, Henry, in 1593. Evidence of thought, especially if it is critically opposed or even tangential to the dominant authorities in church and state, and thus 'criminal', had to remain obscure. As was abundantly clear to himself and his family, Donne would not make a name for himself by being an 'individualist', at odds with or deviating obviously from accepted authoritative norms of behaviour and belief. In an age of overt censorship, when writers faced the severest penalties for their 'subversions' or crimes, it is perhaps not too surprising to find Sidney writing that strangely paralogical phrase: 'Now, for the poet, he nothing affirms, and therefore never lieth'.[11] Neither affirming nor denying, lying, the poet may seem to be 'saying' nothing at all, but rather merely obscuring.

Donne, I shall argue here, had reasons for producing deliberately obscure and secretive texts. He was concerned, broadly, to secrete away the transgressive criminal or critical thoughts which form and trouble his writings. It is important to stress, then, that this is not an attempt to reveal the 'truth' of Donne's *Life, Mind and Art*;[12] rather it is an attempt to release Donne's texts into their full obscurity, so to speak: to make them *difficult*. 'Undoing' the texts does not discover the truth of Donne's meaning, but rather produces an understanding or knowledge which stresses the very difficulty of 'meaning' or 'intending' for a writer such as Donne in the late European Renaissance.

Writers in this epoch were obscure to themselves: neither affirming nor denying substantive propositions directly, they simply could not know the full extent and implication of what they were writing; and nor can we. Textuality, in a post-Copernican universe, is radically historical: texts, and more specifically meaning (as both noun and verb), are conditioned by their historical mutability or changeability, a changeability which is written into their very structure. That is to say that texts are always already palimpsests: any act of writing in a secular age produces not a stable text, but rather a text which is subject to change, to superscription, subscription and transcription: interpretation and self-interpretation, in short. Donne's texts, then, are not only the scene of a crime, in the sense that they are conditioned by transgressive heterodoxy, if not heresy; they are also the theatre of an impersonal but cultural agon, a scene of their own self-criticism, imbued with several layers of meanings, each commenting critically on themselves and on the other layers of meaning. The texts are divided against themselves, obscure and secretive, criminal and critical.

In reading such texts, then, this criticism takes its place among the palimpsest layers of Donnean textuality. It does not demystify Donne as person or character, and to that extent it is not an *ethical* criticism.[13] Rather the criticism here takes its place among the poetry's own self-criticisms, dividing or undoing it more and more, but weaving itself into the poetry's textuality and thus *adding* to the layers of the palimpsest, making any hope of finding or recognizing an 'original' text, or source of authoritative meaning for the text, seem a lost cause. It thus, perhaps paradoxically, makes these texts more obscure: in short, it mystifies.

Such criticism is unethical in other ways. Firstly, it replaces ethics in criticism with the more consequential reading of the cultural politics of late Renaissance Europe as they form specific configurations in Donne's writing. But, secondly, the criticism is unethical in its tendency towards the condition of another 'criminality'. For the contemporary criticism of an avowedly secular text, in order to offer any enlightenment or knowledge, must work on the text precisely as if it were a papyrological fragment. It must recreate the text in a certain sense: but that means that it must proceed by introducing a principle of changeability or contamination into the text itself, just as that text is conditioned by secularity or historical mutability. Criticism, then, can proceed by performing the 'criminal' act of modifying the evidence, *changing* the text.

This is not as extreme as it may sound when it is recalled that the very status of *the* text is what has always been in question in hermeneutics: the words on the page have *always* been seen as a shadowy representation of a more real, more fundamental or more perfectly pure (innocent) medium or text. The revelation of such a purer medium may depend precisely upon changing the words on the page; in a weaker form this is known as 'textual emendation'. Such a mode of criticism is, as I shall show in the ensuing pages, strikingly appropriate to the texts of Donne, texts which are themselves saturated with precisely this kind of criticism and criminality.

John Donne, undone

The argument of this study falls into three sections. It moves from a symptomatic reading or investigation of a psychology, outlining the limitations and problems of that psychology, through an interstitial repudiation of the image of Donne as poet of individualism, into a symptomatic reading of a cultural crux between a competing theology and ideology, and of Donne's position within that crux or crisis.

With the Copernican revolution in astronomical thought, there occurs a fundamental 'displacement' of the Earth and of the privileged position accorded humanity. Centrality and stable certainty are lost, and the human now finds herself or himself in a condition of 'exile' or 'error', like an erring or wandering star in the universe: the time is ripe for the writing of a *Paradise Lost*. Temporality, a 'fall' into secular history, is the corollary of this spatial displacement; and the human now lives in and through time and change, through difference, rather than in a hypothesized realm of 'eternal verities' or transcendence, totalizing identity. The relation of poetry to history also changes: the mediation of proverbial truth is replaced by a writing which takes its place in a more relativist conflict of interpretations. Donne contrives to circumvent historical change and its inevitable result, death; but even as he resists his post-Copernican historicity, his poems reveal themselves to be caught up in historical change as part of their very existence and status: they enact the structural modification of themselves, making what was text into palimpsest, scene not of stable meaning but rather of precisely the opposite: change of meaning. The poems can be seen to demand their own re-reading or repetition structurally, and they thus form themselves into palimpsests with a function of secular mutability as part of their fabric.

Science, then, poses certain problems for Donne; but, in the specific guise of the telescope and manipulation of perspective, it is enlisted as an ally in another struggle against death and change, this time identified as woman. The mutability of historical change is characterized in much of the poetry of the period as a specifically 'female' phenomenon. The struggle against history and death moves for Donne on to another plane, where he struggles against a threat to the purity and authority of masculinist order posed by female promiscuity. The scopophilia encouraged by the telescope enables the construction of a masculinist epistemology, for it is instrumental in allowing Donne to gain a metaphorical control over the mutable environment, understood in terms of a female body which is itself analogically construed as a 'female landscape'. Ostensibly the result is a seeming male victory and a celebration of masculinist desire and epistemology. But this is complicated by the fact that the principle of 'female mutability' is seen simultaneously as the very principle that conditions metaphorical language and poetry itself. Thus the mutability which Donne counters in terms of a female fickleness or promiscuity returns in its shape as the linguistic source or tongue of poetry itself. His writing, 'saving' him at one level, damns him coterminously at another: the poetry is conditioned by a female principle of authority at the very instant when Donne claims a masculine victory over woman and her historical condition.

Given such historicity, the 'present' itself becomes difficult of access, and impossible to identify. This poses an aesthetic problem of mimesis for Donne, for 're-presentation' becomes complicated by the 'revolutionary' nature of the present as such. Mimesis or representation is seen to involve an aesthetic labour of transformation and, inevitably, *hypocrisy* in terms of (mis)representation is the result. Clearly this also affects the notion that Donne is representing himself in the poems. The historicity of a secular, post-Copernican universe ensures that any individuality in Donne is either purely hypothetical or hypocritical; more accurately, it is not a given but something which is, if desired, to be struggled for. The interstitial chapter 4 below shows that Donnean hypocritical representation can never represent 'identity', but rather can only betray or reveal Donne's 'differences' from himself.

The final section (chapters 5 to 7) locates Donne within a wider cultural context still. One way to counter historicity is to retreat fully into theology; but this, given Donne's history as a Roman Catholic in a Protestant England, is also fraught with difficulties and necessary obscurities. Donne contrives to write a poetry which has the status of prayer, by constructing texts in which there is a mute or obscured 'scene of recognition' or 'scene of nomination' between himself and God: the texts, at one level, become a secret focal point for the theatrical meeting of Donne and God. Through the manipulation of the rhetorical device of antonomasia, Donne keeps God's 'address' to the poet inarticulate, mute; he thereby contrives to make the poems into a kind of focal point around which other names, and by implication the name of the reader, can also be recognized or 'called' to this theatre. He thus tries to 'orchestrate' the theatre of an *ecclesia*, and the texts become the site of a congregation around an implied, but unpronounced name.

The linguistic change which informs the poetry is now also mediated in terms of a spiritual change, or rather in terms of the change between spiritual and secular. As a result, the major conceit is that the texts become the locus of a transubstantiation, and at one level this is construed as a materialization of the Word. The material 'body' of the poems can now be named through its various *aliases*: not only Christ himself, but also Ann More, Thomas More, Elizabeth Drury and, very importantly, *Mary* the 'bearer' or 'medium' through whom the Word is materialized, realized or enacted. The poetry is written under such signatures or aliases, and, with the hint of Mariolatry here, it reinstates some doubt again about Donne's theological position.

The study proceeds then towards an examination both of theological and secular criminality, showing Donne's texts to be, in a sense, 'failed' confessions. It is part of the point of the book that what is being 'confessed' cannot be known (even, of course, to the confessor); but, by way of a critique of Fish's reading-responses,[14] I am able to suggest that Donne's texts produce a 'catholic' spirit of guilt in their reading, together with a necessity, but impossibility, of confession to some crime. Undoing Donne simply expands the concerns of these texts, obscures and mystifies them and makes them available for re-reading. Revision, however, simply produces more obscurity in its turn around the texts and depends upon more and greater 'critical criminality' being exercised upon the texts. Confession to such a crime, as the study shows, cannot be truthful; while perhaps seeming to be 'sincere', it remains 'hypocritical', and thus yet another transgression, yet another conflict with authority or with the authorized version, an analysis interminable, an interminable historical struggle whose end remains, alas, obscured. This, then, proposes itself as the first critical, even criminal, word on Donne.

Notes

1 See A.J. Smith (ed.), *John Donne: The Critical Heritage*, London, Routledge & Kegan Paul, 1975.

2 T.S. Eliot, 'The Metaphysical Poets', in T.S. Eliot, *Selected Essays*, London, Faber, 3rd edn, 1951; reprinted 1980. For a list of all important publications of Donne's poems prior to Grierson's 1912 edition, see Smith, op. cit., Appendix A.

3 See, e.g., Janet Batsleer, Tony Davies, Rebecca O'Rourke and Chris Weedon, *Rewriting English*, London, Methuen, 1985, 19 and *passim*.

4 Eliot, *Selected Essays*, 286, 287, 290.

5 T.S. Eliot, *The Sacred Wood*, London, Methuen, 1920, 53-4; but cf. *Selected Essays*, 292-3 on Donne as 'individual', unlike Marvell.

6 Herbert J.C. Grierson, 'Introduction' to Herbert J.C. Grierson (ed.), *Donne: Poetical Works*, Oxford, Oxford University Press, 1929, reprinted 1979, xxxv; J.E.V. Crofts, 'John Donne: a Reconsideration', in Helen Gardner (ed.), *John Donne: A Collection of Critical Essays*, Englewood Cliffs, Prentice-Hall, 1962, 82-3. This attention to voice is positively obsessive in twentieth-century criticism of Donne. Some examples are noted in the chapters following this introduction, but the briefest glance at some of the standard and even not-so-standard criticism of Donne offers corroboration of the belief in a presence of Donne's 'voice' and the attendant recuperation of Donne's *ethos*, personal character or individuality. See, e.g., J.B. Leishman, *The Monarch of Wit*, London, Hutchinson, 1951; 6th edn, 1962, reprinted 1967, 166: 'What is really important is to attend carefully to the tone of voice, the inner vibration: that, ultimately, is the only means of determining the degree to which what I may call Donne himself is present in any poem'; Wilbur Sanders, *John Donne's Poetry*, Cambridge, Cambridge University Press, 1971; reprinted 1979, 8: 'I think that foothold is to be found where Dr Leavis found it – in that extraordinary Donne *voice* which ... effortlessly transforms the kind of attention we are prompted to give it, so that (as Leavis has it) "we read on as we read the living" ... I mean that quality of utterance which implies, indeed creates, a body of experience and a "life" in a sense more important, perhaps, than the biographical. It is the *life* that one is attending to when, like a dominant presence in a room full of chatter, Donne

detaches himself from the surrounding loquacity by an individual vibrancy and directness'; F.R. Leavis, *Revaluation* (1936), reprinted Harmondsworth, Penguin, 1972, 18–19: 'utterance, movement and intonation are those of the talking voice ... the subtleties of Donne's use of the speaking voice and the spoken language are inexhaustible'. I cite Leavis and Sanders in consort like this to draw attention to the means by which an attention to voice and perhaps rather a literal 'fascination' by this 'dominant' voice turn readily into an ethical or moral criticism of a hypothetical 'life' and personality. For more of the same kind of fascination, see, e.g., Joan Bennett, *Five Metaphysical Poets*, Cambridge, Cambridge University Press, 1971; N.J.C. Andreasen, *John Donne, Conservative Revolutionary*, New Jersey, Princeton University Press, 1967; Louis I. Bredvold, *The Religious Thought of Donne in Relation to Medieval and Later Tradition*, New York, Macmillan, 1925; Pierre Legouis, *Donne the Craftsman*, New York, Russell & Russell, 1962; Earl Miner, *The Metaphysical Mode from Donne to Cowley*, New Jersey, Princeton University Press, 1969; Charles Monroe Coffin, *John Donne and the New Philosophy*, New York, Columbia University Press, 1937; Una Nelly, *The Poet Donne*, Cork, Cork University Press, 1969; A.J. Smith, *Donne: Songs and Sonets*, London, Edward Arnold, 1964; reprinted 1979; James Winny, *A Preface to Donne*, London, Longman, 1970; revised edn, 1981. This is but a brief sample of some of the more influential, and still widely read, studies of Donne which turn from attending to voice towards attending to person. Of work undertaken in what might be called 'conventional' (non-theoretically informed) criticism, the only striking exception to this mode known to me is Donald L. Guss, *John Donne, Petrarchist*, Detroit, Wayne State University Press, 1966, 108, where the critic reads this 'voice' as gesture: 'his lyrics are not descriptions of delicate, evanescent plays of feeling. They do not define private sensation – reactions to the sadness of rainfall, the sensuality of a rose, or the horror of a city street. Instead, they make public gestures, and produce social effects – comforting or mocking a lady, for example. It is, then, a mistake to reduce Donne's verse to a private flow of sentiments and fancies'; yet even Guss falls into the error of seeing some of the poems as an 'attempt at honest self-knowledge' (pp. 148–9) and thus again tends towards the ethical mode.

7   Eliot, *Sacred Wood*, 58; Samuel Johnson, 'Life of Cowley', reprinted in John Wain (ed.), *Lives of the Poets: A Selection*, London, Dent, 1975, 11; this kind of paradoxicality, or neo-Romantic reconciliation of opposites as a constituent of Donne's poetry (if not of poetry generally), also made him a particularly appropriate poet for the explication and elaboration of American New Criticism.

8   See Sissela Bok, *Secrets*, Oxford, Oxford University Press, 1984, 286, notes 6 and 7; and cf. the work on secrecy and narrative by Frank Kermode in *The Genesis of Secrecy*, Cambridge, Mass., Harvard University Press, 1979; and his 'Secrets and narrative sequence' in W.J.T. Mitchell (ed.), *On Narrative*, Chicago, University of Chicago Press, 1981.

9   The term 'matrix' is borrowed here from Michael Riffaterre; see, e.g. Riffaterre, *Semiotics of Poetry*, Bloomington, Indiana University Press, 1978.

10 See Paul de Man, *Blindness and Insight*, London, Methuen, 2nd edn 1983, especially ch. 7.

11 Philip Sidney, 'Apology for poetry', reprinted in Edmund D. Jones (ed.), *English Critical Essays: XVI–XVIII Centuries*, Oxford, Oxford University Press, 1922,

reprinted 1975, 33; this is paralogical because the status of the 'Apology', as 'poetry' or 'philosophy', is itself uncertain, according to the definitions of poetry and philosophy offered within the text.

12 The reference is to John Carey, *John Donne: Life, Mind and Art*, London, Faber, 1981.

13 The Greek word 'ethos' signifies 'nature' or 'disposition' in the sense which equates most nearly with our own notion, a humanist notion, of 'character'.

14 See Stanley E. Fish, *Self-Consuming Artifacts*, Berkeley and Los Angeles, University of California Press, 1972 for a full delineation of the specific mode of reader-response criticism and its effects on the act of reading, not to mention the reader, with which I take issue in ch. 7 below.

Problems and paradoxes

1
Displacement and eccentricity: the struggle with history

At the still point of the turning world. Neither flesh nor
        fleshless;
Neither from nor towards; at the still point, there the dance is,
But neither arrest nor movement. And do not call it fixity,
Where past and future are gathered. Neither movement from
        nor towards,
Neither ascent nor decline. Except for the point, the still point,
There would be no dance, and there is only the dance.
I can only say, *there* we have been; but I cannot say where.
                    (T.S. Eliot, 'Burnt Norton', in *Four Quartets*)

1

Shortly before he died in 1543 Nicholas Copernicus published his treatise, *De Revolutionibus*, a work which had been gestating for some thirty years in his researches. The single most important aspect of this work is its replacement of a geocentric model of the universe with a heliocentric one. Not only was the work *about* the revolutionary motions of astral bodies, it was also 'revolutionary' in itself in its effects on human self-awareness and imagination. The idea of the Earth's movement, spinning on its own axis, was not entirely new. Copernicus indeed claimed some degree of authority for his propositions in the writings of ancient astronomers and philosophers: 'Certainly Heraclides and Ecphantus the Pythagoreans, and Nicetus of Syracuse (in Cicero) were of this opinion, making the earth revolve in the middle of the universe'.[1] What was fundamentally new in the work of Copernicus, however, at least for the

European philosophy of the sixteenth century, was the fact of his decentring the earth itself; and subsequently, the impact of *De Revolutionibus* was felt primarily as a threat to the credibility of humanity's special relation to God and the world. In a geocentric, anthropocentric world-model, it is easy to lend belief to the notion that the universe is made, by God, for the delight of humanity or for the exercise of human ingenuity appreciated by God; basically the world is ideally considered as a potential paradise, the place in which the human animal or human consciousness can possibly find fulfilment and happiness. The Copernican propositions disturb this complacency in their implication of a *number* of possible worlds or 'centres' in the universe:

> Since, then, there is no objection to the mobility of the Earth, I think it must now be considered whether several motions are appropriate for it, so that it can be regarded as one of the wandering stars. For the fact that it is not the centre of all revolutions is made clear by the apparent irregular motion of the wandering stars, and their variable distances from the Earth, which cannot be understood in a circle having the same centre as the earth. Therefore there is more than one centre.[2]

In the Latin version, as Copernicus wrote it, the phrase for 'of the wandering stars' is 'errantium syderum'. To 'wander' in this sense is the same as to 'err' or to 'deviate' from a 'correct' path. The 'error of a planet', indeed, is the distance between the position in which astrological computation theoretically locates it and that in which empirical observation discovers it; as if the planet has 'wandered' from its rightful place. This linguistic fact is of crucial importance. Since the Earth is now in a condition of 'error' or wandering, it is no longer simply the case that the human being can, by accident, fall into mistaken ways; rather, error becomes the fundamental condition of being human on the Earth at all.

To the classical *nychthemeron*, the diurnal motion of the Earth spinning on its axis, Copernicus adds two further kinds of movement. The more important of these is the 'error' of the Earth as it wanders around the sun in his new heliocentric model of the universe. But the motion which he calls *declinatio* also figures largely in the intellectual imagination of the sixteenth century, especially in the guise of millenarian concern about the entropic dissolution of the world. But error can also be understood as symptomatic of this *declinatio*.

Inspired by Marcus Vitruvius Pollio's treatise, *De architectura*, the Florentine artist and theorist of architecture, Leon Battista Alberti, had formulated the notion that the most perfect, most divine, form is that of the circle. This idea was dominant in astrological thought, and, in the Copernican system, the trajectory of the Earth around the sun was kept regular by being construed as the description of a circle. While 'wandering', the Earth was, at least symbolically, held to be not in 'error' for Copernicus, because its circular movement was a realization of perfection itself. When Tycho Brahe read *De Revolutionibus*, he underlined the phrase cited above, 'ut possit una errantium syderum existimari'; there is no additional marginalia at this point, as if Brahe simply considered the notion of 'erring' as important or accurate in itself. Brahe in turn taught Johannes Kepler, who entertained the idea of error in all its aspects; and it was Kepler who further corrected the Copernican system, arguing that the trajectory of the planets was not the perfect circle at all, but rather a 'declining' form of the circle, the ellipse. By 1609 then, when Kepler had explored this error, the intellectual imagination of Europe must have been in some slight consternation at these signs of decline or entropy in the condition and position of the human. One clear symptom of this particular malaise might be the ease with which Spenser could introduce Error as a personified character in his *Faerie Queene* in 1590; according to the *Oxford English Dictionary*, this is the first such prosopopoeia involving this figure. Error, at the turn of the century, was fully realized as a condition of humanity, the space itself reserved for the human consciousness.[3]

There is a clear theological danger in this Copernican revolution. According to the accepted theology, Scripture explicitly controverted the ideas of the Earth's motion and of the sun's stability; and the church authorities stressed dogmatically the centrality and primacy of the human on Earth in the divine order of things. When Giordano Bruno of Nola took the Copernican system and its implications seriously, incidentally questioning the exegetical dogma of the church thereby, he was, predictably, charged with heresy and burnt at the stake. Discretion in these matters was clearly called for; indeed, some rhetorical manipulation of *De Revolutionibus* itself seemed necessary.

Andreas Osiander attached a prefatory address 'To the Reader on the Hypotheses in this Work', without Copernicus's permission, in which he stressed the purely 'theoretical' nature of the text. Osiander was at some pains to have the authorities consider the text as if it were a work of poetry. He claimed that its use was simply as a tool for interpretation of the appearances of heavenly motions, and that it bore no more direct reference to the facts of the matter or to truth. Through this strategy, Osiander tried to reduce thesis to hypothesis. The system was merely 'a way of putting it', in the Eliotic description of poetry.[4] It was to be received as a poetic or metaphorical explanation, a 'reading' of the appearances of celestial figurations. In short, it was a 'philosophy of *as if*',[5] a fiction:

> Nor is it necessary that these hypotheses should be true, nor indeed even probable, but it is sufficient if they merely produce calculations which agree with the observations.... And if it does work out any laws – as certainly it does work out very many – it does not do so in any way with the aim of persuading anyone that they are valid, but only to provide a correct basis for calculation. Since different hypotheses are sometimes available to explain one and the same motion (for instance eccentricity or an epicycle for the motion of the Sun) an astronomer will prefer to seize on the one which is easiest to grasp; a philosopher will perhaps look more for probability; but neither will grasp or convey anything certain, unless it has been divinely revealed to him. Let us therefore allow these new hypotheses also to become known beside the older, which are no more possible, especially since they are remarkable and easy; and let them bring with them the vast treasury of highly learned observations. And let no one expect from astronomy, as far as hypotheses are concerned, anything certain, since it cannot produce any such thing, in case if he seizes on things constructed for any other purpose as true, he departs from this discipline more foolish than he came to it.[6]

In the text as presented to the public, this prefatory material, unsigned, could have passed for the writing of Copernicus, the avowed author of the rest of the book. This is important in a consideration of Osiander's strategy. Three main points follow from his transformation of the text from thesis to hypothesis, from series of referential propositions to 'mere' poem or model for reality.

Firstly, and perhaps most obviously, the philosophical content and status of the work are defused. That is to say, its importance for real historical actuality is muted; the poem, fiction or model is not, at least at this cultural historical moment, accorded the same status as the philosophical 'proposition' or statement and is reduced to the level of sophistry or rhetoric rather than logic.[7] It thus 'matters' less and is of less material historical significance: in short, it is not read 'seriously'.

Secondly (and this is a positive point countering the negativity of the first), it thus circumvents some of the harsher vagaries of censorship. A poem, deemed to be affirming nothing or not directly referring to the real historical world, might stand a greater chance of passing safely through the hands of the censoring authorities than would a more 'pertinent' document, like a philosophical tract which is deemed to make referential propositions.

Following on from this, thirdly, the 'text' with its now dubious status is publishable. But what is it now that is published? For the 'poem', a supposedly harmless fabular model or allegory of 'as if', is allowed to be scrutinized by the public consciousness. But this 'poem' contains, as it were, another 'text', that of the philosophical tract whose status is now confused with the poem. In other words, a document which is 'saying the unsayable', so to speak, manages to have itself articulated and disseminated under the guise of the harmless 'poem'.

There is a fourth, and extremely important, corollary of this. Once the text is published, it is the reader, not the writer, who is faced with the *angst* of choice in interpretive procedure. The problem of 'many authorities', a problem which biblical exegetes had already confronted, thereby forcing the theological Reformation into historical eventuality, is realized now for the reader of the 'secular', philosophical or, indeed, poetic text. Either we can privilege the preface of Osiander, masquerading as an authorial intention advising us to treat the text lightly, as poetry, or equally we can choose to interpret the text actively in order to reveal or betray its full revolutionary importance in 'the words beneath the words', the philosophical or historical text made accessible through this publication of a 'poem'.[8] The hermeneutical responsibility of the reader, faced with the problem of 'many authorities', now becomes central.

One way of considering this is to suggest that Osiander's preface constitutes an interpretation of Copernicus's treatise to some extent; but this interpretation, especially when placed alongside the 'original' treatise, makes a completely different work of that basic text. An analogy can be drawn to biblical interpretation. Kermode argues that the gospels are to be arranged in order: Mark came first, followed by Matthew and Luke, and then John was in a tangential relation to all three. The relation between the fables told and their secret senses is brought to the fore here. Kermode writes:

> Mark is already an interpretation; Matthew and Luke are in large part interpretations of Mark. There comes a point where interpretation by the invention of new narrative is halted; in the present instance that point was reached with the establishment of a canon of four gospels. Interpretation thereafter usually continues in commentary. These interpretative continuities are illuminated . . . by the practice of midrash. By midrash the interpreter, either by rewriting the story or explaining it in a more acceptable sense, bridges the gap between an original and a modern audience. The word derives from *darash*, to probe or examine; however the work is done, whether by fictive augmentation and change or by commentary, its object is to penetrate the surface and reveal a secret sense; to show what is concealed in what is proclaimed.[9]

Osiander's 'interpretive' strategy, changing the status of Copernicus's text, allows publication; but the text now contains a secret message, available to the reader who can adopt this midrashic mode of interpretation of the 'poem' or 'rhetoric' which passed through the offices of the ecclesiastical and state censors. The intellectual authorities, then, allowed this 'fiction' or 'poem' about the world to circulate, unaware, for a time at least, of its revolutionary seeds which would later come to fruition.

Parallel to Osiander's dissolution of monological truth into the potential conflict of multiple interpretation, there comes also a loss of stability in the intellectual consciousness, as a result of the Earth's 'eccentricity' or new decentred status. With the Earth now, at least metaphorically, in orbit around the sun, humanity loses its erstwhile stable point of reference, the point from which it apprehended the universe in an assured indubitable way. Put simply, the universe is no longer our exclusive domain; we too, now, are among the unstable uncertainties of the world and are radically involved in what Blumenberg calls 'theoretical curiosity',[10] the quest for stable certitudes and knowledge. Paradise, then, is lost: the human is exiled from an Edenic 'home' at the centre of the world. Error and Mutability enter to dominate the poetic imagination; and these prosopopoeias are understood as the determinants of human disease, human entropy and the gradual but cosmic dissolution of all life. According to Spenser it is mutability itself which brings the possibility of death. In the *Two Cantos of Mutabilitie*, Spenser identifies Mutability as female and has it that she is a deviant from the laws and regularity of nature, justice, policy.

> [She] wrong of right, and bad of good did make,
> And death for life exchanged foolishlie:
> Since which, all liuing wights haue learn'd to die,
> And all this world is woxen daily worse.[11]

Our 'motions' are symptomatic of our decay: such an idea was to come to fuller development in the 'excremental vision' of a writer such as Swift, but it played an important part in the writings and imaginations of Donne and his contemporaries.[12]

The 'spatial' revolution effected through the Copernican text brings about three main intellectual effects. In the first place, displacement of the human is understood as a prime condition of existence. Not only have we been displaced from centre to periphery; we are also, further, being continually displaced on our circumferential trajectory, for the Earth is in various and continual motions. Secondly, we have entered the age of a really secular history. Displacement is irretrievably linked to temporality. The Earth's movements, of course, were instrumental in bringing about a correction in the conception of the temporal process itself in the subsequent adoption of the Gregorian calendar.[13] After 1543 we have 'fallen into history', into secularity. Displacement demands temporality, and history, as its corollary: in order to establish some sense of relation among our many different spatial locations, we require a dimension of time, *saecula*, as a fundamental link. The human now lives in and through time.

This fall into history, however, brings with it the possibility of error, in the forms of instability, uncertainty and relativity: the relations between person and place, text and context, event and situation, person and person, or 'I' and 'I', are no longer fixed or assured. Correspondingly, there follows the third major consequence of the Copernican revolution. With the human habitation now best identified as the house of Error, Truth as monological and given fact is replaced by the conflict of interpretations and of their authorities. Poems, indeed all texts, potentially, are released into obscurity, as it were, and hermeneutic is problematized at the centre of all 'literal' transactions, all writing and reading.

In some respects, then, 1543 might be isolated as some, admittedly vague, beginning of the modern age in Europe. Koyré locates this year as one of intellectual revolution: 'On est tenté de considérer cette date comme signifiant "la fin du moyen âge et le commencement des temps modernes".' ('It is tempting to think of this date as signifying "the end of the middle ages and the beginning of modern times".')[14] The reason offered for this assertion depends on the idea which I am here calling displacement: 'c'est seulement depuis Copernic que l'homme n'est plus au centre du monde et que le Cosmos n'est plus ordonné autour de lui' ('it is only since Copernicus that man is no longer at the centre of the world and that the Cosmos is no longer ranged about him').[15] Blumenberg also locates the beginnings of 'modernism' at roughly the same historical moment; more precisely, in the confrontation of Nicholas Chrypffs of Cusa with Giordano Bruno of Nola. The unrestricted expansion of theoretical curiosity (broadly understood as epistemological enrichment) is a primary characteristic of modernity, according to Blumenberg; and its development owes much to Copernicus:

> The century of the Copernican reform of astronomy manifests not only a sudden change in the evaluation and justification of theoretical curiosity with respect to its object, which had been accentuated by the discrimination against it, but also the self-confirmation of theory's claim to precisely what, on the premises of the ancient physics and cosmology, was supposed to be naturally withheld from the reach of knowledge.[16]

According to Blumenberg, it was not until Nietzsche that philosophy had a full articulation of what is at stake in this inception of modernism. The existential construction of order in the universe becomes the fundamental theme of the post-medieval human, and

> After the kind of delay characteristic of the philosophical explication of historically effective motives in consciousness, Nietzsche formulated the situation of man in the 'disappearance of order', abandoned by natural providence and made responsible

for himself, but he did so not in order to express disappointment at the loss of the cosmos but rather to celebrate the triumph of man awakened to himself from the cosmic illusion and to assure him of his power over his future. The man who conceives not only of nature but also of himself as a fact at his disposal has traversed only the first stage of his self-enhancement and self-surpassing in the self-assertion of his modern history. The destruction of trust in the world made him for the first time a creatively active being, freed him from a disastrous lulling of his activity.[17]

Even before Nietzsche, the particular situation announced here had been enacted in the death of Bruno who, like Kepler, read Copernicus according to midrashic prescription and took the philosophical import of the work very seriously indeed. Both these thinkers went beyond the Copernican model with their own 'critical interpretations' of the text. Bruno came to understand nature as an everlasting metamorphosis, the antithesis of stable allegorical modes of thought, and for him

Movement . . . is necessarily the fundamental character of what exists, and the distinction, which was essential for the Aristotelian cosmology, between the central body at rest and the bodies in motion on peripheral paths has lost its meaning for Bruno. Here Bruno presses beyond Copernicus, who had still only replaced one central body at rest with another.[18]

Bruno's 'heretical' interpretation of the Copernican text led to his execution at the hands of those competing authorities, the church exegetes. While the modern age since 1543 has not seen this kind of resolution of the problem of many authorities adopted as an overt norm, still a mode of 'excommunication' from the institutions wherein power is vested has frequently been the lot of the 'theoretically curious'.

The Nolan conception of existence as constant movement or displacement makes the modern human condition a state of 'exile'. In this condition of exile which eccentricity, displacement or error forced upon the modern human, we might also see the beginnings of a modern secular poetry, with an indeterminacy of reference and reception as its historical condition. Blanchot, considering the modernist writings of the twentieth century, comments that exile as such is the very condition of poetry:

Le poème est l'exil, et le poète qui lui appartient appartient à
l'insatisfaction de l'exil, est toujours hors de lui-même, hors de
son lieu natal, appartient à l'étranger, à ce qui est le dehors sans
intimité et sans limite . . . Cet exil qu'est le poème fait du poète
l'errant, le toujours égaré, celui qui est privé de la présence ferme
et du séjour véritable.[19]

('The poem is exile, and the poet who pertains to it belongs
thereby to the insatisfaction of exile, is always outside herself or
himself, outside of a native place, belongs to the foreign, to that
which is the alien without intimacy and without limit . . . This
exile which the poem is makes the poet a wanderer, always lost,
she or he who lacks a steady presence and a genuine abode.')

Error and exile from a stable centred home, then, is the condition of
modern, historical (secular) poetry. Radical indeterminacy is the
subsequent condition of writing. The notion of a stable self, like a
'home' to which the 'erring' poet could return and discover stable
truth, is now endangered. Not only is returning a physical
impossibility (secular time cannot go backwards), but even if it
were to be contrived as a metaphorical possibility, home would no
longer be there: it too would have 'erred' or moved on. As
Blumenberg writes, 'History knows no repetitions of the same;
"renaissances" are its contradiction'.[20] Thus selfhood, in the form of
a series of self-indentical 'I' or first-personal self-constructions,
threatens to disintegrate; the 'I', strictly speaking, cannot ever
repeat itself and therefore cannot establish a Self which transcends
each individual, historical instance of the 'I'. This may appear to
be unappealing for humanist criticism; but paradoxically it is the
very condition on which modern secular writing depends.

Intellectual history in Europe after Copernicus becomes a series
of attempts to recentre and restabilize the universe and, more
particularly, the individuated human self at its centre. Anxiety
about displacement was not successfully contested until perhaps
1637, when Descartes wrote his *Discours de la méthode* and
Méditations, thereby constructing an epistemological model of
philosophy in which truth reappeared and based itself on the
centrality and primacy of the once dubious, but now assured, self.
From the *cogito ergo sum*, Descartes contrived to reinstate truth or
certainty, in the specific form of a God as guarantor of such truth

and its accessibility; and he also strove to make the human individual the centre of the world thereby, the still point around which all the world moved and which gave the external universe its meaning.

Three dates demand attention, then. In 1543 the 'poetic text' of *De Revolutionibus* was published. Next, 1600 has Bruno taking seriously the philosophical import of this 'poem', through his midrashic interpretation of its secret message. The subsequent execution of Bruno deterred Galileo from revealing his position on the controversy at this time. In 1637 there was a recovery of sorts of the anterior position of stability and truth, with Descartes's recentring of the human individual self, at least in metaphysical if not in astronomical or physical terms. It was precisely in the midst of this period of ferment that the young intellectual, John Donne, began his writing career.

When it began to be seen that some 'heretics' were taking Copernicus as more than a poet, a conservative reaction began. This had already started at around the time Donne was born, in 1572, and continued into his late twenties and thirties at the turn of the century. With the threat of inquisition in the air across Europe, the safest intellectual position to adopt might seem to be a kind of silent scepticism. That is to say, it might appear to be wiser to use the Copernican text *as a poetic model* while professing nothing, or even ignorance, about the divine scheme of things, leaving such knowledge to the church and its Gnostics.

Donne, it should be recalled, was a Roman Catholic in a Protestant England; his early relation to the Roman church must have been conditioned to some extent by its reaction to interpretations and public reception of the Copernican tract. Poetry, however, understood as a series of 'agnostic' and indeterminate approximations to an inaccessible original truth, might offer a useful way out for the intellectual who wants to write at all in Donne's situation. The radical scepticism of Montaigne, with its own midrashic self-interpretations and critical modification of his own texts, is perhaps the most obvious exemplification of the attitude I am isolating here:

> Et si j'eusse a dresser des enfans, je leur eusse tant mis en la boucche cette facon de respondre /// enquesteuse, non resolutive //: 'Qu'est-ce a dire? Je ne l'entens pas. Il pourroit estre. Est-il

vray?' qu'ils eussent plustost garde la forme d'apprentis a soixante ans que de representer les docteurs a dix ans, comme ils font. Qui veut guerir de l'ignorance, il faut la confesser. /// Iris est fille de Thaumantis. L'admiration est fondement de toute philosophie, l'inquisition le progrez, l'ignorance le bout.[21]

(And if I had to bring up children, I would put this kind of phrase on their tongue /// an inquiring, rather than resolute, kind of speech//: 'What should I say? I don't understand. It could be. Is that so?' so that they would rather appear as learners still at sixty years old than as sages at ten. Whoever wants to recover from ignorance has first of all to admit their ignorance. /// Iris is the daughter of Thaumas. Amazement is the start of all philosophy, inquisition is its progress, ignorance its end.)

It was in the face of these historical, cultural and intellectual eventualities that Donne began to write. Revolution, displacement, secularity, eccentricity and the theoretical problems of the status of writing itself all conditioned his output and seemed to propose a poetic stance of speculative scepticism.

Place and time, then, and their by-product, relation as such, become crucial factors in shaping Donne's writing. Eccentricity has long been understood as a striking element in his poetry. The by now well-worn quote from Carew's 'Elegie' perhaps began the popular vogue of Donne as an 'odd' but refreshingly original, even wilfully revolutionary poet:

> The Muses garden with Pedantique weedes
> O'erspred, was purg'd by thee; The Lazie seeds
> Of servile imitation throwne away;
> And fresh invention planted[22]

This is usually taken to mean that the corpus of Donne's poetry introduced something novel into the arts of verse. But it implies something more basic: oddity, eccentricity and deviation from existing models are important certainly, but perhaps even more important is the element of deviation and eccentricity which is structurally integral to Donne's texts. The poems have an element of difference, deviation from themselves, so to speak, actually within themselves. This is to say that the model for Donne's verse looks rather like the Copernican text with its preface by Osiander attached. Like that text, Donne's poems may seem to say one thing, but often potentially release or reveal many other meanings, more or less obscure; and such meanings, of course, may even be concealed from Donne's own consciousness. Rather than this intentional consciousness being at the centre of the Donnean poetic text (which would make it a fiction like that proposed by Descartes), we have instead to witness the exile of such a consciousness from the centre. What the *text* means is as important as what Donne might have meant in writing it.

It will thus become difficult to isolate and identify any configurations in the writing as specifically 'Donnean'. Much of what is produced in an interpretation of Donne's writings will depend upon the historical and ideological constructions located in the texts by their readers. Moreover, Donne differs from himself, as it were, from text to text as well as within each text. Otherwise he would appear to be extremely repetitive, establishing a 'new' style of poetry and endlessly repeating or consolidating it, in such a way that his monopoly on the style would render that style a surrogate signature, an 'advertisement for myself', in Mailer's term.[23] The model I offer here, then, is of a Donne who is rigorously sceptical, endlessly self-critical, posing more questions than answers, more 'paradoxes and problems' than assured and clear monologic propositions or statements. Donne, like Copernicus before him, demands to some extent that the reader adopt the 'theoretically curious' and dangerous position of the midrashic interpreter, wary of the possibility of the 'concealed offence'[24] in Donne's writings, especially given their 'revolutionary' intellectual provenance.

2

In an examination of the Christian root metaphor, 'God is love', from the Johannine writings, David Tracy argues against what he sees as a 'literalist' interpretation of metaphor. He complains that the traditional preacher, exegete or theologian 'feels free to speak or write all too plainly about the "real" meaning of these . . . first Christian scriptural texts'; for too long 'parabolic metaphors have often been considered mere substitutions for some literal (ethical, conceptual, dogmatic, or political) meaning'.[25] But metaphor, he argues, is not merely ornamental addition to or covering of some basic ideational content; rather it is integral to content itself. He isolates some 'tensions' in the phrase 'God is love', and writes:

A first tension was found within the words 'God' and 'love' and, thereby, *between* the words 'God' and 'love'. That tension itself was a clue to the tension between a deceptively literal inter- pretation of the statement 'God is love' (e.g., 'The First Cause of all reality is our loving friend') and a metaphorical interpretation (e.g., 'God, a God of mercy and justice, of love and wrath, *is like* agapic love'). Moreover, the 'is like' is clearly a metaphorical 'is like': the resemblance is *produced by* the redescriptive power of the metaphorical language; the resemblance is not simply a descriptive account of an observed empirical reality. Indeed, the inclusion of the metaphor 'wrath' along with the tension within the word 'love' (*eros* and *agape*) already indicates that in a straightforward 'literal' relational sense 'God' *is not* 'love.' . . . The statement 'God is love' does not say literally what God is but *produces* a metaphorical meaning for what God is like.[26]

In a similar way, Donne's writings are not to be construed 'literally' as transparent self-explicatory statements. Rather, working in the mode of metaphor and poetry, they work to produce metaphors demanding what Tracy calls a 'tensive' response; in short, the poems demand hermeneutical mediation or interpretation. But the adoption of the metaphorical, anti-literal mode of writing in Donne's poetry and prose is of some more immediate relevance in relation to those revolutions in space and time which dominated his contemporary intellectual world. One, perhaps rather crude but at least de-mystifying, phenomenological conception of metaphor is offered by Jean Ricardou, who succinctly describes metaphor as 'the shortest distance between two points'.[27] This is a useful way to describe the efficacy of the metaphorical, poetic approach to writing for Donne. Donne makes a virtue of his metaphorical ability to control space and time. Many poems offer examples of his fictional contractions of the world into the space of a bedroom, or of a lover into an eye, or of his expansion of himself and lover until they constitute an entire world between themselves.

'The Sunne Rising' demonstrates this kind of metaphorical sophistry at work. One of the things the poem is 'about', indeed, is the rise of the sun, its triumphant ascent to centrality. Clearly the poem works to contract all space into the area of the bed or room of the lovers, and it displaces them from their position of the merest peripheral 'accident' to that of the necessary 'universal'; they become the world and occupy the same position of centrality as the sun. They become, in short, the still point around which all else is supposed to revolve, and around whom all time passes, while they remain in some kind of position of supposed transcendence of history itself.

Firstly, the importance of the sun seems to be reduced; it exists in relation merely to the lovers in bed, a kind of voyeur peering through a chink in the curtains or window. This is the first apparent reduction in the purview of the sun, for the space it occupies is significantly reduced; its multiple rays are reduced to the simplest thin and single shaft of light. This reduction is further consolidated in the humanization of the sun, and its conformity with the parameters of a human body in the implied comparison of sun and lover:

> Thy beames, so reverend, and strong
> Why shouldst thou thinke?
> I could eclipse and cloud them with a winke,
> But that I would not lose her sight so long:
> If that her eyes have not blinded thine . . .[28]

In this prosopopoeia, the conjunction of sun and lover reduces the sun to human size. Correspondingly the speaker also 'grows', in inverse proportion to the spatial reduction of the sun. This metaphorical poem now demands to be apprehended in (at least) two ways: as the contraction of the sun's space (and therefore as a reduction of the space of the universe), and as a transmutation of the space occupied by the lovers, most clearly the bedroom, into the space of the universe itself (as they become heavenly bodies capable of producing eclipses). The single most fundamental point at issue is that the space is relativized and made mutable.

The poem continues the line of spatial manipulation by converting the body of the woman into a map, a representation or metaphorical sign of the whole world. East and west are yoked together, coming to a fulcrum point in the figure of the female body, now 'both the 'India's of spice and Myne'. The world, thus, not only provides a metaphorical intersection of its two extremes, but also makes this intersection a place of trafficking, commerce, a cross-roads and microcosmic market-place for the exchange of the world's riches. It is important to recognize that the woman, in these contractions, is inscribed with mercantile metaphoricity: her riches, even her 'identity', are those of the market-place. She is thus tacitly understood as being herself fundamentally mutable, the symbol of exchange itself. Further, while she thus 'contracts' the world to her, the male seems to grow in status:

> Aske for those Kings whom thou saw'st yesterday,
> And thou shalt heare, All here in one bed lay.

> She'is all States, and all Princes, I,
> Nothing else is.

The woman may comprise the world, but the man is its ruler with its riches at his disposal. The world and its riches are contracted into the space of the female body; commerce with that thus becomes trafficking with the world. Sexual relation fades into commercial relation here, and the female herself becomes mediated as a symbol of the market-place itself, her body a 'crossroads' symbolizing exchange. However, since this writing seems to depend upon the operations of metaphor, it might be apposite to suggest that in the very text in which Donne contrives to assert a stable male control of a fickle and changeable world and its mutable women, there is nonetheless a tacit dependence upon the female, at least upon the female symbolically understood as the 'principle of exchange' which permits or even generates the construction of the text. The demonstration of male centrality and power depends upon the primacy of this symbolic female. All the spaces in the poem – body, eye, bed, room, world – remain interchangeable, in obedience to the principle of exchange or 'crossing' which dominates the metaphorical text.

There is an important corollary of this. In the manipulation of space as we have it here, the progress of time is halted. At a moment which I have characterized as the 'fall into history' in intellectual terms, this poem dramatizes a kind of triumph over history itself, a movement from secular or profane into sacred time, to borrow terms from Eliade.[29] The poem opened by asking the sun 'Must to thy motions lovers seasons run?' It provides an answer by arresting the motion of the sun, and by transposing the position of peripheral lovers to one of centrality and stable rest. If time is the corollary of movement, the triumph over the process of history comes from the arresting of that movement. But at the moment when such a victory over secularity is supposedly achieved, there is also a tacit admission of the fall into history resulting from the Copernican revolution. Perhaps the basic exchange in the metaphorical text here is that between Earth and sun, centre and circumference. It might be argued that the poem is a critical response to that 'poem' written by Copernicus (and Osiander), a reworking of the tract in lyric genre.[30] The organization of the poem is such that the sun becomes central and centred, and the world with its lovers becomes 'eccentric'; it is the struggle against such eccentricity that the poem celebrates. This requires further explication.

Dorothy Stimson praises Copernicus for his modern and independent achievement: 'his great book', she writes, 'is a sane and modern work in an age of astrology and superstition'.[31] But at the time when Copernicus's argument was slowly attaining acceptance as a poem which nonetheless had material, historical and cultural significance, as poems do, astronomy and astrology were still confused. The confusion is most evident in the desire of astronomers to be able to predict the movements of celestial bodies. In such a facility of 'pre-diction', some apparent degree of control over the temporal process is of the essence. The heavens, at the time of Donne's writing, posed at least as much of a threat to the human consciousness as they do now. The unpredictability of earthquakes and similar disasters was feared; and at a deeper level of conscious-ness (superstition), any disruption or 'irregularity' in the heavens became a portent of bad days ahead. Gloucester in *King Lear* offers the precise contemporary gloss on this:

> These late eclipses in the sun and moon portend no good to us. Though the wisdom of nature can reason it thus and thus, yet nature finds itself scourg'd by the sequent effects: love cools, friendship falls off, brothers divide; in cities, mutinies; in countries, discord; in palaces, treason; and the bond crack'd 'twixt son and father. This villain of mine comes under the prediction: there's son against father. The King falls from bias of nature: there's father against child. We have seen the best of our time: machinations, hollowness, treachery, and all ruinous disorders, follow us disquietly to our graves.[32]

Regularity was required if the human was to feel safe in such a hostile, or potentially troublesome, world. Whatever regularity could be discerned in celestial motions was instrumental in lending the human an illusion of control over the events of nature:

predictability was tantamount to apprehension. The threat from the skies and their irregularities, at a time of millenarian fears, was also linked to the human's abject helplessness in the face of ignorance about the whims of an all-powerful, but essentially unpredictable God. Quite simply, this was a contemporary articulation of a fairly perennial fear of the single undisputable fact of nature, the passage of historical time which brings death to each individual organism. Astronomical knowledge, which lends credence to the possibility of astrological predictability, was therefore valuable as a means of foretelling, and thus seemingly 'controlling' or at least apprehending, the arbitrary future of historical fact itself.

In 'The Sunne Rising' the Copernican discoveries are enacted. The sun, whose sphere of influence has already been simplified into a mere strip of light, has its circumferential movement contracted; the circle it describes becomes smaller and smaller, until it finally 'homes in' on the central point of the lovers in bed:

> Thine age askes ease, and since thy duties bee
> To warme the world, that's done in warming us.
> Shine here to us, and thou art every where;
> This bed thy center is, these walls, thy spheare.

Such a spatial reduction of movement, of course, is tantamount to the arresting of the sun on its diurnal round. As a consequence, historical time comes to a halt, which is the apparent desired effect of the speaker in rehearsing the poem at all. The manipulation of space in this poem's metaphorical terms, like the manipulation of space in that other text, *De Revolutionibus*, effects a kind of temporal revolutionary moment. But while the Copernican text enacts the revolutionary transmutation of 'sacred time', a kind of transcendent negation of temporal process itself, an 'eternity' into secular history, Donne's poem articulates a reactionary change of historical time back into eternity: 'Must to thy motions lovers seasons run?', he asks, and the answer is that they do not run at all, but stand still, and forever, according to the sophistries of the poem.

Crucial to the reading of this poem, there is another kind of metaphorical exchange operating, focused on the *word* 'Sunne' itself. The title of the poem contains a fairly blatant pun. Mahood has indicated that 'the quibble on "sun" and "son" is one of the most characteristic in seventeenth-century religious poetry';[33] and, if 'The Sunne Rising', with its transformation of profane into sacred time can still be called a non-religious poem, then the pun is present in some secular poetry as well. For a contemporary audience in one of the coteries in which Donne's poems circulated, the title might indeed promise a religious poem, written on considering the occasion of the Son's Rising: that is, on the Christian resurrection. The much vaunted stridency of Donne's openings, usually understood as simply illustrative of the presence of a 'real, speaking voice', takes on a new dimension of scandal in this light. To refer immediately to the Son/Sun as a 'busy old fool', or to comment 'Thy beames, so reverend, and strong/Why shouldst thou thinke?', is shockingly irreverent, even heretical.

The poem, in moving between two spaces (room and universe) and two times (eternity and history), moves also between two worlds which meet or cross in the punning word 'Sunne'. The poem exists, as it were, suspended between the two meanings of this pun. It is through the metaphorical punning exchange of these meanings that Donne manages to deal with the problematic fact that, in stabilizing the sun, the poem's argument has relegated the poet to an eccentric peripheral position. For Donne is arguing himself into both the stable centre of the universe (the space of the bed) and also, in so far as he has exchanged positions of earth and sun, into the periphery of the universe. Inasmuch as he occupies the position ascribed to the sun, in the central relation embodied by the two lovers in bed, he is at the centre of the world. But in occupying this heliocentric position, and through the pun on sun/son, Donne manages to provide a theological concept of omnipresence which is in fact instrumental in effecting a suspension of meaning between 'sun' and 'Son of God': 'Shine here to us, and thou art every where'. Donne, then, is now nothing more or less than an incarnation or realization in metaphorical terms of the sun itself; in this Copernican revolution, the sun, embodied in the relation of love as a habitation of the space between two people, stabilizes, and the Earth is 'everywhere' on its peripheral trajectory. Donne too is now, safely, 'everywhere', for this is the position not ascribed so much to the astral sun as to the divine Son.

The poem *is*, then, about a resurrection of sorts. Humorously, it is about Donne's own 'resurrection', for it is he, after all, in the position of the sun/son, who should be rising. In his self-displacement from bed, Donne as the rising sun, there comes a hint of Donne as incarnation of the Son of God, through the metaphorical exchange of the pun; and there is also the idea that he and the lover, in their relation of love, embody or incarnate (which here might mean propagate) the whole world. The space of the world is coterminous with that of the bodies of the lovers: self-propulsion on their part thus becomes the force which motivates or animates, even populates, the entire world. By eccentrically removing himself to the periphery, in accordance with Copernican precept and also with the idea of making himself a being 'everywhere', Donne assumes not simply the position of a primal Adam before the fall into history, but also that of the *primum mobile* in the conventional understanding of the cosmos. Time, history and the secular existence of the entire world are now all contrived to be in the power of Donne, all dependent upon his absolute priority.

The proto-cinematic technique of the opening, in which the reader is propelled inwards, with the sun, towards the focal point of the lovers and from the universe outside as it were, works further to involve the reader in this process. Donne has control not only over the sun and history, but also over the reader in a sense, who is manipulated all the way through the text. The poem as a whole, and as a readerly experience, is located firmly at what might be called a 'revolutionary moment'. This moment here is the moment 'between' sacred and secular history, a moment which can, aptly enough, be articulated in Christian thought in the Christian resurrection, which was a moment of seeming reversal of time and transcendence of historical process through the entry into eternity. In the poem such a moment is seen to be dependent, in earthly terms, upon the organization of space or, bluntly, relation between two lovers, and upon some kind of resurrection in the material body, a resurrection which effects some kind of transformation of that body.

Resurrection is articulated in the poem, then, even if in an apparently perverse way. But in a sense there is a perfectly orthodox theological motif here. The resurrection has the effect of waking the two lovers into a new day, a new birth or new order of existence (and many other poems are set at precisely this same moment: consider 'Breake of Day', 'The good-morrow', 'The Dreame' and so on). In such a revolutionary moment their love relation is seen to comprise an entire world, and their spatial position is firmly at the centre of this brave new world. They are, in their amorous motions, supposed to be an articulation or incorporation (incarnation) of the 'Sunne Rising' or the resurrection of the Son. In orthodox manner they thus incorporate the myth of Christ as their centre. However, there is an important political corollary to this. In so far as the particular relation between the two lovers, explicitly in the private space of a domestic bedroom, becomes a microcosmic organization on which the whole world, and its population, depends, the poem can be seen, in its theological orthodoxy, to be establishing an ethics of privacy and domesticity as its 'normative' basis. A model of the Christian, nuclear familial unit becomes the implicit norm for the historical organization of human relations. The assumption is then that only such an organization can offer sufficient protection against the march of time and the historical progression which brings human death.

There are at least three consequences of what must be seen as a 'recuperation' of the revolutionary threat of the Copernican poem. Firstly, revolution as such has become theologized, as a kind of spiritual reawakening to be found, presumably, in a secularized version of a eucharistic 'communion', in the affective individualism which produces the 'communion' of the amorous 'couple'. Secondly, the revolution is further domesticated; it thus becomes a non-historical event and a privatized, asocial event. What was no less than a kind of 'world-revolution', at least in intellectual terms in Copernicus's writing, has become privatized and removed from the spheres of social history. Thirdly, Donne himself, as poet, assumes a vast authority, in the form of the metaphorical power of self-resurrection. The 'sacred' love at the domestic centre of this new macrocosm is to be realized, as in many other poems, in a carnal manner; that is, it is to constitute a literal incarnation. This kind of resurrection might thus be understood as being the revolutionary moment of the discovery or production of maleness, in having the (male) flesh stand upright. An explicit statement of this is to be found, of course, in 'Elegie XIX: Going to Bed':

> and though
> Ill spirits walk in white, we easly know,
> By this these Angels from an evil sprite,
> Those set our hairs, but these our flesh upright.[34]

This struggle with the passage of history is no mere whimsy or insignificant poetic device, but is rather of crucial importance in an understanding of some of the oddities of the writings of Donne and his contemporaries. The fall into secular time is a fall into differentiation. The world is fractured into a series of discrete entities, dissolved from some supposed transcendent state of primal and eternal unity. With the condition of unity threatened, the conflict of civil war appears as a possibility: difference and dissent become dominant conditions of consciousness. Further, those 'units' with which the human consciousness had organized the world, such as nations, are now also under threat of fragmentation.[35]

As I described it, this means that the human subject, consciousness itself, the first-personal 'I', is now threatened with its own dissolution, in turn, into a series of instantiations of subjectivity. Where before there was a 'self' which, in its transcendence of mere historical accident, formed a nucleus of certainty, guaranteeing the identity (sameness) of all these 'I's, now it becomes the case that there is no such assured certainty of identity. Instead of a self understood as some kind of mystic 'presence', there are only 're-presentations' of this self, which now begins to assume, conceptually, the status of mere construction. This now is the experience of living in time, in secular history; and the struggle against it is an attempt to reconstitute or reconstruct some quasi-eternal or essential transcendent 'presence' or 'self' which will guarantee personal and individual self-unification and identity.

3

Given that this fall into history has made re-presentation the axiomatic condition of an assumed selfhood, it follows that there will emerge a notion of history as pessimistically entropic. Each subsequent representation of 'I' can now be regarded as a kind of fading image of some original transcendent unity; the passage of time, then, is a constant deviation away from this central origin or source, in eternity or sacred time. The construction of the domestic unit, as we have seen it in 'The Sunne Rising', is an example of a poetic manoeuvre which tries to combat such dissolution; the poem strives toward the construction of an individual and unified position for the poet himself, now regarded or represented as the (male) central and dominant figure in the world. But just as the sun winds itself down in ever decreasing circles in that poem, until its sphere is reduced to less than its own volume, so also history and its material artefacts, or even its material makers, the human beings who generate history, are also thought of as being in a state of corruption, dissolution, disease and decay.

In 'An Anatomie of the World: the first Anniversary' Donne relates this directly to the 'new philosophy', and he reiterates the same sentiments as Gloucester in response to the 'trepidation of the spheres' which the new philosophy, and indeed Donne's own poetry, has brought about:

> And new Philosophy calls all in doubt,
> The Element of fire is quite put out;
> The Sun is lost, and th'earth, and no mans wit
> Can well direct him where to looke for it.
> And freely men confesse that this world's spent,
> When in the Planets, and the Firmament
> They seeke so many new; they see that this
> Is crumbled out againe to his Atomies.
> 'Tis all in peeces, all cohaerence gone;
> All just supply, and all Relation:
> Prince, Subject, Father, Sonne, are things forgot,
> For every man alone thinkes he hath got
> To be a Phoenix, and that then can bee
> None of that kinde, of which he is, but hee.[36]

In this brief passage there is a recapitulation of the concerns which are crucial to 'The Sunne Rising', and which dominate much of the poetry not only of Donne but also of his contemporaries. There is the primacy of error, the entropic decay of the world and nature, the fragmentation of a primal transcendent sacred unity into historical serialization, the struggle to establish new formations of human relation, and the phoenix-like reconstruction of the isolated individual as the new basic social unit.

More pertinently here, though, this passage makes it clear that history itself is regarded with suspicion and pessimism, which might be one reason why Donne and others are interested in circumventing it. In effect, however, the presence of the phoenix serves to illustrate that Donne does not manage entirely to transcend the secular age of modern history, but rather simply transforms his understanding of that historical process. In place of a continuous serialization of time, Donne provides an image of history as a discontinuous series of deaths and rebirths, dyings and risings. This history paradoxically turns out to be in some measure composed of the same kind of 'revolutionary moments' (albeit theologized) of resurrection as were found to dominate 'The Sunne Rising'. In order to circumvent the ultimate corruption and decay of the body in history, Donne models temporality on a series of 'feigned deaths', a series of radically discontinuous re-beginnings, re-presentations of the instant of death followed immediately by rising, rebirth. If death can be repeated, as in the mythic mystery of the phoenix, then Donne might appear to be in control of death, rather than at the mercy of its historical necessity. Secular life is accordingly converted metaphorically, in many poems, into a series of deaths and resurrections. The result of this clearly is the production of power, authority and self-determination; quite literally the determining or delimiting of the spatial and temporal boundaries of the reconstituted individual self.

Donne is adept at controlling space and time so as to make his 'present' self into a being everywhere and of every moment: omnipresence from one act of representation. He can make the space between himself and a lover equivalent to the space between two continents; a tear can become an entire ocean, as in 'A Valediction: of weeping'; sixty years becomes a mere second, as in 'The Anniversarie', and so on.[37] This kind of manipulation of space and time is integral to many of Donne's *Songs and Sonets* and permeates the rest of his poetry as a fundamental structural aspect not of imagination as such, but rather of the relation between imagination and incarnation, a relation between *logos* and *ergon*, word and enactment.[38] What is at stake here is often the demonstration of the power of the word, the power of the word to act, understood both rhetorically and theologically. That is to say, of course, that the very activity of writing these texts is for Donne an exploration and establishment of his own individualized 'power of the word' or *authority*. According to Blumenberg, some notion of self-assertion and self-determination is a constituent part of the definition of the modern (post-medieval) consciousness. It is perhaps no great surprise, then, that Donne should hold such a fascination for self-consciously 'modernist' poets like T.S. Eliot at the turn of the twentieth century, for in some respects he offers one of the first models of modern or modernist authority in English.

One understanding of being 'modern' is being 'up to the minute' or, as it were, living not so much for the day as for the morrow. In 'The good-morrow', Donne wrote a poem which demonstrates that,

Displacement and eccentricity 41

no matter what degree of sophistry he uses to circumvent historical process, the writing, articulation or rehearsal of the text itself nonetheless constitutes a historical act and an entry into modern, secular history and temporality. The poem is another of those texts set at a 'revolutionary moment' of awakening, enlightenment or regeneration. But two contradictory impulses seem to be at work in the poem, and it is in the conflict between these that Donne's 'struggle against history' can be most clearly seen. On the one hand there is the moment of novelty or welcomed revolutionary change which the poem seems to celebrate:

> I wonder by my troth, what thou, and I
> Did, till we lov'd? were we not wean'd till then?
> But suck'd on countrey pleasures, childishly?
> Or snorted we in the seaven sleepers den?
> T'was so; But this, all pleasures fancies bee.
> If ever any beauty I did see,
> Which I desir'd, and got, t'was but a dreame of thee.[39]

On the other hand, there lingers a desire for stability. Speaker and addressee might be awakening, in the terms of the metaphor, to a new morning of love, a liberating new relation; but they are also waking to a situation of paralysis, arrest or imprisonment:

> And now good morrow to our waking soules,
> Which watch not one another out of feare;
> For love, all love of other sights controules,
> And makes one little roome, an every where.

In the situation mapped out here, the lovers stare at each other, but become trapped, caught in the power of each other's eyes. They are, as it were, fixed and held fast in this new relation: if one little room is an 'every where', then there is no reason to leave this cramped space. The 'revolutionary' change then is actually one which forestalls the possibility of any further subsequent change; and so there are the two contradictory urges, towards change, and towards stability. As the souls recognize each other, the look becomes one of literal 'apprehension': they 'apprehend' each other both in the sense of coming to understand and recognize their 'true', valid inter-relation, and also in the sense of holding or imprisoning each other. The situation, if you will, is an arrested revolutionary moment. This apprehension comes despite the text's apparent rejection of (moral) apprehension. The line 'Which watch not one another out of feare' is ambiguous. It might mean that the souls do not stare at each other after all, their gaze being promiscuously wandering or erring; alternatively (or simultaneously), it suggests that they *do* watch each other, but not out of feelings of fear and jealousy. This second reading is corroborated by the following lines, which suggest that there is no need to look beyond each other; the space they inhabit is the only reality or world, 'an every where'.

The poem is in some respects an attempt to overcome fear, but its sole manner of doing this is to inscribe 'apprehension' as the mode of relation of these two lovers, in their 'revolutionary' renaissance. They 'grasp' each other, thus preventing further revolutions; the 'revolutionary moment' can merely be reiterated precisely, thus forestalling any more fundamental change or movement towards other partners, other spatial and temporal relations. The two lovers are to wake together every morning, and all 'good morrows' are to be a strict repetition of this one. The lovers are imprisoned, cramped into the tiny space constituted in the crossing of their eyes, that space between them which constitutes their 'dwelling', the little room of their domestic privacy. As in 'The Sunne Rising', this contracted space implodes, like a black hole, bringing within its confines an entire alternative universe from the supposed 'other side' of reality, the non-historical transcendent sphere from the dark side of the moon. The space occupied by the two lovers thus becomes an area defined as the locus of revolution as such. It is in their space, in the fact of their establishment of such conjugal space in the 'crossing' of their eyes or paths, that the implosion/explosion of space occurs. Mobility of space then and this new history to which they give birth in their moment of recognition of each other seem to be dependent upon the anteriority of their establishment of relation and of the spatial configuration produced in their crossing or trafficking with each other.

How to reconcile a revolutionary moment with the paralysis which seems to condition it? One might suggest that in the revolutionary moment the struggle against history has been won, and the lovers have moved from secularity into eternity. But this would be to miss much of the point of the text as text. The suggestion in the poem seems rather to be that the revolutionary moment and its repetition is the determinant and constituent of love. Love thus becomes defined implicitly in terms of a continual renewal of the love-relation, a continual reiteration of the same spatial configuration which engenders the love in the first place: that is, the lovers are always to waken in the same bed, staring at the same eyes, every subsequent morning. The 'covenant' of their relation is to be rehearsed, re-negotiated continually. Continual, but repeated, revolution is the primary factor in this human relation; there is to be a turning to each other endlessly, but always as if for the first time.[40] If this is the case, then the transcendence suggested by the text becomes impossible, for there can be no 'essentializing' of either partner in the relation. Every repeated meeting will be a first, revolutionary one; but the revolution is always therefore incomplete, and a state of transcendence never finally attained.

The poem thus dramatizes the discovery of a world, tantamount to the unveiling or generation of the world. Such a moment is itself a reiteration of the mythic primal moment of creation itself, whether this be understood in terms of the physical 'big bang' or in theological terms as expansions and contractions of God.[41] Their moment of love or recognition repeats this kind of implosive/ explosive contraction/expansion into promiscuity, while at the same time supposedly harnessing all the elements thus disseminated into cosmos from chaos. As in 'The Canonization', they build themselves 'in sonnets pretty roomes'.[42] The argument, though, is inverted. Rather than their activity being a secondary or derivative imitation of the 'real' or 'original' creation of the world, it becomes instead that very originary generator of the world itself. They are a kind of primal Adam and Eve, before the fall, setting about the population or generation of an entire universe. To this extent they are *proles*, themselves their own offspring; for they populate this world with repeated mirror-images of themselves, representations of themselves in their explosive self-expansion:

> Let sea-discoverers to new worlds have gone,
> Let Maps to other, worlds on worlds have showne,
> Let us possesse one world, each hath one, and is one.

> My face in thine eye, thine in mine appeares . . .

The lovers reduce into the space of the glassy eye itself. This is the precise moment or scene of recognition, the moment of opening the eyes. But the problem is that in opening them simultaneously, they see only a reflection of the self, and not another person at all. The Other is entirely reduced and subsumed as a function of the Self's own self-recognition, self-constitution. The Other becomes merely the instrumental mirror which allows the fractured subjectivity of the historical 'I' to cohere into an individuated entity. The Other is so apprehended by the Self here that it has no effective existence at all, except in dependent relation to the Self which the poem strives to generate. This is to say, however, that within the structural frame of this poem there is not a situational relation between two characters at all: in this poem there is but one Self generated.

Further, in accordance with the spatial mutations which the poem typically offers, a synecdoche reduces this Self as its own 'heart'. When they look into the mirror-eye, that primary lens required for the telescopic manipulations of space and time which organize the text, they see that 'true plain hearts doe in the faces rest'. To be more precise, there is not, strictly speaking, even one person here. Like a prefiguration of some Jim Dine paintings, there is the primacy and centrality of the heart, a heart which becomes a metaphor of relation, of a spatial configuration or, in short, a symbolic 'scene of recognition'. But even in such a scene of recognition, the heart/self is actually discovered to be somewhere else, elusive and erring into the eye of another. Such 'promiscuity' or eccentricity, the intermingling which constitutes the moment of recognition, is understood to be the stuff of historical life itself:

> What ever dyes, was not mixt equally;
> If our two loves be one, or, thou and I
> Love so alike, that none doe slacken, none can die.

Change or displacemental promiscuity, then, is the very condition of the eventualities of the revolutionary moment which the poem celebrates. Moreover, this kind of change or revolutionary moment is integral to the reading of the text. The poem is an instance of 'revolution', a moment of 'good-morrowing' or beginning in a new and transmutational way to establish the relations of time and space (here seemingly domestic privacy) which makes up the human social condition. It is, as the title suggests, an address, a 'good-morrow' to the reader, in the attempt to construct the space of the human heart as the scene of a mutual recognition, mutual address. 'Good-morrowing', according to the interpretation of the poem which I am constructing here, is the very foundation or ground of such humanity. This is to say that the secular existence of human consciousness, the waking from a kind of dream, illusion or false consciousness to some alternative, historical reality, is not something which happens once and for all, as it were.

The entry into history, which here is tantamount both to the construction of *proles* and to the entry into social relation and the space of human communication (even of 'communion', as in 'The Sunne Rising'), is to be constantly reiterated or re-enacted. History is not an assimilation of 'facts of the past'; rather history, according to the implications inferred from this text, is always to be made and is the precise arena within which any human action or relation or communication can take place. As such, then, the 'good-morrow' is never completed. Rather, such a bidding or address is, of course, primarily a phatic invitation to the establishment of social relation, an invitation extended to another human in the attempt to make human recognition and to find a ground of human response and socio-historical responsibility. In fact, of course, what this now 'revolutionary' phatic noise demands in conversation is precisely its own repetition; it asks for 'good-morrow' as a mirrored acknowledgement of itself and its speaker. The poem, in this sense, is now clearly merely the first part of a real historical dialogue. Although there are not two persons in the poem in terms of its content, as I explained above, it nonetheless remains structurally 'dialogical'. It constructs the space, or symbolic heart, within which historical humans can come to exist in social relation. And it demands its own repetition in response to itself. This criticism, of course, is but one mode of response. More fundamentally, it requires its own rehearsal or reiteration: it demands to be read, and re-read.

The poem thus radically enters the modern historical sphere of secularity, and Donne loses the struggle against history in a sense. In secularity, to generate social relation and maintain the possibility of human life for the speakers of the text, and perhaps even to maintain the possibility of communication itself, 'The good-morrow' has to be repeated, reproduced and represented: it must itself form its own *proles* or offspring. The space of its reproduction is that between the text and the eye of the reader. 'Good-morrowing' is not only constitutive of the scene of recognition in the spatial organization of secular social humanity; it is also constitutive of the very activities of writing and reading themselves which demand their own self-rehearsal and construct their own *proles*. Literary activity here does not refer us to the realm of eternal verities and values such as some supposed 'transcendental love', but remains rather a firmly historical activity.

The poem thus becomes a manifestation in writing of the revolutionary principles of the post-Copernican philosophy. It eccentrically spins away from itself and reverberates in its relations with the sphere of a reader who is the real historical speaker of the text. This is a demonstration of the fundamental dilemma in the struggle with history. Donne contrives to negate historical progression by fixing both himself and his reader at the same, endlessly repeated instant: in principle, there is no historical movement away from the scene of recognition elaborated here. Speaker and reader seem to be frozen, like stills from the narrative progression of a film. But, at the same time, paradoxically, it is precisely as Donne contrives this manoeuvre that narrative is implied and history admitted. For the repetition of the text can never be entirely faithful; every re-reading of the text deviates in some way from its model. It is the degree of deviation or eccentricity, the displacement of the model in its revisionary repetition, which marks the poem out as historical *event*, rather than mere substantive text. In the displacement resulting from the change of speaker, the change of informational consciousness which invests the text with significance, there is not only an admission of history, but even a shaping of history.

As Blumenberg would corroborate, history knows of no strict repetitions: even the most closely verisimilar restatement of a text works to establish not sameness, but the fundamental series of differences and differentiations which constitute historical event and activity. Donne's struggle to contain history works paradoxically as a means of producing history, allowing us to produce our own difference from the implied speaker of the poem. This instates the historical as fundamental to our own condition; for the speaker of the text is precisely its reader. We are thus establishing displacemental differention and eccentricity, a 'critical difference', as the condition of our existence. A struggle against history, even in writing/reading, becomes simply a struggle with and in history; and, correspondingly, the control of meaning for that history cedes place to the production of its meanings.

As Mehlman argues, there is a close relation between revolution and repetition: repetition, while striving to forestall change, in fact works to establish it.[43] More pertinently here the production of meaning in the activity of re-reading which is axiomatic to poetry like 'The good-morrow' depends on a series of deviations and divergent repetitions of that text. As we rehearse the text, we rehearse it always in the voice of the Other; that is to say, displacement within ourselves as we read or repeat the poem negates the possibility of stabilizing its meaning on a stable 'us', 'I', 'reader', just as much as it denies the possibility of stabilizing meaning on a 'central', 'unified', 'stable' 'consciousness' of an 'individual' called Donne. The text becomes a raw material demanding our repetition for the construction of its historical meaning. Such a repetition is a labour working to transform the text, and to put transformation incontrovertibly at its core. As we rehearse, and now transform, the text, there is a fundamental sense in which we must 'change' it: 'exchange' is the principle controlling the possibility of reading the poem at all.

It is thus no longer a question of what 'Donne' says, nor even strictly of what the text says (both Donne and text are silent); rather it is a question of what we, the *proles* of the text, can say, and how we can construct historical meaning from working upon the raw materials of the text. What we seem firstly to construct is ourselves as historical, differential, 'displaced' entities. Accordingly any meaning we might establish for the test is not dependent upon the stability or centrality of our own consciousness, for it too has been decentred and has a principle of difference, or criticism, as its founding component.[44] Self-criticism, then, is one basic product of this kind of writing/reading; and this might seem appropriate, of course, to a cultural moment which I have characterized as an age of scepticism. Donne, like Montaigne, produced texts which are radically unstable, open to change, critically sceptical: fundamentally, *historical*. It is this intellectual formation which is most productive and appropriate for a consideration of the poetry of Donne. Indeed his entire writings might usefully be considered as a confrontation of a genuinely secular moment with an essentialist, proverbial mythic and religious orthodoxy in thought. As one of the first 'modern' writers, the construction of a historical self becomes crucial to the texts and their interpretation.

48 *John Donne, Undone*

Notes

1 Nicholas Copernicus, *On the Revolutions of the Heavenly Spheres* (trans. A.M. Duncan), Newton Abbot, David and Charles, 1976, 40; cf. 'Letter to Pope Paul III' in this same volume, 25-6, which adds Philolaos as another such authority.

2 ibid., 46.

3 Edmund Spenser, *Faerie Queene*, 1, i, 13; in Spenser, *Poetical Works*, ed. J.C. Smith and E. de Selincourt, Oxford, Oxford University Press, 1912; repr. 1979. In approximately sixty years, then, the beginnings of the impact of the Copernican revolution are being felt; as 'revolutions' go, this one is fairly gradual, but insistent. Cf. Thomas Kuhn, *The Structure of Scientific Revolutions*, Chicago, University of Chicago Press, 1962, 2nd edn enlarged 1970, and his *Copernican Revolution*, Cambridge, Mass., Harvard University Press, 1957.

4 T.S. Eliot, 'Four Quartets' in *Complete Poems and Plays of T.S. Eliot*, London, (Faber and Faber, 1969), 179.

5 Hans Vaihinger, *The Philosophy of 'As If'* (trans. C.K. Ogden), London, Kegan Paul, Trench, Trubner, 1924, *passim*.

6 Andreas Osiander, 'Preface' to Copernicus, op. cit., in Copernicus, ed. cit., 22-3.

7 See Wilbur Samuel Howell, *Logic and Rhetoric in England, 1500-1700*, Princeton, New Jersey, Princeton University Press, 1956.

8 See Jean Starobinski, *Les mots sous les mots*, Paris, Gallimard, 1971, for a rationale of this mode of hermeneutic as construed by Saussure. On the subject of 'many authorities', see Jeffrey Stout, *The Flight from Authority*, Indiana, University of Notre Dame Press, 1981.

9 Frank Kermode, *The Genesis of Secrecy*, Cambridge, Mass., Harvard University Press, 1979, x; it should be pointed out, though, that the primary position accorded to Mark here is being forcefully challenged, as Kermode himself parenthetically admits, ibid., 30.

10 See Hans Blumenberg, *The Legitimacy of the Modern Age* (1966) (trans. Robert M. Wallace), Cambridge, Mass., MIT Press, 1983, *passim*.

11 Spenser, op. cit., 395. Consider, in this regard, the extensive use made in Shakespeare, for instance, of twins, doubles and mistaken identity.

12 See Swift's scatological attacks on Enthusiasm in, e.g., *A Tale of a Tub*, *The Mechanical Operation of the Spirit*, and his concern for excrement and defecation in all of his writings. Cf. Norman O. Brown, *Life Against Death*, Connecticut, Wesleyan University Press, 1959, for a full exploration of this 'excremental vision' in Swift. Among Donne's contemporary writers, Spenser again makes a clear excremental joke in *Faerie Queene*, 2, ix, 32; and Herbert's 'L'Envoy' closes *The Temple* with an explicit allusion to farting, suggesting that the entire book is but breaking of wind.

13 Pope Gregory XIII reformed the Julian calendar in 1582. Sosigenes, who had calculated the calendar's regularities for Julius Caesar, had overestimated the length of the year by about eleven minutes. By the sixteenth century it was substantially out of synchrony. Gregory's intention was to restore the vernal equinox to the date (21 March) it had at the Council of Nicaea (AD 325), and the Copernican model and subsequent researches enabled this.

14 Alexandre Koyré, *La révolution astronomique: Copernic, Kepler, Borelli*, Paris, Hermann, 1961, 15.

Displacement and eccentricity 49

15 ibid.
16 Blumenberg, op. cit., 361. It should, however, be noted that Blumenberg criticizes the concept of 'secularity' (in Part 1 of the book) and 'epochal thought', 478.
17 ibid., 139.
18 ibid., 571.
19 Maurice Blanchot, L'espace littéraire, Paris, nrf, Gallimard, 1955; repr. 1982, 322–3.
20 Blumenberg, op. cit., 596; cf. ch. 7 below.
21 Michel de Montaigne, Essais in 3 vols (1580–95), Paris, Garnier-Flammarion, 1969, vol. 3, 242. The solidus in the text marks the various revisions which Montaigne made to his text in subsequent publications. There is an ambiguity here in the notion that (perhaps theological) 'inquisition' is 'progress' – though a progress towards ignorance.
22 Thomas Carew, 'An Elegie upon the death of Dr John Donne', repr. in Helen Gardner (ed.), The Metaphysical Poets, Harmondsworth, Penguin, 1966, 143. It might, of course, be asked whether this is itself a 'new kind' of poem; if it is a clichéd model of elegiac verse, perhaps Donne's example was not as successful as Carew's poem ostensibly claims.
23 See Norman Mailer, Advertisements for Myself (1961), reprinted London, Panther, 1968. Donne might thus appear to be not so much 'Modern' as 'post-Modern', in the manner of Motherwell, Law and so on. Cf. Leslie Feidler, 'Archetype and signature: a study of the relationship between biography and poetry', Sewanee Review, 60 (1952), 253–73; Jacques Derrida, 'Signature event context' in Margins of Philosophy (trans. Alan Bass), Brighton, Harvester Press, 1982.
24 See Kenneth Burke, Philosophy of Literary Form, Berkeley and Los Angeles, University of California Press (1941), third edn, revised, 1967, 51ff.
25 David Tracy, 'Metaphor and religion: the test case of Christian texts', in Sheldon Sacks (ed.), On Metaphor, Chicago, University of Chicago Press, 1979, 90.
26 ibid., 103.
27 Jean Ricardou, Nouveaux problèmes du roman, Paris, Seuil, 1978, 106.
28 Donne, 11.
29 See, e.g., Mircéa Eliade, Le mythe de l'éternal retour, Paris, nrf, 4th edn, 1949, passim. Cf. chapter 7 below on 'returning' and repetition.
30 See Harold Bloom, Anxiety of Influence, Oxford, Oxford University Press, 1973, 94: 'The meaning of a poem can only be another poem'; and cf. all of Bloom's writings on poetry and revisionism.
31 Dorothy Stimson, The Gradual Acceptance of the Copernican Theory of the Universe, New York, Baker and Taylor, 1917, 28.
32 William Shakespeare, King Lear, 1, ii.
33 M.M. Mahood, Poetry and Humanism, London, Jonathan Cape, 1950, 26.
34 Donne, 107.
35 See, e.g., David Trotter, The Poetry of Abraham Cowley, London, Macmillan, 1979, 8.
36 Donne, 213–14.
37 Donne, 23.
38 See Hans-Georg Gadamer, Dialogue and Dialectic (trans. P. Christopher Smith), New Haven, Conn., Yale University Press, 1980, ch. 1. Cf. Kenneth Burke, passim on the theorization of the 'dramatistic'.

39 Donne, 7.
40 For more contemporary mediations of this, see, e.g., Eliot, 'Four Quartets', and John Berger, *G.*, London, Weidenfeld & Nicolson, 1972.
41 See Blumenberg, op. cit., Part 4.
42 Donne, 15.
43 See Jeffrey Mehlman, *Revolution and Repetition*, Berkeley and Los Angeles, University of California Press, 1977, for a theoretical sophistication of this point; and cf. chapter 7 below.
44 Cf. Barbara Johnson, *The Critical Difference*, Baltimore, Johns Hopkins University Press, 1980, ix and *passim*.

2

The problem of women: authority, power, communication

We were woken by someone knocking on the door, then half opening it. Sunlight slashed through. He withdrew when he saw we were still in the bunks. . . . I pushed up, but she held me by the shoulders, so that I had to stare down at her. I sustained her look, its honesty, for a moment, then I turned and sat with my back to her.

'What's wrong?'

'Nothing. I just wondered what malicious god made a nice kid like you see anything in a shit like me.'

'That reminds me. A crossword clue. I saw it months ago. Ready?' I nodded. '"She's all mixed up, but the better part of Nicholas" . . . six letters.'

(John Fowles, *The Magus*)

England . . .
From out her pregnant entrails sighed a wind
. . .
Sooner than you read this line, did the gale
Like shot, not feared till felt, our sails assail;
And what at first was called a gust, the same
Hath now a storm's, anon a tempest's name.

(John Donne, 'The Storm')

1

Donne's basic impulse in his various manipulations of space and time is to merge the secular word of his own writing with the incantatory Word of sacred Scripture. A transhistorical authority, the very possibility of writing (as opposed to speaking) at all, is linked in this with the search for secular power and control over the fundamental elements of human existence: space and time. But this space and this time are, historically and geographically, inhabited. Donne, then, actually has to work to assert some mode of authority both in and over his circumambient environment, the Other of his imagination. This Other is most frequently characterized as Woman.

Woman, as an 'other space' or 'elsewhere', as it were, presents Donne with some outstanding problems. His own authority as an identifiable individual is threatened by the possibility of a promiscuous displacement of his writings in the process of their rehearsal or reading/interpretation. Just as woman is, in the poetry and its ideology, archetypally 'adulterous', there is the fear, it would seem, that communication as such is potentially adulterous; and what is adulterated most is Donne's own imagination or intentional consciousness: his determination of meaning or, more fundamentally, his construction of meaning for himself in relation to the Other environment.

Fixity of meaning and 'successful' communication become translated in the poetry into the terms of fixing or stabilizing the woman, imagined as the locus of promiscuity and uncertainty. It is as if the Other was no more or less than an empty space, a container of sorts, into which Donne pours his 'influence', his words which are supposed to shape the Other in an imagined repetition of his own image. This extremely crude model of communication, thoroughly discredited in fact though still maintained as valid by much criticism, gives Donne a convenient analogy or metaphor. 'Embracing' the woman becomes tantamount to 'encompassing' or shaping, describing and 'informing' a circumscribed meaning. The manoeuvre, such as I explain it here, is fundamentally 'colonialist'. That is to say, faced with the threat of dissolution or even attack at the hands of the (ideologically imagined) woman, locus of promiscuity, Donne does not retreat; rather he embraces the threat (the woman) and moreover assimilates or appropriates it as his own. The Other, as threat, is domesticated and converted into an aspect of the Self and thus rendered harmless, 'colonized' or appropriated and controlled. In the present chapter I shall relate the control of space and time to this important question of 'the problem of woman' for Donne.

2

'The Flea' is a poem which demands attention in this context. After 1590 the flea and the microscopic world it inhabited, its own proper space, as it were, became more open to human visual perception. Not only could people feel the presence of the flea in their space; now they also began to have visual access to the tiny world it inhabited and could scratch out an ode or two on it. Donne would have been interested in the visual capabilities, or 'visions', of Galileo and a number of Dutchmen. The telescope, which had been in existence at least since 1590 and which had been on the open market as a 'toy' since 1604 in Middelburg, Holland, was a vital instrument in the imaginative perversity of Donne. Distant places could be brought from their location elsewhere, in the realm of the Other, towards a position in the universe within our grasp, the universe of the Self. Alien objects could be domesticated and made to reflect or construct a Self. More pertinently for present purposes, the use of the telescope relativized the phenomena of space, distance and differentiation, awaiting Einstein's much later articulation of this in the principle of relativity. The practical use of the telescope also led to the replacement of the eye for the hand, ocular for tactile verification of the facts of material existence (hence the cogency of Othello's demand for 'ocular proof' of Desdemona's infidelity).[1] This is important both for art and for science. In scientific terms the possibility of a rationalizing theory, albeit still dependent on empirical ocular verification, becomes available. For the arts the notion of mimesis as supposedly precise attempts to recreate the real with a kind of *trompe-l'oeil* art-form becomes genuinely artistic (on the assumption that there can be no *trompe-l'oeil*; the eye is not deceived) and genuinely conventionalized. Eventually seeing was believing; and, as in 'The Good-morrow', looking was apprehending.

Telescopic vision plays an important part in the organization of 'The Flea'. As in poems discussed earlier, there is a principle of mutability and transubstantiality of spatial and temporal relations at work in this text. The flea begins as a small insect:

> Marke but this flea, and marke in this,
> How little that which thou deny'st me is ...[2]

But as it sucks on speaker and lover in the poem, it changes in size and stature, assuming a posture strikingly analogous to the tumescent penis of the speaker, and swelling in response to this sucking with an influx of blood:

> And pamper'd swells with one blood made of two,
> And this, alas, is more then wee would doe.

Just as the telescope had enabled a shift from the primacy of the tactile to that of the visual, so also the coming of print to England had marked another shift, this time from the aural to the visual. It is worth noting at this point that in Donne's contemporary script and in early printed editions of the poems the letter 's' often took the form of the 'long s', making it look very like an 'f'. In the lines just quoted, the notion of the flea 'sucking' the lovers opens the poem, thanks to the primacy of the visual orientation to the print, to an immediately titillating ambiguity.[3] This indeed may even be responsible for alerting a reader to the seemingly odd analogue of flea as phallus, swelling into erection with blood.

In any case the flea, as penis or not, changes shape once more, swelling to include not two, but rather three lives: 'Oh stay, three lives in one flea spare'. In this there is a more or less explicit theological reverberation: 'three lives in one' is a clear reference to the notion of the Trinity. But this contributes to a positive explosion of space here, for the flea, as an analogue of the theological Trinity, has now metaphorically expanded to accommodate the entire created universe (this being the 'proper' space of God). But then a contrary movement happens, and the flea beomes a mite smaller again, reduced to the space of 'you and I'. This, however, is far from the end of these mutations. Telescopic variations then render this space into that of a bed, followed by expansion into marriage temple; but this 'temple' might itself be a euphemism for the vagina and thus a contraction working to complement or 'consummate' the heterosexual relation in the poem. Then the space becomes that of the ambiguous nunnery or monastery, 'nunnery' here, as in *Hamlet*, connoting both religious house and brothel:

> Oh stay, three lives in one flea spare,
> Where wee almost, yea more then maryed are,
> This flea is you and I, and this
> Our mariage bed, and mariage temple is;
> Though parents grudge, and you, w'are met,
> And cloysterd in these living walls of Jet.[4]

This final notion of the flea, as 'living walls of Jet', not only makes the space of the flea an extremely ambivalent area, but also suggests an image of the insect itself varying in size as a condition of its continued existence: the process of breathing in and out, 'living', renders the size and space occupied by the flea indeterminate. Further, in line with the earlier analogue of flea and phallus, the image becomes one suggestive of a repeated swelling and detumescence of the phallus, itself pulsing with the same blood as that which inhabits the flea.

There is in this progression, then, a self-repetitive and self-reflexive motion, contractions followed by expansions and vice versa. Such a movement, of course, with exactly the same resultant perspectival effects, is precisely the kind of movement offered by the use of the telescope. The first telescopes were simply a tube with two different lenses or eyes at each end. But, as we might expect, these were of limited use, especially with regard to focusing on objects situated at varying distances from the perceiver. It did not take long, however, for the necessary developments to be effected in the perfection of the machine, and Galileo rapidly excelled in the production of the new instrument. Instead of making a whole series of tubes of varying lengths, and making the lenses detachable, Galileo came up with the idea of constructing a telescope made from two interlocking tubes. Moving one tube back and forth within the other then made it possible to focus on a wider range of distant objects. In a letter to Antonio de' Medici of 7 January 1610, he wrote:

> It would be well if the tube could be capable of being elongated or shortened a little (about three or four inches), because I have found that in order to see objects close by distinctly, the tube must be longer, and for distant objects shorter.[5]

The motion back and forth of one tube within another, as a basic form of the telescopic instrument, was rapidly brought into use. It is precisely such a motion which underlies the varying perspectives in 'The Flea'. The world gets bigger as the tube moves one way, and smaller as it retracts: 'apprehension', or control, of the circumambient universe is to be attained from the simple use of the telescope; distant worlds can be brought into creation or can be generated; small worlds, like that of the flea, can be enlarged to constitute a whole cosmos.

It is indeed likely that Donne, with his interest in all matters scientific, would have been aware of the telescope. In fact, it is worthwhile to suggest an image of him here, 'toying' with this instrument which was still considered a plaything despite its pretensions as a serious instrument of knowledge. Such toying might allow the discovery of the sexually suggestive motions of the telescope, reminiscent of the sexual activity which 'The Flea' seems to require. The telescope becomes, for this cast of imagination, an analogue explaining notions of phallic potency. It is through the telescope/phallus that the world can be controlled and known. The analogue provides Donne with an important ideological aspect of imagination: knowledge of the Other is dependent upon scopophiliac and phallic control over the Other. In the case of 'The Flea', what is at issue is the fact of male control of the female, through the telescopic manoeuvres of the phallus in sexual relation.

Moreover, the movement of the telescope, which is what the very motions in the poem enact (the tube moving in and out enables the varied perspectives on flea and world), becomes thereby a kind of prediction of the kind of movement which the phallus strains to attain in the text. In a certain sense then the poem succeeds in hallucinating, if not fully enacting, the desired end of (primarily male) sexual stimulation and movement. A kind of 'prevention' in the Herbertian sense occurs: in asking for the sexual movement, the very elaboration of the 'question' constitutes the fulfilment of its response: in asking for sex, the poet discovers that he has already performed sexually.

'Oh stay' in this context takes on a different sense, as a kind of (verbal) ejaculation which prefigures, but temporarily arrests, seminal ejaculation, retaining a kind of male control in the form of phallic priority and potency. In so far as the poem asks for the kind of movement which its very articulation already brings about, this phallic potency is translated into the terms of male powers of prediction. Knowledge thus becomes mediated as a mode of predictability dependent upon the supposed primacy of the phallus itself, the instrument which telescopically controls its Other, the female 'outer space' of the environment.

Three vital points are to be noted here. Firstly, the telescope offers some kind of increased knowledge of space. Secondly, it works to control space by extending itself into the environment in a sense, and this allows an analogous relation to be established between telescope and phallus. Thirdly, it is instrumental in the acquisition of powers of prediction, authority. The single common element in all these is the relation between knowledge and a certain kind of power. The telescope offers increased knowledge of the environment, and this knowledge in turn offers the possibility of control or power over the environment: the world can be 'apprehended', grasped or contained, at least mentally, psychologically or metaphorically, in language. This increased knowledge depends upon the scientific facts about the telescope; that is, the fact that it allows the extension of the human into the environment. That extension into space is not simply coterminous with the length of the telescopic tube, of course; in fact, it is greatly in excess of the physical length of the machine itself. With the telescope, the viewer, the eye, can be 'here' and yet also, at some imaginative level, can be some distance away from 'here', in the other spaces of the world. Here the analogy of telescope and phallus, vital to Donne, is of crucial importance. For in so far as the telescope is a phallus of sorts, the increased knowledge and control of the world which it offers can be thought of as being dependent upon the primacy of the phallus. It is as if knowledge of the other spaces of the world were dependent on the fact that the phallus can make the human male into a being both here and also everywhere else, 'disseminated' into space and omnipresence.

Two things follow: firstly, the Other is characterized here as always female or at least 'non-male', and this implies a definition of the self or humanity *as* male; secondly, clearly, the kind of 'knowledge' of the Other engendered here is specifically male-oriented, productive of male, or masculinist, power and ideology. This works to suggest that the human self is primarily male, and that anything which does not cohere with this male-oriented notion of selfhood is a 'deviation', an Other or imaginary state against which the self can always define itself, as male or phallic. Clearly, then, this 'knowledge' which neutral science has produced through the telescope is not at all 'neutral', but ideologically loaded in favour of masculinism.

It is not a great logical leap from this to the third point noted above. Since this 'knowledge' is dependent upon the fact and supposed priority of the phallus as a determinant of the human, prediction and knowledge (or control of the future) are also seen to be dependent upon men, not women. Here historical activity becomes the realm of men, and women in this elaboration of science are debarred from historical agency. Having established that knowledge is dependent upon the priority of the phallus in its control or (perhaps carnal) knowledge of the Other or environment, it is clearly easy to predict or control future history in at least one area of human gender-relations: the future will be as men know it, not as women might want it in sexual or, more generally, gender-relations. The knowledge which is produced through this science, at least in its use in a poem such as 'The Flea', is in accordance with a masculinist epistemology and ideology.

There is another more trenchant aspect to this notion of predictability, which clarifies further the relation between (supposedly neutral and scientific) knowledge and power. As I suggested, astronomical knowledge in the late sixteenth century was confused with astrological portentousness. The acquisition of knowledge about the regularities of celestial movements allowed the astronomer to predict, with some certainty, future states of affairs (in the skies if not on the earth). Predictability in this manner becomes a manipulation of time itself. Future eventualities become dependent, in some sense, upon the anterior prediction of the knowledgeable, and thus seemingly authoritative, astronomer or scientist.

This relates to the question of authority as such,[6] which was understood in at least two ways in this late-Renaissance moment. On the one hand, authority can be an anterior body of statements or propositions to which present activity must conform: obedience to 'the authorities' and acknowledgement of the authority of others, predecessors, is fundamental to this notion. 'The authorities' (or authority itself) are understood as unchangeable monument, as it were: authority is the 'facts' which simply condition the way things are (and here it comes close to being conflated ideologically with the state of an essentialist 'nature'). On the other hand, however, authority can also suggest the assumption or inauguration of some supposedly more spontaneous agency, which may even be in discord with the power of the monumental 'authorities'. Here there is often a reaction against anterior authority, an attempt to differentiate a present autonomy from tradition.

The first conception of authority here is tied up with notions of *potestas*, a kind of absolutizing power (and 'nature', of course, is one such ideological formation of this power). The latter notion of authority pertains more to *auctoritas*, which might conform to a prior authority, but only to the extent necessary for the wilful formulation of a new and different historical authority. One such mode of *auctoritas* might be found in the historical construction of a personal identity, different from the mass of nature, through the activity of writing. In terms of writing, *auctoritas* might be aligned with the secular word; and *potestas* is the realm of the sacred Word of theology. Donne, in 'The Flea' and elsewhere, works to conflate these two, to make word approximate to Word. He strives to make his own authority as powerful, absolutizing, anterior, original or primary as that of the divine Word of the creating God. Here we can see the phallogocentrism, as Derrida might call it, of Donne's writing. The authority of this writer becomes dependent upon the centrality of the Logos as understood in theology (the Word that is God) and also upon the *potestas* or potency which is supposedly vested in the erect phallus, as instrument of generation. Clearly the kind of 'knowledge' which is in question here is based upon male power and works to maintain that male power, at least in gender relations, as a historical norm, 'natural'.

Donne's self-satisfying predictions in 'The Flea', for example, contrive to translate his own weak *auctoritas* into the status of the all-powerful Logos, the self-creating, self-enacting, self-fulfilling Word. Prediction is tantamount to the generation of factuality in this poem: *auctoritas* becomes *potestas* and creates, through language, a historical state of affairs predicted by that language. Similarly, in 'The Sunne Rising', a shift of position, from 'Donne' through 'sun' to Son', with a corresponding increase in power and (carnal) knowledge, was effected. In manoeuvres such as these, Donne contrives to make himself a kind of repeated representation or literal incarnation of the Word; there is a theologization of his own position, as he conflates his own historical and material existence with that of God, in the figure of the Word incarnate. The local, historical word is supposed thereby to become equivalent to the transcendent Word; and so, through the ideological construction of knowledge, Donne seems to seek a measure of metaphysical *potestas* allowing him the fullest control of history and of secular temporality. It begins to appear as if the revolutionary moments of transference from the realm of *auctoritas* to that of *potestas* depend upon the whimsical, but phallic, will of Donne, a Nietzschean will-to-power long before the phenomenon was articulated: Donne, then, poses as surrogate theistic source of history, Donne-as-Word.

This will-to-historical-power, if I may adapt the Nietzschean phrase, may indeed be apparent in Donne and may be what is usually mediated as 'ambition'. But, as the 'struggle with history' shows, such power is not to be attained once and for all. Here we might suggest that, thanks to the discontinuity which disrupts historical progression, Donne has forever to repeat his transfer from secular to sacred logocentric authority. The power, then, is dependent upon a series of differential formulations or definitions of the Word, differential articulations of the source of power. That is, Donne has constantly to renew his difference; he has, as it were, constantly to re-produce his phallus as the condition of his ideological power.

But this, of course, works in fact fundamentally to *question* the very notion of a transcendent authority or *potestas* which the strategy in the texts is supposed to effect. Paradoxically, as the poems 'differ' from themselves as an aspect of their structural organization, it turns out that the more Donne writes in this 'ambitious' manner, trying to transform local historical words into theological Word, the more he actually destroys his own acquisition of such a Word. Correspondingly he becomes less authoritative, in the sense that the more he strives to attain *potestas*, the more he reveals the emptiness of his own *auctoritas*. The identity of the writer, usually understood in terms of the unity of an intentional consciousness, is vitiated in these ambitious writings, for it turns out to be always displaced, eccentric to itself: that is, *it is never there.*

Thus the writings work to cast doubt on any notion of Donne's own authority over the texts and their meaning; for there is no identifiable 'Donne', no identifiable or self-identical source or authority determining the meaning of any text. The more Donne writes, the more he has to write, like a Shandean character caught in the double-bind of his own paradoxical situation, struggling to get the author born. The result of all this is to invalidate 'humanist' criticism of Donne, at least in so far as that mode of criticism ascribes identity, authority and meaning to an informational consciousness identified as the individual, 'Donne'. In a sense there is no such thing, for Donne is that which always differs from itself, the text always spinning eccentrically away from any authority. As Rimbaud was later to suggest, 'je EST un autre'; Donne is that which is always the Other (to) himself.

Displacement in the post-Copernican universe, I argued, implies secular temporality as its corollary; similarly this temporality itself implies change. For Donne, in some writings, this notion of change is axiomatic: there is no overlap between distinct elements, especially in the changing historical human self:

> Now thou hast lov'd me one whole day,
> To morrow when thou leav'st, what wilt thou say?
> Wilt thou then Antedate some new made vow?
>   Or say that now
> We are not just those persons, which we were?[7]

These lines, from 'Womans constancy', help indicate Donne's alignment of this changeability or promiscuity with what is characterized as the female Other. Change is not only the founding condition of the struggle for authority and power against the vagaries of history; it is also the ground of poetic writing, poetic authority and its maintenance. The source of such authority, if we carry the analogy between promiscuity and woman to its logical conclusion, turns out to be characterized as female. The Other, woman, becomes the condition of Donne's literary self, those instances of self-authorization through writing. Alongside the ideological contempt for the female there runs what is perhaps the real rationale for such a suppression of this Other: not only a fear of historical death, but a fear of woman, and a tacit acknowledgement that the female is the source of whatever authority Donne appropriates in his poetic attempts at self-construction and at transcending his historical situation in writing. One strategy in dealing with this threat from the female Other is the apprehension or appropriation of the 'female landscape', most immediately, of course, in the phallic apprehension of the female body.

3

In Donne's 'libertine' poetry, women are most frequently described in terms of infidelity and inconstancy. Since I have described such inconstancy as a fundamental component of Donne's 'revolutionary' self-displacing writing, it is not surprising that Donne, *as a writer* or *in the act of writing/reading,* is interested in woman. Woman becomes the very founding condition of whatever (provisional) selfhood or identity Donne can engender for himself. However, criticism has not usually considered Donne's attitude to woman in this kind of light. Most (male) critics seem to have condoned an image of Donne as rakish young cad, an image enjoyable to those who enjoy the flattery of the young 'man of the world'. Thus A.J. Smith, for instance, can remark that poems like 'The Curse', 'The Indifferent', 'Loves Usury', 'The Apparition', 'Loves Diet' and so on strike a cavalier pose of the young man's world 'in which women are mere objects, to be tried, enjoyed, and lightheartedly discarded' – 'by whom?' we might ask. Further, 'the worst indignity it offers is that which diminishes a man's self-sufficiency by reducing him to a humiliating slavery and so sapping his independence'[8] – again, the worst indignity to whom? This, fairly typical, example of the way criticism has dealt with Donne's attitude to women, while thinking that it is merely corroborating the ignorance of woman in the texts, in fact is producing that ignorance for the first time, constructing it. For Donne's text resolutely refuses to ignore woman. This sexist approach to the poetry is in some degree anti-critical, even anti-intellectual, for it refuses to discover anything which is genuinely troublesome or problematic for the masculinist ideology within which it is written. The supposedly 'enjoyable' image of Donne-as-rake requires a more serious critical understanding.

Displacement is important in this respect. Woman, in at least one poem, is mediated explicitly as that Other space which is defined as the very locus of displacement. 'The Anagram' makes of the female body a kind of nature's jigsaw or crossword puzzle (another 'crossing', 'trafficking' or market-place), demanding completion, solution or fixity at the hands or mind of the controlling intelligence of the proprietorial male. This is vitally important to a critical knowledge of how women were understood or mediated by Donne and his society. Feared, as their Other, by the men who were in power, ideologically and factually, women are accorded only the status of 'object' of study and thought; this demonstrates that the real source of this male fear is a worry about the subjectivity of the female, as a consciousness or mode of desire or will which could challenge male authority and domination or masculinist epistemology and ideology. Women, feared as incomprehensible subject in nature, are accorded only the status of object in the 'nature' or ideology constructed by masculinism.

In a slightly different, though relevant, context Turner writes:

'Land' and 'place' are equivalent to 'propriety' – meaning in seventeenth-century English both *property* and *knowing one's place*. The order of the universe, like the structure of society, was supposed to depend on a hierarchy of places from lowest to highest. Place is identity. Things out of place are not properly themselves, and move as living forces towards their natural home.[9]

The woman 'described' in 'The Anagram' is, potentially at least, a microcosmic version of a revolutionary land, a society where interchange of social place is the norm. The woman here is a demonstration or articulation of what would have been seen as a disturbing revolutionary model of a different kind of society, which can then be mediated as an 'unnatural' society in order to protect the interests of the dominant ideology in society as it stands. Such a revolutionary society would be understood as one whose consti-tuents did not 'know their place'. Ambiguity and 'impropriety' thus surround this description and in fact constitute part of the point of the poetic exercise.

It is impossible to say who the woman 'is'; she has no stable identity, no recognizable face or body and can thus go 'unrecognized' or unnoticed. But the poem remains fixated upon this mobile image of the woman and strives to contain, rather than ignore, her. With displacement as her element, she is never 'properly' herself, or even any self. She thus becomes a kind of embodiment of the human condition post-Copernicus, forever searching after centralized, stable identity. The human looks to arrange the displaced letters of her or his constitution into a 'proper' name, a recognizable identity.

On the one hand, this might produce a poetry of 'nostalgia' (*movement homewards*); this would be a mode of writing running counter to Blanchot's notion that all poetry is conditioned by exile. On the other hand, such fracturing of identity might be understood as a 'liberationist' state of affairs, granting the human a suppositious freedom to behave forever eccentrically, without adherence to any kind of stable identity-model, imposed either by individual psyche or by cultural and ideological norms of a society. The poetry produced in these conditions might synthesize both these contra-dictory impulses: desiring the discovery of a stable identity, a house for the poet so to speak, there might still be a recognition of the fact that the human condition remains one of 'exile' from such a home. The poetry resulting from this conjunction of a nostalgic frame of mind with an acceptance of loss and displacement as basic to human consciousness, striving for stability and finality but never attaining it, would be one in which criticism was integral, scepticism was basic, and the notion of self-modifying structural change as a condition of the text's existence *qua* writing would be partly a description of poetry itself.

But women, idealized as an image of this condition of displacement, are put in an odd position. Firstly, their supposed 'inconstancy' makes them elusive; and yet stimulates the desire for their appropriation, as, for example, 'The Anagram' strives perhaps to identify its object firmly. Secondly, what is then desired in this object-woman becomes itself difficult to define, an obscure object of desire: inconstancy and betrayal are welcomed as a potentially liberating image of the state of reality for human consciousness. Donne pursues the elusive woman; but this object of desire, by definition, is itself always changing. This in fact problematizes desire as such. Donne literally does not know (at one level 'ignores') the Other or object of his desire. It is desire in the abstract, without stable object, which is enacted in these texts. The notion of Donne assuredly running after clearly identified object-women and then actually discovering or knowing the women (carnally or otherwise) before himself moving on and discarding the women is not at all borne out by the texts. Exemplification should clarify this.

'The Anagram', which renders the woman as pure text, a 'literal' woman, shifts anagrammatically its own ground. The first twenty-eight lines of the poem work in a fairly conventional mode: the poem which 'perversely' or ironically praises some kind of extreme ugliness or nastiness, as in the light-hearted manner of Tasso, say. However, this 'anagrammatic' woman is suddenly fixed as a different kind of identity in the latter stages of the poem, from around line thirty-four to the end. For example, there is a strange discrepancy between the early comment to 'Give her thine, and she hath a maydenhead' on the one hand, and the lines towards the close of the poem suggesting that even inanimate objects would shy away from genital contact with her:

> Who, though seaven yeares, she in the Stews had laid,
> A Nunnery durst receive, and thinke a maid,
> And though in childbeds labour she did lie,

> Midwifes would sweare, 'twere but a tympanie,
> Whom, if shee accuse her selfe, I credit lesse
> Then witches, which impossibles confesse,
> Whom Dildoes, Bedstaves, and her Velvet Glasse
> Would be as loath to touch as Joseph was . . .[10]

Clearly, by this point in the text, the object of the poem, the woman, has changed: 'now/We are not just those persons, which we were', to recall the lines from 'Womans constancy'. The first part of the poem jocularly makes a perverse case for the social and personal advantages of Flavia and her 'disfigurements'; but the woman in the latter part of the poem does not even seem to be the same person. This, of course, is precisely the point: 'Flavia' is simply one of many possible anagrammatic configurations of the woman's body. This woman, and woman in general, becomes stripped of stable identity, anonymous in fact, in the elaboration of the text.

The moment at which anagrammatic rearrangement is effected here is interesting. Space becomes mobile and elements shift their ground or change places in these lines:

> Love built on beauty, soone as beauty, dies,
> Chuse this face, chang'd by no deformities.
> Women are all like Angels; the faire be
> Like those which fell to worse; but such as shee,
> Like to good Angels, nothing can impaire:
> 'Tis less griefe to be foule, then to'have beene faire.
> For one nights revels, silke and gold we chuse,
> But, in long journeyes, cloth, and leather use.

The most fundamental moment of change here comes in the comparison of women and angels. The 'obvious' suggestion, perhaps, is that fair women *will fall* to worse, like falling angels; but the lines suggest something different. In fact, they suggest a reversal of 'faire' and 'worse': for the fair women are like those which *fell* (past tense) to worse: that is to say, what we call fair is already foul and foul is fair. 'So fair and foul a woman-witch Donne has not seen' is the tenet of the text here. But most importantly, the normal opposition of fair and foul is disturbed.

There is a comparison between temporal beauty, which will fade entropically, and a 'healthy' face, by implication, one 'chang'd by no deformities'. This clearly is an odd thing to suggest about the face of the woman previously described in the text, Flavia's disfigured, 'anagrammatic' face. It is as if the poem is suggesting that the fortuitous falling of the elements in the face (this 'happy fall' of the angelic into materiality), into a figure or figuration which we conventionally identify as 'beauty', is not *essentially* beauty at all; rather it is simply one possible formative arrangement, or figure, of a kind of elemental 'ur-face', so to speak, the formal idea of a face itself. It is a figure of a figure then, with nothing essential, natural or real about it. Further, in so far as it is just one such fortuitous fall or figuring, it is already 'fallen', foul as the fallen angel. Such an arrangement of the face then, any material realization of the face or figure into what is conventionally termed essentially beautiful (large dark eyes, small mouth, white teeth and so on), is already one 'deformity', one 'disfiguration' of the pristine ur-face itself.

There is an element of neo-Platonism here, with these formal Ideas of a face and its poor material representations, or actual historical faces of real people. In using this, the text begins to establish a differentiation between objects and how they appear, faces and figures, or figures and disfigurations. That is, it drives a wedge between the object and the sign which represents it materially. The object here is the Idea of a face; but this is inevitably, in this neo-Platonic situation, disfigured or misrepresented by any single material or historical face. There is the beginning, then, of an attack on what might be called the 'tyranny of nature'. The ideology, enforced by a notion that the present state of historical affairs is unchangeable because it is essential or 'natural', comes under attack; things are no longer necessarily as they seem. This is to say, of course, that 'nature' is not an actual material or historical state of affairs to which we must conform; rather 'nature' is now an area of contention, to be created, historically, through human intervention and action. The realm of these formal Ideas is inaccessible; we have, after all, 'fallen into history', where mutability and change is normative. As such, the notion of a transcendent, eternally fixed state of nature (the most fundamental bolster of all ideologies) comes under attack. The essentialism of nature cedes place, in this stirring of the modern age, to the existentialism of historical activity.[11]

There is a second aspect to this, of relevance to the workings of language. Corresponding to this move from essentialism to existentialism, from nature to history, there is a linguistic shift.

The 'natural' state would be one in which the face is a *self-evident* sign of beauty: the 'sign' of the face reveals *in itself* the essence of the object to which it refers or which it is ('beautiful face' equals 'beautiful woman', for example). The linguistic sign or counter maps precisely on to its objective referent. But it is precisely this which 'The Anagram' and anagrammaticality in language challenge. For in the poem, and specifically in the lines cited, the sign of the face has become extremely unstable, and the object to which it refers, the woman, has in a sense disappeared; or rather there is no single identifiable referent here. 'Fair' is or means 'foul' and vice versa. The struggle with history is coterminous here with a struggle for authority in language, itself a struggle for the construction of historical meaning.

Given that the 'beautiful' face is but one 'falling' of the formal elements of the face in a certain anagrammatized order, 'beauty' itself becomes as much of a 'deformation' or disfigurement as 'ugliness'. It is not, in the poem, so much that an 'ugly' face is a deformation or displacement of some logically anterior 'proper' arrangement of the face; rather that there is no such 'proper' arrangement. There is no figure, only disfiguration. The loss of the idea of 'property' here, closely linked to that of 'propriety' as Turner indicates, is located in the now mobile and radically ambiguous sign or symbol of the woman. That is, woman as such becomes understood here as the very locus of a revolutionary displacement which threatens the notion of individuated 'property' and, more specifically, the property of those identified as singular, recognizable men with their 'proper' names.

This should go some way towards construing an interpretation of the first part of the poem, with its suggestions that the mobility of Flavia's face and identity is a source of verbal and musical profusion:

> If we might put the letters but one way,
> In the leane dearth of words, what could wee say?
> When by the Gamut some Musitions make
> A perfect song, others will undertake,
> By the same Gamut chang'd, to equall it.

The displacement which is the only formal constituent of Flavia's face and identity thus becomes the source of words and music; in short, it is the source of the language of poetry itself. Poetry is founded here, if on any ground at all, on a specifically 'feminine' principle of mutability and displacemental eccentricity. That is to say, it is formulated on a ground, or earthquake, of the indeterminacy of meaning, the inaccessibility of nature and essential truth; and, perhaps more immediately, on the impossibility of identifying a speaker with a supposed intention which her or his words perfectly match or imitate. It is founded not on such an 'origin', but precisely on the loss of origins.

On one level, what is being lamented in the poem is the decay of nature, this loss of access to 'essence' or reality as some transcendent and knowable or recognizable state of affairs. Donne means it, it seems, in writing that ' 'Tis less griefe to be foule, then to' have beene faire', lamenting the decay which temporality, history, enjoins. It is as if the essentiality, the *being* something, is better than existentiality, the temporal change of *becoming*. And yet, according to the interpretation which I am constructing here, Donne cannot simply mean it at all. For the poem is at pains to demonstrate, among other things, that a state of being is itself but one form of becoming. Anything we choose to call a stable essence is always already on its way to becoming something else: essentiality is itself 'magnificent with existence', in the words of Ammons;[12] it is riven with existence, temporal change and difference. 'Flavia' is never the essence of a self here; 'Flavia' is not the limit of her becoming. In a paradoxical sense, this woman is not ugly, but extremely 'becoming', as the text argues despite itself. That is to say, any limit which is identified as the locus of essence (such as 'Flavia') immediately becomes existence once more, and the essential limit is deferred.

In this sense the relation between being and becoming is itself constitutive of the process of history, with its shifting boundaries and limits or 'end-points'. In the poem there is a dramatized enactment of this situation, in the figure of the angel. Angels, in theology, are somewhat ambiguous. They occupy precisely the terrain between existence or secular history and essence or transcendent eternity; and they are thought to occupy the median metaphysical space between humanity and godhead. They are media, then, between history and transcendence, existence and essence, in theological terms. Further, they are the media through whom communication between these divergent realms is effected; and they are as symbols or tokens of exchange between two *topoi*, with no 'proper' space or identity of their own. Like coins and words they have no intrinsic essential value, but rather assume whatever value is imposed upon them by their manipulators. The word 'angel' is itself a slang term at the historical moment under consideration, meaning a gold coin. The fact that an angel is somehow *like* a coin, like money, stresses its status as medium or locus of exchange; and the fact that there can be a slang word at all, of course, incidentally stresses the exchange which is fundamental as a principle of linguistic meaning.

But it is the woman who is described here in terms of 'angels', mutable symbols of exchange with no inherent value in themselves and worth only what their owners or manipulators determine. Just as the capital of money or the status of the angelic give identity through their realization as 'property' (meaning either land or some metaphysical quality in the human), so also women here become tacitly acknowledged as an element which is instrumental in providing an identity for their 'owners' or manipulators, men. Women, in the terms of the poem, are indeed like 'angels' in so far as, like 'Flavia' and her personal variations, they have no fixed or subjective human identity, no 'property' in any sense, but become identified, appropriated, by the men (here Donne) who depend on them for their own identification as male property-owners, men of substance, material or real men, as it were.

Since women are, according to the tenets subscribed to by the text, evanescent or changing by definition, the poem becomes a vain attempt to deal with the threat of female promiscuity, female subjectivity and female desire. The male tries to control these through the institution of marriage; but this itself is tainted with failure, for the 'fair' woman attained becomes immediately, in the married state, a different object of desire, becomes 'foul'. The object of desire here constantly shifts and cannot be repressed entirely, but returns to haunt the male. Moreover, the fundamental threat here stems from the possibility of a female desire which might dissolve the stable 'property' of the male by promiscuously leaving him or casting desire on another. Woman, then, although necessary for the construction of a male identity according to this ideology, is simultaneously a threat to such male stability. Most specifically female subjective desire threatens the nameable identity of the male; that is, she threatens the male proper name with dissolution. Despite the appropriative description of Flavia in 'The Anagram', the woman in question cannot be known or recognized; for she exists, promiscuously as it were, in a kind of crossroads 'between' the two descriptions of her which I outlined in the two sections of the text. She is neither one nor the other; rather the two descriptions are interdependent, and, existing in the mutable difference between the two descriptions, this woman exists in history, temporality or 'difference'. As such, despite the poet's efforts to contain her under the name 'Flavia', she threatens his nominable identity at the very instant when she seems most firmly 'caged', in marriage.

It is possible to find Donne's own signature in the text, but now only in a covert and anagrammatic way, as a kind of attempt to reinstate his own fundamental priority and underlying authority as the owner of this property. The penultimate line is: 'One like none, and lik'd of none, fittest were'. An anagrammatic reading of this offers up Donne's own name as one of the text's possible anagrammatic formulations. This 'One', of 'One like none', is not only repeated in that 'none' but also suggests the third person impersonal, 'one' as a substitute or 'anagram' of 'I'. In so far as it is one 'like none', or perhaps like 'O', it is also suggestively numerical, and thus to be written as the numeral '1', itself like 'I'. Not only is there an echo of this 'one', this 'I', in the line, there is also a clear echo of Donne's own name, in the phrase 'lik'd of none'. Following the text's own advice: 'If we might put the letters but one way,/In the leane dearth of words, what could wee say', we might be tempted to put these letters too 'one' other way. Thus we can discover 'Done' in 'lik'*d of none*', especially since this echo of 'one' is precisely the 'one/1/I' which the initial word of the line offers us, as one engaged with a 'nun'. We have now produced 'I. Done' or 'J. Donne'.

Given that the poem is, as I have indicated, about Donne's attempt to establish his own individuated difference, to make a name for himself as an identity made by differentiation from the Other, then we might now read the line as 'One like none, and like John Donne, fittest were'; For Donne, if he has been successful in these sleights of hand or anagrammatic slips of the pen in establishing his difference, is precisely 'like none'.

If the poem were a 'dialogue of one', a kind of address by Donne to himself, then this 'lik'd of none', meaning 'liked by none', can now fully reveal the line as 'One like Done, and lik'd by Done, fittest were'. That is to say, Donne, in looking for the perfect mate, and also for that mate as antithesis to himself, profoundly different from himself, actually discovers himself as his own desired object. He discovers the 'one/I' to be different from the 'one/I': it is like 'none'. He has been looking at woman to establish himself as different from woman, and hence as the nameable identity or individual 'John Donne'. He does establish that name but immediately discovers the same kind of 'difference' from himself to be integral to this generation of a supposedly stable identity. Now, rather than pursue the Other as woman, he discovers that he is pursuing himself, as his own object of desire. The woman here is subsumed under the form of a representation of Donne himself: she is 'One like Donne', but a Donne who has been 'disfigured'. Pursuing the Other, he finds it already in himself. The female threat, as an element which threatens to undermine integrity, property and the proper, identifiable name of the male individual, is here discovered to be itself constitutive of that individual. Donne, as specifically masculinist writer, is an entropic deviation from, and a disfigured representation of, the logically anterior position of the woman. The poem short-circuits, then, at the moment when Donne manages to write his shadowy signature; for at this moment, when he establishes his differentiated identity as it were, he discovers that he is talking to (or desiring) himself, or at most the Other within himself.

4

The Donnean thesis of 'containment' of the threat of this now thoroughly insidious Other is outlined in 'The triple Foole':

> I thought, if I could draw my paines,
> Through Rimes vexation, I should them allay,
> Griefe brought to numbers cannot be so fierce,
> For, he tames it, that fetters it in verse.[13]

Here the idea is that rhyme, with its semiotic similarities or rhymes which, in echoing themselves, wind back upon themselves ('one like none', 'lik'd of none', and so on), 'encompasses' or harnesses the possible threat of unruly, uncontained grief, or any real historical feeling. It is as if rhyme were supposed to describe a circle isolating the emotion of grief, or its expression, from the secular historical world. Grief is thus to be refused material realization or articulation; and, by implication, it is to be refused real existence, fettered instead in artifice. The grief, no longer enacted, is bound within the poem.[14]

The mathematical compass is a useful instrument in the elaboration of this piece of metaphysical sophistry, for it is a tool which is used to create and demarcate space, 'containing' space (as the poem 'contains' grief, say) and describing a circular boundary which separates (or creates in fact) a realm of difference, between an 'outside' or outer space and 'inside' or inner space. In so far as woman is the threatening Other, she is also the outer space in this configuration; and in so far as she is 'angel' or boundary between Donne's 'inner space' or self and the realm of divinity, she is also the boundary which the compass draws, the circle itself. The notion of assimilating or apprehending an outer space, as in Copernican astronomy, now becomes explicitly sexualized. Woman, an 'outer space', is to be probed; a fundamental displacement of the central authorial male self is to take place such that the female outer space can be incorporated *within* the circle of the self, and thus neutered as a threat. This means that there has to be some metaphorical or metaphysical interchange of positions between male and female in the writing. There is a precise example of such an interchange in what is perhaps the most widely known and discussed 'compass' image of the poetry of this period, in the final three stanzas of 'A Valediction: forbidding mourning'.

The conceit bears fresh and close examination. Firstly, it is useful to relate it to what is perhaps the most 'intrusive', the least readily recuperable, and most difficult stanza in the entire poem. This is the stanza referring to Copernican revolutions, earthquakes, and the fact of displacement or decentring of the self as a fundamental concern:

> Moving of th'earth brings harmes and feares,
>> Men reckon what it did and meant,
> But trepidation of the spheares,
>> Though greater farre, is innocent.[15]

This stanza makes some sense on its own but, coming where it does in the poem, it looks like a disturbing change of subject and direction, a 'movement' of the ground on which the poem seemed to be elaborating itself. As such, it enacts the fact of eccentricity or displacement within the text at an early stage. It becomes a more crucial stanza for the poem when we arrive at the closing conceit, when the writer remarks that 'Our two soules' undergo no breach, but rather simply expand, and:

> If they be two, they are two so
>   As stiffe twin compasses are two,
> Thy soule the fixt foot, makes no show
>   To move, but doth, if the'other doe.
>
> And though it in the center sit,
>   Yet when the other far doth rome,
> It leanes, and hearkens after it,
>   And grows erect, as that comes home.
>
> Such wilt thou be to mee, who must
>   Like th'other foot, obliquely runne;
> Thy firmnes makes my circle just,
>   And makes me end, where I begunne.

Criticism has usually read this as a tribute to female constancy, in the face of the literal extravagance, 'wandering outside', of the male; as such it becomes a hymn to male dominance in heterosexual relation. But this meaning is fraught with inconsistencies and difficulties. It might be useful to inaugurate a revision of this judgement by commenting that the supposed stable centre, the woman, is not in fact stable at all. The fixed foot, we are told, makes no show of its own to move, expresses no desire to move; but if the other leg moves then this one does too, and without hesitation. The centre does move, as we have already been advised in the stanza on the movement of the earth. That movement, of course, was one which displaced centre on to circumference; is a similar move about to happen here? If so, then centre and circumference are confused, and it becomes difficult, if not impossible, to ascribe one position to the male and another to the 'steady' or 'fixed' female.

The central leg of the compass does move then; and this movement is not just a movement of the leg as such in its activity of leaning, hearkening. Rather it is a fundamental movement of the soul which is at the foot of the compass-leg, as the grammar of the text makes abundantly clear. Thus the 'centre' itself becomes problematic, especially since it seems to be unstable, mobile, and maybe even peripheral, situated on the circumference of another circle, determined by the position of its partner-leg. This would suggest almost that the legs of the compass are interchangeable (as in fact they are); it is difficult to assign each person in the relation a clear position, difficult to say which leg represents which person in the poem. Centre is circumference, as it were, because decentring or displacement has been established as an organizational principle in the poem's mapping out of the earth and of more general spatial relations, or 'context'.

The compass, in both mathematical and geographical usages (for there are at least two kinds of compass), is instrumental in mapping out a world; and it is such a world, as ever, that these Donnean lovers are supposed to compass or 'contain'. Their relation is a circumscription (and perhaps a circumcision therefore) or 'containing' of the entire world, as suggested in the elaboration of the figure of the circle. But, in the drawing of that circle, two stages at least can be distinguished. In the first place, the compasses are together, and erect; in the second stage, the legs of the compass are prised apart, separated, opened out to allow the description of the circle. This suggests an analogy between the legs of the compass and human legs, either opened in walking (as the (?) male partner walks) or opened in sexual activity (and thus like (?) female legs). There is, in this, a confusion of the gender of these legs; there is, perhaps, an interlacing of the legs in the act of sexual congress suggested in the opening of the legs. In such a congress, of course, the legs themselves may constitute a circle, as the legs of one partner encircle the body of another. In the seemingly heterosexual relation which the poem may figure, we might expect that it would be the female legs which would thus comprise the circle, around the body of the male. But the poem suggests precisely the opposite and has it that the legs of the male describe the circle (in walking and thus 'describing' the circle). Something has happened then. We can locate precisely where this strange gender-displacement occurs. The lines:

> Thy firmnes makes my circle just,
> And makes me end, where I begunne

are radically ambiguous, especially if the reader bears in mind the fairly explicit sexual overtones of the text. The fundamental ambiguity here concerns the implied speaker of the lines: male or female? If we suppose that the poem is entirely spoken by the male, then the sexual suggestions here begin to make the relation appear to be homosexual. The firmness of another penis makes the 'circle' of this male speaker just: this could either be the male circle hinted at already in the notion of circumcision, and 'ending where he begun';

would perhaps be in seminal ejaculation; or, alternatively, this circle could be the anus, used as a pseudo-female genital organ, and in this, 'ending where he begun' might suggest the male's return to the female Other at the centre of his Self. But these readings may seem too contrived. It is apposite to suggest, in fact, that the gender of the speaker of the poem changes at this point; the 'male' speaker discovers the 'female' as constitutive of his authority. Hence the firmness could be the erect penis, the 'stiff leg', as it were, and the circle could be the vagina; and the 'ending' becomes in this the female orgasm, experienced 'where I begunne', that is, where 'I' was born in the female womb or genitals.

In some manuscript versions of this poem, its title suggests that it must be spoken by a male to a mistress; but there is nothing within the text itself to necessitate that. Indeed, as I have argued here, it is precisely the question of gender in relation to authority (writing or speaking) which this conceit problematizes. We might suggest that it is spoken by a male, but a male displaced on to the position of eccentric, unstable and peripheral 'femininity' (according, of course, to the poem's own tenets of femininity). That is, it is spoken by a male, but 'authorized' by the Other female which constitutes that male. Donne has, as it were, literally incorporated the female threat, assumed and assimilated it within his own body. As in 'The Dissolution', Donne contrives to write a poem in which 'My body then doth hers involve';[16] and such 'involution' is an attempt to circumvent the possibility of the revolution effected by female pro-miscuity, an 'eccentricity' or extravagance which threatens his own 'proper placement' in a position of sexual, and literary, authority.

5

Fundamental to this entire project, in the metaphorical acts of 'communion' or communication which the verse celebrates or fantasizes, are two phenomena: the exchange of positions of speaker and addressee; and the hyperbolical expansion of the self in space and time. For example, the Valedictory poem under discussion, 'forbidding mourning', stressed the fact that as the two lovers move away from each other, there will be no separation but, on the contrary, an expansion of themselves sufficient to make them the inhabitants of all the space available between them:

> Our two soules therefore, which are one,
>   Though I must goe, endure not yet

> A breach, but an expansion,
>> Like gold to ayery thinnesse beate.

As the speaker moves away, the compass draws not a perfect circle, but rather an infinitely expandable ellipse; and if there is a return homewards, then the geometrical shape traced by the poetic compass is precisely hyperbolical. Further, the speaker's movement away becomes an expansion of the self such that all the ground s/he covers, the world described by the compasses, becomes an aspect of the speaker's identity. Movement across or through space becomes a process of inhabiting, or the appropriative colonization of that space. This conspires to render the potential opposition of the Other utterly neutral, harmless to the Self. In fact, it conspires to negate the very existence of the Other, by assimilating it entirely under the Self. The notion is encapsulated in these lines from Brooke's 'The Soldier':

> If I should die, think only this of me:
>> That there's some corner of a foreign field
> That is for ever England. There shall be
>> In that rich earth, a richer dust concealed;
> a dust whom England bore . . .[17]

Donne, like Brooke here, confronts the moment of separation, individuation and death with the assertion of vital identity. Faced with the threat of 'alien' space, Donne identifies it as himself, assumes it as himself and thus neutralizes it, at least metaphysically.

This incorporation of 'outer space' is part of a struggle to 'contain' death, quite literally, in the struggle with history: Donne tries to control the potentially entropic dissipation of life. In other areas the same kind of hyperbolical expansion aids the struggle against other forms of entropy. For instance, 'Loves growth' strives to demonstrate that love grows inexorably from year to year, without ever receding; even winter brings, not death or decay, but rather an addition to love in this inflationary exercise:

> And though each spring doe adde to love new heate,
> As princes doe in times of action get
> New taxes, and remit them not in peace,
> No winter shall abate the springs encrease.[18]

'Lovers infinitenesse', like this poem, also adds this further temporal sophistry to the counter-entropic exercise. The lover would have all the heart of the mistress, meaning by that not only all 'present' affection (understanding 'present' both spatially and temporally), but also all past and all future potential affection. But in this temporalized expansiveness or acquisitiveness, there is a deferral of the realization of such affection: 'Yet I would not have all yet,/Hee that hath all can have no more'.[19] The compass-leg, as it were, has to expand more and more, again hyperbolically 'encompassing' more and more potential affection. This kind of exponential self-expansion is one of Donne's most basic counters against the prevailing millenarian mood in which there is despair at the envisaged or imagined decay of the world. Further, the fact that the poet never reaches satiety, never comes to a moment when the future can be attained, as it were, means that such a millenarian 'end' of all things, i.e. death, is itself metaphorically deferred. The future, repository of entropy and death, is made an aspect of the present, and so there is the continual production of more and more futurity. This is itself tantamount to a denial of future history and is certainly a denial of the possibility of death.

Self-expansion such as this is mediated in terms of the interchange of positions, for example, of speaker and addressee such as I described it in 'A Valediction: forbidding mourning'. The same manoeuvre operates in poems such as 'Aire and Angels', 'The Dampe', 'The Dissolution', 'The Extasie' or Elegy 4, 'The Perfume'. In 'Aire and Angels' the male speaker exchanges positions with the woman, but with this woman understood metaphorically as angel; and thus the fundamental exchange of positions is of human with divine. This radical exchange then is effected through what might be termed a 'scene of exchange', a crossing-scene or trafficking-scene, here constituted by a woman who has herself already been metaphorically exchanged for angel. In 'The Dampe' the damp in question expands and suffuses all who look upon the image of the poet's lover, carved in his heart; and in this there is another such 'scene of exchange', for the image offered when the poet is looked upon is precisely that of the lover and not the poet at all. 'The Extasie' abounds in spatial confusions of the lovers it attempts to describe and circumscribe, with their eye-beams crossing, hands cemented, bodies intertwined and so on. In 'The Perfume' the poet expands in space as the odour of his perfume strays from his own body across space and is perceived elsewhere. This perfume then becomes a prime agent of self-betrayal, or self-revelation (the reproduction of the self elsewhere), rather like 'the spider love' in 'Twicknam garden', which is another 'enclosed space' to be incorporated by the poet as he becomes a spirit or genius of the place, a metaphysical space without real discretionary boundaries.

The most explicit articulation of these 'colonialist' tendencies, these incorporations of the Other space, usually the alien space of the body of woman, is, of course, Elegy 19, 'Going to Bed', a poem which extrapolates from the traversion of the female space or body in Elegy 18, 'Lovers Progress'. In Elegy 19 Donne explicitly relates the space of the alien female body to be overcome with that geographical space which demands colonization: 'O my America! my new-found-land'. The woman here becomes another space, demanding, through the simple fact of her alterity, to be incorporated, assimilated and controlled by this 'inner space' of the self speaking. This inner self, actually a form of self-presence, is frequently called the 'intelligence' of the 'sphere' in the Donnean lexicon and in imagery of the human constitution or body. Such a mediation, of course, allows the mediation of the self as a consciousness, present to itself ('intelligence', self-knowledge and so on), living in a space which is to be related to that consciousness for its reality or realization (the 'sphere'). The sphere is a realization, in three dimensions, of the image drawn by the ever expanding compass and is related to that.

In Elegy 19, however, not much attention is given to the body or space of the woman, as has been noted before. Carey comments, for instance, that 'He hardly seems to see the girl, though his appraising eye dwells on the clothes she takes off'.[20] It should be added to this, as an important corollary, that we as readers do not see this girl either: her very ontological status is in some doubt. Firstly, she is conceived in the unrealistic terms of an entire cosmos, her body perhaps as some kind of geometrical 'encompassing' of the world:

> Off with that girdle, like heavens Zone glittering,
> But a far fairer world incompassing.[21]

The removal of the girdle becomes a breach in the integrity or 'purity' of the circle or world described by or coextensive with the body of the girl. The *girdle* 'contains' the *girl*, and the breach made in this girdle to 'produce' the girl becomes tantamount to a breach in the body of the girl herself, tantamount to the opening of the girl's legs, her 'compass'. The linguistic suggestion here, in the play between 'girdle' and 'girl' is meant to suggest that the word 'girl', the supposedly pure and naked 'girl' produced in the rupturing of the 'girdle' is already, in a sense, at least linguistically impure, mixed up promiscuously, anagrammatically, in another word or object. The opening of this 'compass' or world, and the subsequent re-encompassing not of the girl herself but of the male in the circle described by the embrace of the girl's legs, constitutes the enactment of the rupture of the 'girl' (both word and person) in the breaking of her hymeneal boundary. This is, of course, precisely a 'colonization' or 'inhabiting' of the space of the woman by the foreigner, the male writer; it is also an adulteration of the space of the girl, seen already in the adulteration of the word 'girl', supposedly purely contained within the 'girdle'. She also becomes, thus, the man's 'girdle'.

As she removes more and more clothing, however, she begins to disappear, paradoxically, behind a mound of clothes. Woman as woman disappears, that is, to be replaced either by the clothes themselves ('girl' lost under 'girdle', say), or by a series of metaphorical replacements or euphemisms for the body:

> Your gown going off, such beautious state reveals,
> As when from flowry meads th'hills shadow steales.

At this point the woman and her body have been replaced by a kind of 'female landscape', thus becoming a microcosmic conception of the world of America or, more precisely, Virginia, a supposedly 'virgin' land. Once more this 'Virginia', a supposedly 'virgin' space, has already been adulterated in its *linguistic* appropriation or naming, even before being more fully 'raped' by its invasive foreigners. That is, the language in which the 'exploration' of the new world, of Virginia, virgin and woman is framed already produces a notion of the satisfactory rape or appropriation of the woman: the 'girl' is an adulterate form, when 'produced' from her 'girdle'.

The progressive 'covering' of the woman continues, as she metamorphoses into ghostly angel and then, significantly, precisely into the form and figure of the male speaker himself, who has by now successfully colonized or appropriated the space of the 'alien' woman:

> Licence my roaving hands, and let them go,
> Before, behind, between, above, below.
> O my America! my new-found-land,
> My kingdome, safeliest when with one man man'd,

> My Myne of precious stones, My Emperie,
> How blest am I in this discovering thee!

Here, the movements of the hand, its 'displacements', make it into the hand of a priest in the act of blessing. (An analogue which clarifies and substantiates this is in *Othello*, 2, i, when Cassio welcomes Desdemona into Cyprus, saying, 'Hail to thee, lady! and the grace of heaven,/Before, behind thee, and on every hand,/Enwheel thee round!') 'Blessing' itself is etymologically related to notions of marking with blood in order to hallow, and it comes close to the activity of marking with a name, identifying or, in Christian theology, baptizing. This demarcation of identity, however, this giving of a name to the woman, 'America' (or Virginia) works to establish the primacy of the nominator (the 'parent') over the nominee (the 'infant' who, literally, is refused a voice). This female 'America', then, is dependent upon the primacy of the male 'England' or Donne for its identity.

The priestly hand of Donne converts sexual foreplay into the activity of blessing, thus assuming a power and primacy with regard to the woman/infant from the outset. The lines then offer a hymn not only to individualistic monarchy (a form of despotism perhaps) but also offer a praise to the primacy and potency of the male, and specifically to the authority of the male voice, as vocal nominator. As this woman/space becomes a kingdom, isolated and individuated *like* the isle of Britain (and thus like a sailing vessel, being struck not by a bottle but by the male phallus and being named, blessed and identified in that act), we are told that she is 'man'd'. This can simply imply 'piloted', led and controlled, which is bad enough; but it also means 'gendered male', that is to say, woman as woman or self-identifying subject disappears, and woman as merest adjunct of Donne's own maleness takes her place. Her voice, her ability to speak, is lost under his nominating voice; she remains 'infant', Donne's 'baby'.

Paradoxically she becomes precisely that adjunct of Donne which identifies him as male, the phallus. Moreover, the act of blessing suddenly becomes a blessing of Donne himself, at his own hand so to speak, as he writes, 'How blest am I in this discovering thee'. For the 'thee' who is discovered here is the displaced 'I', that is, the male speaker, Donne himself. The woman has become more and more covered up, while what is 'dis-covered' is maleness. The woman has become the imaginative instrument by which Donne identifies, names or blesses himself as male. In this 'colonial' eradication of the Other space of the woman, Donne's text begins to assume an aspect of auto-eroticism, which stresses the failure of communication with the Other, woman, and which also highlights the fact that the new-found-land, if it is an island, is precisely that of Donne himself as the isolated, auto-erotic male. Contrary to what Donne may write in his sermons, this man is precisely an island. There is no communication between Donne and the woman in the text: not only does the woman not speak or respond, she also quite simply disappears, goes under cover and Donne is left talking to an aspect of himself. The Elegy is instrumental in 'isolating' Donne, as a clearly individuated space, itself described as the phallus.

The priestly blessing becomes a more distinctly secular blessing when Donne prepares to 'stamp' or 'impress' the woman with the image of himself which she has now become. His 'boarding' of her is supposed to be like the impression of the king's image cast upon a base metal, thus transforming this 'bastard' metal, 'validating' it and legitimizing its status. Such a stamp is meant to confer value on the coin or metal by identifying it as an aspect of the king's wealth, an image or imagination of embodiment of the king as symbol. The value of the woman, by analogy, becomes itself dependent upon that of her 'owner' or appropriator, the poet who has rendered the woman harmless, reduced her to the level of symbol or anagrammatic word. She becomes, in short, an image or representation of the appropriative male Donne:

> To enter in these bonds, is to be free;
> Then where my hand is set, my seal shall be.

Here then the male derives worth and identity in terms of the amount of fetishized 'outer space' or Other space which he has appropriated and reduced to the level of the merest incarnation of himself. The woman is such an incarnation here, an embodiment of (at least part of) Donne, as the instrument of the revelation of Donne's phallus. This opens the way a little towards an understanding of the poem as a study not in exchange, but in hoarding; a study not in sexual relation but rather in auto-eroticism, masturbation, talking to the isolated self. Moreover, this hoarded value is imputedly derived from the supposed priority of masculinity itself, from the supposed centrality of the phallus. The male is understood as the stable point of reference, the Self which explores, exploits and determines the boundaries and worth of the Other, here the space of the female body; such a determination, of course, reflects back as a determination of the worth of the Self, identified in terms of a mass of fetishized and appropriated objects, 'property' or 'properties'. The woman, as woman, has no value in the poem: she does not, in fact, even appear. She becomes 'worthy' only when 'man'd'; that is, either controlled by one man (thus identifying that singular man, paradoxically), or 'granted' the possession of the phallus, as if the act of sexual commerce were simply the male 'giving' the phallus into the body of the woman who receives the 'gracious' gift.

What is revealed in the poem is not woman at all; it is rather a male striptease, as becomes clear in the closing lines:

> cast all, yea, this white lynnen hence,
> There is no pennance due to innocence.
> To teach thee, I am naked first; why than
> What needst thou have more covering then a man.

At the close of the poem, it becomes clear that it is Donne who has been disrobing, and Donne who is here exposing himself. The woman is but the literal extension of the phallus, representing the phallic erection and also occasioning its revelation. What is being sought by the poet is recognition of his maleness, recognition of his phallus, and an acknowledgement of the power which its potency is supposed to give him. This Other woman then equates with the clothing which normally keeps Donne covered, and through which he presents himself (at the same time hiding himself), or presents an image of himself, to the world. The fetishism which treats the woman as 'angelic' coin, supposedly carrying the image or imprint of Donne into social currency or worth, also reduces Donne to the status of the merest image, the simplest representation. But he is no longer a representation of a Self, transparently revealed in the representation; rather he is a representation of the 'coin' which endures, fixing an image to which he must conform. He is imprisoned on the coin or representative token of himself and thus makes of himself an island devoid of exchange and communication with the Other, society at large. Exchange-value is, as it were, replaced by sexual-self-ab-use-value. Donne is left, after his eradication of the woman as Other, to bless himself and his own genitals, stripping himself in a futile attempt to lay bare the 'difference' of woman from himself, and yet progressively covering that Other space of the woman with his own phallic maleness: 'What needst thou have more covering them a man?'

This covering, apart from its ambiguous value hovering between senses of 'over-laying' and 'copulating with', has another ambiguity of relevance here; who is being 'covered'? Donne's self-exposure 'covers' the woman, at least in the sense of reclothing her or hiding her once more behind a pile of clothes or a phallus. But it also 'covers' the male speaker present, in that the text is a 'recovery' or re-covering of Donne in both the figure of the erect phallus (recovered, not disfigured anymore) and also in the imagistic 'coined' representation of himself which the woman has become.

This analysis of the poem begins to expose what is a basic issue in writing which is 'revolutionary' in the manner described in the present study. The fact that neither Donne nor the woman, the two main protagonists of the text, is 'presented' to us, underlines the difficulty of the notion of mimetic representation. In a mutable world where nothing ever stays in place, where the 'present' is always on the move and noumenal objects are being 'recovered' for humanity, the notion of 're-presentation' is fraught with troubles. The present becomes difficult of access, for it has always displaced, transformed or 'covered' itself before it can be repeated or represented.

This difficulty is made all the more trenchant in the activity of writing or constructing stable messages for communicative activities. Not only has the sender of the message always displaced herself in the temporal act of enunciation of the message, but also the addressee is in a similar state of flux or displacement. The poem called 'The Message' is a case in point. In this text there is a shift from the idea of the message as transaction demarcating two positions as 'sender' and 'addressee', towards a notion of the text itself as a 'scene of communication' or meaning. That is to say, 'The Message' almost demands to be read in a phenomenological manner: it is not an actual record of a message transacted between two human communicators; rather it is itself the scene which demands to be 'activated' and raised to the status of meaningful message by a reading subject. 'The Message', in short, is the medium which offers the message that we, as readers, must construct 'The Message' or at least some meaning through it.

One reading of 'The Message' could suggest that the speaker of the poem demands the return of eyes and heart from a lover who has spurned the advances or 'messages' of the speaker:

> Send home my long strayd eyes to mee,
> Which (Oh) too long have dwelt on thee ...

> Send home my harmlesse heart againe,
> Which no unworthy thought could staine...[22]

These are the opening gambits of the first two stanzas; but an important point is that this perhaps seemingly clear message is rapidly confused, for each stanza immediately contradicts the message or order, demanding that the addressee retain the eyes and heart. Further, the text suggests that the eyes and heart are really now 'proper' to the addressee. This seeming change of mind (perhaps already a change of heart) is then *re*-controverted once more, as the final stanza recapitulates (or represents) the first message, marking a second change of mind in the poem. First: return the eyes and heart to me. Second: no, retain them, they are properly yours. Third: return them:

> Yet send me back my heart and eyes,
> That I may know, and see thy lyes ...

This reading, which appears to be straightforward, still exposes some problems with the notion of the message (the poem) and its transmission, or transposition from one person to another, sender to addressee. There are, in fact, difficulties with what is the poem's own displacement in this act of transposition. 'The Message' gets displaced, misplaced, lost; and both 'The Message' and the message change at various points in the text, producing something that is self-modifying, even self-contradictory.

Another mode of reading attends to this difficulty. The reading suggested above depends upon an untenable theory of communication of messages, which goes as follows: sender, A, is a kind of receptacle informed by an ideational message or content which she then 'pours' into a similar, but empty, receptacle, the consciousness of the addressee, B. B would then be identified with A (that is, their consciousnesses would comprise precisely the same 'information'), and a supposed successful communication would have taken place. But there is error here. In so far as B 'successfully' receives the message from A, then B 'becomes' or is identifiable with A. That is, A has now communicated a message not to a different consciousness, that of B, but rather to the same consciousness, A itself. Clearly communication does not work like this, in poetry or in any historical situation. The message is rather always adulterated by 'interference', and specifically by the informational consciousness (never empty) of the addressee, or reader. At the most simple level, this means that a sender of a message has always already taken into account its possible reception by an audience. The reader or addressee (B) is never the 'empty' receptacle of a message or 'influence' but has an active informational consciousness which contributes to the understanding or interpretation, that is, to the meaning, of the message. In the poem under discussion, this is dramatized in terms of the interchangeability of sender and addressee. The reader, as addressee, becomes the sender of another 'message': that is, the reader beomes the sender of a transformed (displaced) text of 'The Message'. The sender requests the return of eyes and heart; however, these are the property of the addressee (at least since they were received by her). This is the organizational principle of the first two stanzas. The notion of self-modifying change, which was important in the naïve reading of the poem given above, now becomes structurally integral to the working of the text. If the eyes and heart are really the property of B, the addressee, then who is the real sender and who the real addressee of the request? Only B, the supposed addressee, can actually send this message, logically, now. So the poem is not a statement followed by a contradictory response (in the text's 'changes of mind'); rather, the text is itself already a 'response' from the addressee to an anterior 'Message'. 'The Message' has already shifted its ground, displaced itself or got lost, even before we come to read the text. Further, the reference of the speaker (both sender and addressee, it seems) to the 'lyes' of her correspondent complicates the issue, not to say the message, even more. The 'response' which this poem now is (for it can no longer be read as an 'original' statement or sending of a message) is a response to a statement of an anterior 'Message' which is already fundamentally mendacious, a lie or falsehood anyway. The 'original' of 'The Message' thus really is lost and begins explicitly to disappear from recuperability.

In so far as the sender and addressee interfuse or change positions in this reading, something happens to the activity of communication or 'messaging'. In short, individuation is lost – 'who is who?' – and the original of an informational or informing consciousness which supposedly determines the single meaning of the message is also lost. Places, hearts, minds and even bodies of the communicants have changed or interfused. 'The Message' is a dramatization not only of its own loss, but of the activity of communication as such, conditioned now both by 'exile' and by 'loss'. The kind of adulterous promiscuity which is the condition of communing here, with its necessary infidelity to an 'original' (but lost) message (which was a lie in any case) becomes axiomatic to this poetry. The message is self-changing and thus always inevitably a lie, a fiction which, if it ever attained to truth, could do so only by circuitous routes of fiction, metaphor, euphemism and so on. 'The Message' is never clear, in this poem or anywhere else: all poems are released into obscurity. That is to say, the message, like the objects of reality, cannot be innocently represented. The title of this poem, for instance, promises us a message which the text refuses to provide. The attempt to represent 'The Message' has to fail, for the message or the poem changes in its historical elaboration, articulation or dramatization of its own realization. As Herbert might phrase it, instead of our having the possibility of a purely represented or repeated message, other messages, not to mention messengers, 'weave themselves into the sense' of the poem.

As is clear even from this poem, the representation of the message, its repetition as the third move in the series of changes of heart and mind, is not a 'simple' or innocent representation. When 'The Message' to return the eyes and heart is reiterated once more towards the close of the poem, it means something entirely different from the 'initial' meaning of the statement in its first appearance in the text. For by this point in the poem the sender or author of the message is the character identified earlier as B, the recipient or reader of the initial propositions. Clearly, then, the sense of the message differs from its first appearance. For instead of A asking for the return of eyes and heart, we now have B asking for the eyes and heart of A, which, supposedly, B already has. That is to say, the poem does not ask, at this stage, for the return of a gift; but rather asks for the making of a gift. This 'Message' has fundamentally changed, differed from itself in its own elaboration.

The poem, then, is not the innocent representation or repetition of a message; rather it is better described as a 'scene of communication', a crossing where there is a *production* of a message, the construction of some kind of meaningful proposition or message. But, since the message articulated in the interpretive reading of the poem has fundamentally changed from the message supposed to be originally constitutive of the poem, the single most important point about the text is that it has, in some sense, to be 'betrayed'. It has to be adulterated by the subjective agency of the reader, whose consciousness is invited to inform the text or message phenomenologically. This is but one aspect of what I call 'the failure of representation' in Donne, a factor which goes far towards helping us understand why the notion of hypocrisy is so important in this poetry.

Notes

1 This is also related to the impact of print culture. The transformation from the direction of orality to the indirection of print is *like* the movement from ear/hand to eye described here. See Walter J. Ong, *Orality and Literacy*, London, Methuen, 1982, for a full examination of this.

2 Donne, 36.

3 See Mark Roberts, 'If it were Donne when 'tis done . . .', *Essays in Criticism*, 16(1966), note 9, p. 328.

4 Donne, 37.

5 Quoted in Ernan McMullin, *Galileo, Man of Science*, New York, Basic Books, 1967, 277; cf. picture of telescopes, figure 4, between pp. 274–5.

6 See my *On Modern Authority* (forthcoming) for a full examination of this subject.

7 Donne, 9.

8 A.J. Smith, *Donne: Songs and Sonets*, London, Edward Arnold, 1964, 47; cf. Wilbur Sanders, *John Donne's Poetry*, Cambridge, Cambridge University Press, 1971, 9ff., and John Carey, *John Donne, Life, Mind and Art*, London, Faber, 1981, 9 and 107, for some similar examples

9 James Turner, *Politics of Landscape*, Oxford, Basil Blackwell, 1979, 5–6.

10 Donne, 72ff.

11 See Hans Blumenberg, *Legitimacy of the Modern Age* (1966), (trans. Robert M. Wallace) Cambridge, Mass., M.I.T. Press, 1983, *passim*.

12 A.R. Ammons, 'Still', in *Selected Poems 1951–1977*, New York, Norton, 1977, 41.

13 Donne, 15.

14 The poem, though, points out that the rehearsal of verse, its oral articulation, actually *releases* the grief into history. Cf. chapters 3 and 7 below.

15 Donne, 44.

16 Donne, 58.

17 Rupert Brooke, 'The Soldier', reprinted in Jon Silkin (ed.), *Penguin Book of First World War Poetry*, Harmondsworth, Penguin, 1981, 2nd edn, 81.

18 Donne, 31.

19 Donne, 17.

20 Carey, op. cit., 107.

21 Donne, 107.

22 Donne, 39.

3
Crisis and hypocrisis:
the failure of representation

> Each mortal thing does one thing and the same:
> Deals out that being indoors each one dwells;
> Selves – goes itself; *myself* it speaks and spells,
> Crying, *What I do is me: for that I came.*
> I say more . . .
>
> (Gerard Manley Hopkins,
> 'As kingfishers catch fire')

> If all things be in all,
> As I thinke, since all, which were, are, and shall
> Bee, be made of the same elements:
> Each thing, each thing implyes or represents.
> Then man is a world . . .
>
> (John Donne, Satire 5, 'Thou
> shalt not laugh in this leaf, Muse')

1

For Donne the new philosophy had called all in doubt. After the Copernican revolution, or perhaps even during it, the paradisical world of essences had been lost for the human. The human was expelled, as it were, from a paradise in which all elements 'knew their own place', and where everything was 'proper'. In Donne's texts things continually threaten to move out of any possible 'proper' place, or even lack such a place to begin with. This is of relevance to another change in human consciousness, which came with the advent of print culture. Some years before Copernicus produced his tract, Gutenberg and Fust had printed the *Forty-Two Line Bible* in Mainz (1448); and William Caxton brought the techniques of print to England in 1477. This had a profound effect on writing and poetry.

The myth of Paradise connoted two interconnecting sentiments. It was a place or state of being in which objects and persons were entirely 'present to themselves'. That is to say, there was no danger of there being a discrepancy between appearance and reality; things *seemed* entirely and purely or faultlessly as they really *were*, and we could strive, as proto-Arnoldians, to 'see the object as in itself it really is'. To phrase this in existentialist terms, everything and everyone was in the condition of the *en-soi*. The myth of this paradise *lost* ushers in a discontinuity between what a thing might be in itself, *en-soi*, and how it appears or what it might be for others, *pour-autrui*. The corollary of this, of course, is that the conscious human can no longer rest entirely successfully as an essential object, *en-soi*, but now becomes fully and historically existential, *pour-soi*. Thus desire or at least some potential sense of 'in-completion' or 'imperfection' becomes the condition of human consciousness and activity; and this, of course, corroborates the nostalgic myth of paradise lost. This is the sense of Blumenberg's notion, already cited, that the human now becomes 'creatively active' and 'freed ... from a disastrous lulling' of her or his activity.[1] In this desire, which can be considered as a gap between consciousness and its objects, there is the beginning of the Eliotic notion of the seventeenth-century's 'dissociation of sensibility', which may indeed have been 'aggravated by the influence of the two most powerful poets of the century, Milton and Dryden', but which was already, *contra* Eliot, a problem for Donne. Eliot wrote that

> Tennyson and Browning are poets, and they think; but they do not feel their thought as immediately as the odour of a rose. A thought to Donne was an experience; it modified his sensibility.[2]

But this simply raises the problem of the 'immediacy' of such experience. For if Donne's sensibility is modified by the thought, then how can there be an identity or sense of self-presence in the Donne-before and the Donne-after the thought. It is not the same Donne who is aware of having had the thought/experience as it was who in fact underwent the thought/experience. There is, with the ushering in of this kind of existential self-consciousness, a negation of the possibility of the human consciousness ever coinciding with itself, of ever being 'present' to itself.

This question of immediacy links the creative and historical activity of the existential consciousness to the second connotation of a paradise-myth. For, according to at least one notion of what was lost with the expulsion from paradise, ease and clarity of communication, the immediacy of contact between communicators, was paramount. In Milton's *Paradise Lost* Adam asks about the difference between human and angelic communication:

> 'Love not the Heavenly Spirits, and how their love
> Express they, by looks only, or do they mix
> Irradiance, virtual or immediate touch?'
>   To whom the Angel, with a smile that glowed
> Celestial rosy-red, Love's proper hue,
> Answered: 'Let it suffice thee that thou know'st
> Us happy, and without Love no happiness.
> Whatever pure thou in the body enjoy'st
> (And pure thou wert created) we enjoy
> In eminence, and obstacle find none
> Of membrane, joint, or limb, exclusive bars;
> Easier than air with air, if Spirits embrace,
> Total they mix, union of pure with pure
> Desiring, nor restrained conveyance need
> As flesh to mix with flesh, or soul with soul'[3]

In the state of paradise lost, however, such immediacy is unavailable; the human consciousness cannot even be immediately present to itself but has to construct itself through the medium of language, linguistic self-understandings. Similarly all forms of human communication are now *mediated*; and the specific mode of mediation which is becoming dominant in the seventeenth century is alphabetic writing fixed in print.

Oral speech or, more generally, sound, is radically historical; sound exists only as it is always already going out of existence. But, as Ong writes, the alphabet (and alphabetic writing) 'implies that matters are otherwise'.[4] It implies that in the material realization of the abstract alphabet, the typographic font, there is the entire range of linguistic possibilities there before us, simultaneously and permanently in space. This is to say, writing is historical in a very different sense from speech. The alphabet, further, implies that a word is an *object*, and not an *event*; the written word is understood as a 'thing' in some sense, while the oral word is a participant in a historical situation organized between two communicators. In the movement from chirographic writing (manuscript) to typographic writing (print), between, say, the time when Donne circulated his manuscripts and Herbert constructed his texts, such an 'objectification' in language can be seen clearly. Consider Herbert's proto-concrete poetry, in poems such as 'The Altar' or 'Easter-Wings', where the shape of the words on the page supposedly represents the material shape of the objects of the altar or wings. This is an extreme example; and, although Donne has no such 'concrete poetry', still his texts have been affected by their status as chirographic exercises.

One of the advantages which alphabetic writing has over pictographic or ideographic 'script' as a means of communication is that it can determine with more precision how a reader will either vocalize or silently read the written text. But although it determines precisely which words are received, as it were, it has, paradoxically, much less control over the *meaning* of those words. Words may be 'objects' when written, but there is a clear dislocation between the objective status of the word and that of its referent. One cannot sit on the word 'chair', for instance. The word then does not so much re-present its objective referent as much as point to its material absence. The written word here is dislocated from its object; the meaning of the word, like the 'meaning' of the object, its essence, is not, as it were, present to the orthography of the word; the word is not *en-soi*. Thus the written word comes to have a greater degree of indeterminacy of meaning with respect to its referential value. Whereas a spoken message, an event in which I *say* 'I have eaten the plums that were in the icebox' seems relatively free from ambiguity, given the fact that it is a historical event in a specific communicative situation, that 'message' becomes radically multivalent when written, devoid of the presence of a historical speaker and addressee:

> I have eaten
> the plums
> that were in
> the icebox

and which
you were probably
saving
for breakfast

Forgive me
they were delicious
so sweet
and so cold.[5]

Similarly we have already seen how the words of the message shift
in Donne's poem, 'The Message', say. The desired, but lost,
immediacy of contact between person and person, consciousness
and consciousness, word and referent, becomes apparent as one
fundamental condition of Donne's *writing*. The mediating word is
not all it may seem; it does not so much re-present its referent as
either fail to represent it (are Williams's plums simply fruit or are
they symbolic of something sexual, and so on), or simply indicate
its *absence*, not any form of its presence or presentability.

From this moment in history, then, the human consciousness is
split or fragmented in a very specific way: 'I' can never fully coincide
with 'I' or 'myself'. That is to say, the question of the historical and
spatial notion of the 'present' becomes problematical. And this
being the case, there are difficulties in a writer *writing* what she or
he means to *say*; it is impossible to 're-present' the self, to state or
express the single consciousness in full authenticity. As Polonius
has it:

> Your bait of falsehood take this carp of truth,
> And thus do we of wisdom and of reach,
> With windlasses and with assays of bias,
> By indirections find directions out.[6]

This is, of course, the culmination of a speech which exemplifies
the very indirect mode of discovery of a truthful proposition which
it (indirectly) purports to establish.

A mimetic problem is the result of this for poetry. Carey remarks
what is almost a commonplace of Donne criticism, that Donne's
visual, mimetic imagination is not a dominant factor in the
continued popularity of the poetry: 'We don't go to him for flowers,
pastoral . . . nor does he love the English countryside'. But this lack
of a representation of exterior reality is immediately replaced, for

Carey, by a supposedly more worthwhile and more direct revelation of 'the structure of his imagination': 'The physical characteristics of the girl he's supposed to be talking to don't concern him. Nor does her personality: it is completely obliterated by Donne's'.[7] But if mimesis is problematic, by definition, given the intellectual state of the contemporary consciousness, then it is no easier to represent oneself than it is to represent the external world; the problem is that one cannot know what is to be represented, since one is refused access to what is present.

What Carey calls the structure of Donne's imagination, most other critics have called the tone of his speaking voice. Most seem to agree with the notion that Donne presents himself forcefully and with vitality in his writing; and the aspect which is presented most clearly is the voice. Thus Eliot could write that there was 'a direct sensuous apprehension of thought' in Donne; Leavis commented that 'utterance, movement and intonation are those of the talking voice'; and R.G. Cox, for a final typical instance, valued Donne for the 'speaking voice that strikes us in the Songs and Sonets', where 'The effect is always that of hearing a particular tone of voice rather than of merely following words on a page'.[8]

In comments such as these, the notion of the presence of the poet is being vaunted: Donne is valued because he is in some sense present before us, like a contemporary poet giving a reading. But even if this were in any way acceptable, it would have to be pointed out that what is present before us at such a rehearsal is not the essential poet as such, but the *representation* enacted by the existential *performance* of the poet. In this sense there is no great ontological preference in having Donne there rather than oneself as reader; there is no logical value attached to the presence of the poet in such a situation. The implication of the criticism cited here, though, is that even if Donne has failed to represent the countryside or material reality, at least he has managed successfully to represent himself and his own voice: he is 'present' to us in and through the writing. He is supposed to have converted the mediacy of writing into an angelic immediacy of communication such as was fantasized by Milton.

Donne himself seems to have been fascinated by such a notion; many poems are testimony to his obsession with the 'present' as a philosophical and metaphysical problem. One of the most persistent traits of his writing is the attention accorded to speculations on ideas of identity and duration, two forms of 'self-presence'. Before enjoying representing himself, Donne seems to have examined, in a critically rigorous manner, the question of the present in the writing. It may indeed prove to be the case that there is some resurgence of 'voice' through the mediations of Donne's written texts; but such a voice is not simply a presentation of the consciousness of Donne. Rather, what is at stake in these texts is the determination of the text as 'event' rather than 'object'; that is, what is at stake is the historicizing of the activity of reading or rehearsing the poems.

2

The poems are frequently organized around a moment which might be called the 'revolutionary present'. That is to say, they are arranged around a moment of transposition from one state of affairs to another, most simply understood as a moment of the putative 'present' sandwiched between an imagined future and a posited past. This is most evident in the first two lines of the first Divine Meditation, thus:

> Thou hast made me . . . [past tense]
> . . . And shall thy work decay? [future tense]
> Repaire me now . . . [present tense]

But the same kind of instant is repeated in many of these divine poems:

> Oh my blacke soul! now thou art summoned
> By sicknesse . . .

> This is my playes last scene, here heavens appoint
> My pilgrimages last mile . . .

> What if this present were the worlds last night? . . .⁹

Some poems also draw attention to their 'present' occasional status, to the supposed moment of their composition. Examples include 'Upon the Annunciation and Passion falling upon one day. 1608', 'Goodfriday, 1613. Riding Westward', 'To Mr Tilman after he had taken orders', and, of course, the Anniversaries ostensibly commemorating the life and death of Elizabeth Drury. But the 'present' instant which poems such as these are meant to memorialize seems to be evanescent to the point of non-existence. Divine Meditation 6, 'This is my playes last scene', is a fine example of the difficulties of locating a 'present' moment with any degree of precision.

This poem builds itself initially on one of Zeno's paradoxes. This paradox states that an arrow, fired at a target, can never reach it. Firstly, it has to travel half the distance towards the target; then half the remainder; then half the remainder again, and so on. There can never come a point, according to this mathematical sophistry, when the distance to be travelled will be nought; for nought can never be the half of any number. Divine Meditation 6 opens at a point where a final mile towards a destination can be fractured in much the same kind of way. Starting from what seems to be the end, the 'last' mile or stage in the journey of life, Donne rapidly contrives to make this end an end at all. He moves on to the last inch, and such a measurement as this can also be open to the same sophistry: it too can always be fragmented or halved, made to defer the final point of arrival at the destination of death. The paradox is established both in terms of space and time:

> This is my playes last scene, here heavens appoint
> My pilgrimages last mile; and my race
> Idly, yet quickly runne, hath this last pace,
> My spans last inch, my minutes latest point . . .

Clearly the poem is set at a moment of extremity; but the final stage of this extremity is always deferred. However much Donne may reduce the length of his time remaining, he never finally reduces it to one precise instant. Any such 'instant' in fact covers a measurable length of time and has a real duration: the 'present' moment is, to say the least, as difficult of access as is human consciousness in the instant of death.

But there does seem to be some temporal mutation here, in the movement from these 'last' moments towards a putative future, beginning in the line, 'Then, as my soule . . . takes flight'. The articulation of this transposition is interesting and instructive. From the series of attempts to locate and identify a definite present moment, Donne passes to a meditation on definiteness itself, in its guise of death. Approaching the instant of the final present, the final remaining moment of life, the poet has suddenly come upon it and revealed it:

> And gluttonous death, will instantly unjoynt
> My body, and soule, and I shall sleepe a space,
> But my'ever-waking part shall see that face,
> Whose feare already shakes my every joynt:
> Then, as my soule, to' heaven her first seate, takes flight,
> And earth-borne body, in the earth shall dwell,
> So, fall my sinnes . . .

Here, in the closer and closer approximation to the 'last moment',
the finality of the 'present' and self-enclosed moment of death at
which the poem is ostensibly located, there is a sudden projection
forward into the temporal mode of the 'after-life', the after death.
That is to say, the poem moves from the past history of a life
instantaneously through to a futurity in the 'after-life'. It is this
instant of change, the present, which is, by definition, mutable and
evanescent, the scene of change itself. From seeing death as a future
event, there is an instantaneous (and non-appearing) moment
which transports us to the moment when death has happened. As
Saint Augustine had meditated, the instant when a person is 'in
death' is impossible to locate; for the person is always either 'before
death' or 'after death', and in between these two instants which
encroach on each other's territory the instant 'in death' disappears.
The same can be said of the passage of time from the past (before
death) to the future (after death) as in this poem: but the present,
like the instant of death, has thus been sophistically erased. The
'present' moment of the poem's setting then is best regarded as a
'revolutionary moment'.

The identification of the moment of the present and the moment
in death is of interest in both Donne and Augustine. It is almost as if
the present were to be understood as a moment of revolutionary
death and rebirth; but such a rebirth, of course, can only be into the
subsequent moment of another possible death, to be followed by
another rebirth, and so on. The progress of historical time becomes
radically discontinuous here, a series of more or less perfectly
repeated (or 're-presented') instants, with no necessary or continuous
connection linking them. Moreover, each such moment of representation attempts to represent, or more precisely to create or
generate, an always absent 'present' moment. The present as such
remains inaccessible in this schema; all that remains is a series of
representations, whose original has been lost. This is exactly akin

to the dislocation already noted between, say, word and referent in the age of print. In this writing there are no objects, only words; or, in more precise Saussurean terms, there are no signifieds, only signifiers. But this need not imply a rejection of the historical significance of the texts. Indeed, on the contrary, it opens the possibility of regarding the texts as potential *events*, rather than as mere fetishized self-present objects. As signifiers, they demand to be 'enacted', to be made to signify in the event of interpretation. There may be no access to any suppositious 'Truth', conceived of as the clear presence of the contents of Donne's consciousness; but this does not deny the possibility of meaning; more specifically, of the action of meaning as an interpretation is constructed.

A perfect example of what is going on here is 'A Lecture upon the Shadow', in which a 'reading' of the shadowy marks on the ground strives to construct the presence and eternized present moment of love between two persons; from the 'absence' which the shadows are, there is implied, in the constructive reading of them, the presence of the lovers. In the *Songs and Sonets*, the counterpart of 'A Lecture upon the Shadow' is 'A Nocturnall on S. Lucies day'. This latter poem concentrates, like Divine Meditation 6, upon the discovery or laying bare of a present moment, the moment of the year's midnight which becomes understood as the moment of death and rebirth which the shortest day (the briefest moment, the evanescent 'present' instant) symbolizes. While this poem is set at 'deep midnight', 'A Lecture upon the Shadow' is set at a kind of high noon of love, another briefest moment, according to the text, which contains both life and death. Both poems are overtly concerned with shadows and with representation as such. In the case of the 'Nocturnall', the poet is a shadow or representation of the state of dying itself.

If we equate the moment of death with the moment of the present, as both this poem and Divine Meditation 6 encourage us to do, then the poet in the 'Nocturnall' can be understood as striving to be a representation of the present; a representation of his own 'presence'. The moment of the year's midnight, an equivalent of the 'last moment' of Divine Medition 6, is described in a series of concepts of entropic exhaustion and downward motion. Then 'all these seeme to laugh,/Compared with mee, who am their Epitaph'. This makes the poet a verbal manifestation, or shadowy and textual representation of the death of the year itself; he is the presentation of the present moment of death and thus becomes some kind of death of death. This is ambiguous, and productively so in the poem: as the death of death, the poet becomes the epitome of death, and represents the essence of 'deathness' in death; but, theologically, this also works to defeat death in the sense reiterated in Divine Meditation 10 where, as at another midnight:

> One short sleepe past, wee wake eternally,
> And death shall be no more; death, thou shalt die.[10]

In the 'Nocturnall' the poet conceives of himself as a shadow of death or representation of death; and this mere fact of rep-resentation is instrumental in the 'negation' of death, the act of 'absenting' it from reality. The poet here is in a position analogous to the shadow which has to be read in the 'Lecture'.

Interestingly, the first thing to mention about this poem, the 'Lecture', is that, if it is indeed set at the moment of high noon, then there is no shadow upon which the poet can exercise the sophistries recounted in the text. The shadow, in fact, is itself absent, not there at all; this 'present' moment is itself characterized by 'absence' in this sense. But the present moment of noon, of course, is so evanescent as to be virtually non-existent, and thus in fact there can be, indeed must be, shadows there to 'read'. Such reading, however, is now to be carried out in the less secure, less clear shades of fore- and after-noon.

The opening words of the poem are a plea for fixity in the face of this: 'Stand still'. This, however, is precisely the problem. The lovers cannot 'stand still', except through all sorts of contrivances, like those in 'The Sunne Rising', say, to make time and history stop or to negate the effects of its passage. The fact of the matter, of course, in this 'Lecture', is that history does not stop. The moment of noon is precisely like the moments of 'lastness', death or the present; it is easy to identify time as 'before death' or 'after death', 'before noon' or 'after noon', but it is impossible to locate and identify the instants of death or noon themselves. For such a moment to be identifiable, to have 'identity', it would have in some way to endure: there would have to be at least two self-identical instants. And if this were the case, the instantaneity of the present, noon or death, would be vitiated. One of the points of the poem lies here: the fullness of love or the purity of love is unattainable or unidentifiable, for the moment of clear mutual recognition cannot endure. If we allow the pretence that the text of this poem happens instantaneously at noon, then the gambit suggested is that love lasts only for this putative duration of the poem itself. 'Stand still' becomes a command determining the desired reading or 'Lecture' of this shadowy text.

But this is simply the first of the many problems here; for the poem admits of temporal progression in itself, passing from morning to afternoon, from one kind of shadow to another. If the poem starts at the moment of noon (assuming that it could be isolated), then it finishes in the afternoon, a time when the shadows work upon the lovers to deceive them. This affects the reading or interpretation of the poem. For the text is, in a sense, its own reading; the shadows are representations or signs of the lovers, and our reading of the text is fundamentally the same activity as that of the poet, 'lecturing upon' or reading shadowy marks which suppose the 'presence' of two lovers. These shadows are, in effect, the hieroglyphic marks on the written page, left as the trace of noon, the trace of the presence elsewhere and in another time (and thus the absence) of the lovers. Fundamentally these marks are duplicitous, like the afternoon shadows, and our eyes 'blind' to the supposed presence which disappears away from them.

As a black mark which represents, iconically, the human body, the shadow is also an extension of that body into the surrounding space. The 'Lecture' then follows a movement of spatial reduction followed instantaneously by a kind of counter-expansion; the shadows are reduced and then re-expand or re-present themselves, but in another direction and to a slightly different end. This is exactly the usual kind of spatial mutability which I have already revealed as an important factor in the organization of Donne's texts. Here the poet 'reads' the hieroglyphic shadows and interprets them, builds a poem upon this reading. If there are shadows to be interpreted, of course, then the poem cannot be set at the moment of noon. The fact that there are shadows, black marks to be read and to comprise this lecture, indicates that the moment of noon, the present of a desired standing still, comes and goes instantaneously. Further, the activity of reading and the 'Lecture' itself, as a reading of the shadowy marks, must be duplicitous, imperfect; for the very presence of the shadows guarantees the impossiblity of clarity and Truth or sincerity:

> So whilst our infant loves did grow,
> Disguises did, and shadowes, flow,
> From us . . .
> Except our loves at this noone stay,
> We shall new shadowes make the other way.
> As the first were made to blinde
> Others; these which come behinde
> Will worke upon ourselves, and blind our eyes.[11]

This reading then, this 'Lecture', is a reading of the shadows based upon the blindess of the poet; it is hardly to be relied upon as a clear representation of a factual state of affairs. There is more to reading, and more to representation, than the poem expressly suggests.

Once more, then, presence gives way to representation. The poem moves from one examination of the representation of the forenoon selves of the lovers to an examination of another representation in the afternoon; and this investigative lecture is based either upon a desire to deceive others (us, the readers) in the forenoon shadows, or to deceive the lovers themselves (in their blindness) in the afternoon. There is, that is to say, no 'presentation' of the lovers here; they are barred from existence in the present. At noon, there is no evidence of their presence at all, for there would be no shadow; but there is a hieroglyphic shadow, the trace of a duplicitous voice, which in asking 'Stand still' enters the historical realm and denies the possibility of stillness and presence. All that remains in the text, then, are shadowy representations, counters of the lovers, which comprise duplicity, misinterpretation as central to their 'legibility' or legitimacy. The moment of the pure meeting of two clearly individuated, unshadowy selves does not take place. Even at the imagined moment of perfect clarity, at noon, there is no stillness, for the lovers 'tread' the shadows; they do not 'stand still'. The poem itself thus becomes a shadowy 'afternoon text', as it were, a duplicitous scene of misreading.

The moment at which the poem is set can be characterized by *crisis*. Its mode is, precisely, the critical, as the poet performs a critical interpretation of the shadowy hieroglyphics which the lovers produce (or which the poet himself generates, either as a representation of his body, or as a representation of his voice). But it should be noted that the shadowy text upon which the poet performs the critical interpretation is not the product of a singular individuated consciousness or imagination; rather it is already double, produced by the 'society' or intermingling promiscuity of two lovers, the very negation of the principle of 'brave clarity' which the poem seems to want to vaunt. More fundamentally still, it is produced by the mere fact of relation, of social existence, in the relations between the humans, the earth, and the sun as source of light and shade. The text invites the reader to partake of and confuse these relations; for while the poet in the poem regards the carnal shadows (so imagined), the reader of the poem regards the poet as himself a shadow, in the hieroglyphics of the words here written. The most important point, then, in this self-doubling, self-duplicitous poem, is that this critical text is *hypocritical*.

In Book 2, chapter 10 of the *Deffence et illustration de la langue francoyse*, Joachim du Bellay traced the etymology of *hypocrisie* back to a Greek source which he claimed to subtend the meaning of *pronunciation*. This is linked to a more acceptable etymology which traces the word back directly to *hypocrisis*, meaning the acting of a part (*hypo* = under; *krino* = I judge/decide). Donne's text is hypocritical in some ways relevant to this. Firstly, it is itself a critical reading, a lecture; and moreover it is a lecture or critical reading of itself. Thus there are, in our reading of the text, at least two acts of pronunciation or critical reading going on one under the other. Secondly, it is clearly concerned, at the merest level of content, with the notion of falsity and duplicity in proclamations of love and, more basically, with questions of such duplicity or imperfection in communications between lovers or human individuals. Thus it is about 'hypocrisy' in its more conventionally understood sense, as the opposite of sincerity. Thirdly, the very enunciation, or pronunciation of the poem, as an act which occurs in time and denies the possibility of standing still, becomes itself not so much a criticism as a hypocriticism or hypocrisis. For the reading, based upon shadows, must take place in the arena determined by those shadows, an arena of blindness and duplicity according to the text. This activity of integral reading then is fundamentally hypocritical, duplicitous and a necessary 'betrayal' of the text itself.

The text becomes paradoxical and problematic in the sense that its very articulation (the very act of reading it) changes its meaning and status; here, as in Du Bellay, enunciation is hypocrisis. We are now faced with a situation in which there is no originary presence which will authorize or validate any representations; there are, however, representations nonetheless, but now of an always absent (though perhaps implied) presence. No wonder Donne pleads: 'Stand still'. Further, the very fact of representation, in its most basic guise as rehearsal or repetition (reading) of the text, constitutes the fundamental act of hypocrisy, a kind of deformation or transformation of the text.

I argued earlier that the original stability of a centralized home seemed to be lost forever to Donne; here we see that the concept of a stabilized text, reliable shadowy hieroglyphics whose transparency will make their recuperation, interpretation or reading self-evident and self-justifying, now also begins to disappear. The notion of a text as a self-present, self-sufficient entity or objective 'verbal icon' is lost; the text as we receive it has only the status of hypocritical representation. There is no stable product, no text which is complete and sufficient in itself whose 'integrity' we can supposedly only understand from a position which transcends the historical and objective specificity of the text. The text now does not exist apart from its rehearsals; but in the repetition of the text, in its articulation or reading, another text or representation is always being produced. As readers of the poem, we are fundamentally Baudelairean 'hypocrites lecteurs'. Quite simply, the poem lies, does not or indeed *cannot* 'say what it means'. 'What it means' depends upon its hypocritical articulation, its critical reading; that is to say, it depends to a large extent upon the historical moment and situation of its reproduction, of its (necessarily) hypocritical articulation.

One problem in this text, with its explicit request or desire for clarity and sincerity in human amorous communication, is that this hypocrisy seems impossible to avoid. For the hypocrisis is wound up with the fact of duplicitous, shadowy, representations of an origin which is not in fact there. Yet the desire for representation and its implicit corollary, repetition, are axiomatic to the text. In asking 'Stand still', the poet seeks to make the instant of the poem's generation an endlessly reiterable, self-identical moment. Even if the moment were reiterable, representable, I have shown that the representation of it would in fact be misleading, an entropic deviation from the supposed purity of the moment. This paradox is fundamental to the text.

The poem is, as it were, demanding the rehearsal of the same breath of the lovers; demanding that the breath which enunciates the text be endlessly repeated. The poem's 'inspiration' is to be repeated, in order to circumvent the possibility of a final 'expiration' or dying of the love between the partners. That is to say, of course, that if the lovers are to stay together there can be no mere continuity or fluent continuation of their relation; there can only be its repetition, the repetition of its inspiration. This means that they can only attempt to 're-present' themselves again and again. But here, obviously, is the crux. Representation is what the poem claims to avoid at this moment of high noon, when 'to brave clearness all things are reduced', when all there is is pure presence without any shade of representation. But the lovers are condemned to representation, for their existence as presence is lost. Any repetition of the breathy inspiration (any repetition of the articulation in voice of this poem) brings with it hypocrisis as an inevitable corollary and, by implication of that, the separation and failure of the two lovers. Their relation becomes, by definition almost, duplicitous and hypocritical, demanding separation or parting.

There is a difference between the demand for repetition in this poem and that already discussed in 'The Good-morrow'. Both poems are in a sense 'incomplete', demanding their repetition in some way. But the 'Lecture' modifies this slightly. It is not so much that it demands its own repetition as a 'completion' of the scene of recognition imagined in the text. Rather there is the demand that the moment of 'inspiration' be prolonged, and the moment of 'expiration' deferred. In this, then, there is another aspect to the paradox of repetition. For there is a hope, in this deferral of the breath, that the text will not be breathed or voiced. For if the poem were to be completed in this sense, with a reader repeating the movements of inspiration and expiration, or if the text were thus voiced as a 'definition of love' in some Marvellian manner, then it would become a self-destructive text. Its enunciation, the articulation of its inspiration would be tantamount in fact to its expiration (on the breath of another), and this would contradict the very deferral which is integral to the text's demand for stillness.

It seems that this poem requires to retain its status as purely 'written'. So the final and most basic paradox of this text, this 'lecture', is that it demands *not to be read*. The text requires some kind of suspension, in the realm of reading, which will deny the historical articulation of the text on the voice. It asks to be held at the critical moment of inspiration, as if the reader were always 'about to' read the text, offer it a voice, without ever fully enunciating it. 'Stand still' can now be read as a request not to go any further, to stop right here and not read on. It is the suspension of the breathing process which the 'Lecture' demands, whereas 'The Good-morrow' simply demands an acknowledgement that the activity of breathing (inspiration followed by expiration inviting inspiration once more) can carry on indefinitely.

Given this, it seems particularly odd that what many critics can claim to have in these texts is the distinctive tone of Donne's present voice, as a pure mediation (or immediation) of his consciousness. There is no such presence behind or informing these texts of hypocritical representation, as these activities of reading, outlined through the texts themselves, make clear. The 'Nocturnall' at one point even goes so far as to state explicitly the 'non-presence' of Donne at the very instant of the present, the instant equated with the moment of death:

> If I an ordinary nothing were,
> As shadow, a light, and body must be here.
> But I am None . . .[12]

As in the 'Lecture' even the shadows, as some kind of self-present entities or signs, are here called into doubtful question. The 'tone of voice' as a breathy articulation was important for Donne purely as an area of critical inquiry; and what was examined through it was not the notion of the sincerity of the present speaker, the poet (for that very presence was contentious), but rather the fact of hypocrisy, misprision. The breath itself was, for Donne, hypocritically 'misunderstood' or (mis)represented in the metaphors of inspiration and expiration; and by extension the breath and its discontinuous repetitive motion became analogous to theological notions of death (expiration) followed by rebirth (inspiration), and so on indefinitely. The repetition involved here was never simple or clear; it was, rather, always informed by misrepresentation, hypocrisy, and an imagined entropy. Representation failed to 'present' anything; for the present itself was the merest abstraction, non-existent in material terms, like a breath which cannot be felt or heard, the pause between inspiration and expiration.

3

Towards the close of *King Lear* comes the death of Cordelia, a death which Lear and many other witnesses since have found difficult to accept. Lear pleads for a sign that she lives, and the sign in question is to be the representation of her breath (itself an analogical sign for the soul) as it stains, shadows or impresses itself upon a glass. The breath, sign of life, is taken as an indexical icon, to borrow the terms of C.S. Peirce:[13] it both points to the fact of life and is itself the image of life (the representation of the soul, its only apparent manifestation):

LEAR: She's gone for ever.
  I know when one is dead and when one lives;
  She's dead as earth. Lend me a looking-glass;
  If that her breath will mist or stain the stone,
  Why, then she lives.
KENT: Is this the promised end?
EDGAR: Or image of that horror?
ALBANY: Fall and cease!
LEAR: This feather stirs; she lives. If it be so,
  It is a chance which does redeem all sorrows
  That ever I have felt.[14]

Several interesting things go on here. Firstly, Lear looks not for life but for the *sign* of life. That is to say, he looks not upon the 'presence' of Cordelia; rather he attends to the glass or feather in search of the *representation* of Cordelia's life. He looks, in other words, for a representation through which the presence of life in Cordelia is to be inferred. It is as if the breath, in 'stamping' or impressing itself upon an environment, in generating its own image, works like a Donnean coin, to 'validate' (make well) Cordelia here.

Secondly, there is a movement in the scene as a whole from present realities towards (diseased, corrupt, or entropic) imagination. Life as a present reality remains inaccessible to Lear; Edgar wonders if the whole scene before *his* eyes is 'image' of the end; the scene itself, of course, is not real but a representation before the eyes and ears of the audience as theatrical event; the real location of the scene can be identified as in Lear's imagination, and so on. There is a tension established between the real and its image or appearance, reality and imagination, noumenon and phenomenon, presence and representation, in these few lines. In all these binary oppositions, the 'representational' aspect supplants the 'real' aspect; and that which is construed as 'reality' turns out to be really only one specific kind or mode of representation, one imaginary construction among many possible scenarios.

Thirdly, at least within this realm of representation, phenomenon and imagination, there is another movement, from the death to the life of Cordelia. Such a movement can be explained in terms of the representation of the breath itself, as a movement between exhalation and inspiration. Cordelia is spoken of firstly as dead; and then she is revitalized, as it were, in some sense for Lear. She is resurrected in some way as Lear, straining too closely for a sign in the glass, perhaps stains it with his own breath. Then there is doubt once more, in 'If it be so'; and such a reinstatement of doubt threatens to reiterate the whole movement, from death to life to death to life (from exhalation to inspiration and vice versa) once more. This movement from death to life, repeated, potentially endlessly, brings together the notion of the 'present' in time and space and its equation with an instant of death, separation and individuation. This scenario from *King Lear* underlies much of the problematization of the present and its representation in Donne.

The clearest way into the argument here is through Hartman's brief discussion of 'A Valediction: forbidding mourning' in *Saving the Text*,[15] and in particular his comments on the opening stanza of the poem:

> As virtuous men passe mildly away,
>   And whisper to their soules, to goe,
> Whilst some of their sad friends doe say,
>   The breath goes now, and some say, no . . .

Hartman comments that 'The mere breathing space between "now" and "no" is the economy of death as a principle of phonemics, the subtlest "glas".' Further, he remarks (bringing this kind of criticism closer to my own comments above on *King Lear*) that this initial stanza 'hangs the evidence of life on a word, on less than a word, on a vocal inflection or quantity, the difference between "now" and "no"'. The interpretation can be clarified if we proceed more slowly with these lines.

The whisper of the dying person is, as it were, the breath itself, scarcely articulated into a word as such, scarcely able to carry the weight of a word. However, the merest possible breath, the dying breath itself, does manage to 'say' something: it whispers to the soul 'to go'. That is to say, the sound of the breath, the whisper, is articulated or represented as the words 'to go'. There is a substantial equation here, then, between the fact of breath and that of death, going or separation. The whispering text, the shadowy voice or words which are thus produced, are immediately interpreted, within the poem, by the friends who surround the body. In short, they 'represent' the text of these dying words, this dying breath, to themselves in an activity of interpretation. This representation of the dying text does not quite 'get it right'. They interpret the breath as saying 'now' or 'no'. As Hartman comments, it is the merest breath, the merest inflectional difference between these two interpretations or representations which either kill the speaker ('now') or suggest a fight against death ('no'). It is almost as if the most minimal 'inspiration', the most minimal breath, produced the minimal text, 'to go'; and this text is *immediately* subject to deformational or, better, transformational representation. The mourners hear the text differently and thus represent it to themselves differently.

The 'original' or 'present' dying man or men are immediately lost in any case, as the poem continues by shifting attention to the lovers and their own 'feigned death', their own separation. There is a similarity here to the 'Lecture'. In that poem the moment of noon, the critical 'present' which forms the crux of the text, is a moment which is identified by separation: 'and to brave clearness all things are reduced' (it should also be noted, of course, that this individuation is written of as a 'reduction' from a superior or logically anterior state of community). The design of that text is such that the spatial expansion of the lovers into the environment, in the stretch of their shadows, is progressively reduced. Once a base-point is reached, of individuated separation, there is a threatened expansion immediately, with the production of a kind of counter-movement. Such an organization, of expansion and contraction, is one I have indicated also in 'The Flea'; and in the 'Lecture' this movement approximates to the motion of the flea as it breathes, in its 'living walls of Jet'.

It is at a similar crucial moment of the breath, between expansion and contraction, between inhalation and expiration, that the 'Valediction: forbidding mourning' is set. This moment becomes a moment both of some kind of death, and also some kind of minimal activity of representation, in the production of the breathy differentiation between the enunciation of 'now' and 'no'. The breath which differentiates between these two words also distinguished both of them from the minimal text which the dying breath utters or whispers, 'to go'; and even at this level, it must be noted that the words 'to go' are themselves already an interpretation or manifestation or representation of the breath of the dying speaker. A breathy differentiation is announced in these first lines of the poem as a means of deferring death and separation.

More pertinently, there is an equation of the death with the breath. Such an identification of the instant of death (and in its 'feigned' or muted forms, sleep and separation) with the instant of the breath in utterance is very common in Donne's poems. The uttering breath, further, tends to utter or represent such minimal texts as 'to go', 'go', 'so', 'two', 'goest' and by punning extension 'ghost', and so on. To breathe, almost, becomes 'to go', or at least expresses the breath in an expiratory separation. Similarly the production of a text, the production of such an utterance, might become easily analogous to the fact of separation, individuation and a kind of 'feigned death'. The 'voice' or soul of Donne has, as it were, always disappeared from the glassy surface of the text, the mirror which reflects the signs of life or of his breath. But what these texts are fundamentally are signs of *absence*, rather than the presence of the individuated clearly definable author, John Donne.

Death and breath are equated further in poems such as 'A Feaver', where the lines reiterate the same kind of gesture as was operational in the Valediction poem, 'forbidding mourning':

> But yet thou canst not die, I know,
>> To leave this world behinde, is death,
> But when thou from this world wilt goe,
>> The whole world vapors with thy breath.[16]

Understanding 'go' here in a similar way as in 'forbidding mourning', we have the notion once more that 'going' is an equivalent of breathing or, more precisely, of expiring. Further, such a moment of separation instigates the process of entropic representations. If this woman is to 'go', then, as the following stanza makes clear, any other woman will be but a failed representation of her:

> Or if, when thou, the worlds soule, goest,
>   It stay, 'tis but thy carkasse then,
> The fairest woman, but thy ghost,
>   But corrupt wormes, the worthyest men.

This particular 'going' instigates the rhetoric of poetry in the precise form of the metaphors of women as ghost, men as worms, and world as bodily carcass.

But such metaphors, of course, are meant to demonstrate merely the failure of representation, in the loss of the presence of the fevered woman. After such an 'expiration' (and this word conveys both the required senses of breathing out and of dying) on the part of the woman, an expiration which signifies or is her departure and the separation of herself from the world, the possibilities of womanhood are exhausted; any other woman remains only as a kind of ghost or spiritual representation, that is to say, as dying breath, of this fevered woman herself.

In other words, the transient fever which the poem rehearses is, in a sense, cured within the text itself. The threat of the final expiration is overcome in the sophistical re-inspiration (an artificial respiration, so to speak), in the discovery of the 'ghost' which constitutes the continued breath of the fevered woman; she lives on in this sense and in these breaths, or ghosts. Her breath is repeated, and the final expiration deferred; indeed she is in the process not of decay but rather of recovery in the enunciation of the poem. 'Goings' are but 'burning fits' and 'meteors'. She represents herself, in the continued breath or in the ghosts which the world offers. But this makes her, as it were, the ghost of herself, the spiritual representation of her own breath or soul. Once more, the presence is merely ghostly; the woman herself becomes one of the ghosts of the world, one of its representations or manifestations of the archetypal beauty which her body articulates.

Morever, the very relation which has brought this state of affairs about in this stanza is that between the words 'goest' and 'ghost', a relation which could be characterized as rhyme, but which might equally well, and more aptly here, be called 'failed representation'. 'Ghost' repeats 'goest', and *transforms* it; the 'goest' itself returns as a ghostly informant of the word 'ghost' and establishes a critical difference within that very word: 'ghost' now has some kind of difference from itself inscribed into its very meaning. That is to say, there is no 'ghost' present in the word 'ghost': it differs from itself and is itself but a failed representation of the ghostly. But this transformation or failed representation is what keeps the possibility of continued life or breath for the woman in the poem. The first instance of the pun here, in the line 'Or if, when thou, the worlds soule, goest', now echoes with another sense; it is an address to 'thou' as 'world's soul' and, in apposition to this, as 'ghost'. This 'original' woman is herself already a ghost, then, so that, when we discover that other women are but ghosts of this 'original', we discover a potentially infinite regression. For these women are now but the ghosts of a ghost, shadows of a shadow; they are representations not of an anterior presence, but rather of a different representation merely. There are no 'presences' (and, paradoxically, no ghosts), only representations.

Perhaps the most frequent equation of 'going' with breathing comes in poems which make more or less explicit use of conventional Petrarchan idiom, where sighs of lovers at moments of separation are mediated as the final expiration of their souls. This occurs in one way or another in many of Donne's 'poems of departure' as they may be called, and most clearly of all perhaps in 'A Valediction: of weeping':

> Since thou and I sigh one another's breath,
> Who e'er sighes most, is cruellest, and hasts the others death.

or in the 'Song: Sweetest love, I do not go':

> When thou sigh'st, thou sigh'st not winde,
>   But sigh'st my soule away.

There is a clear collocation of the expiratory breath with death in a poem such as 'The Will' which is almost a complete poem of departure, a kind of hugely sublimated euphemism for the final word 'go', a word in which *logos* matches *ergon*, enunciation matches or is performance:

> Before I sigh my last gaspe, let me breath,
> Great Love, some Legacies . . .

This is the opening of 'The Will', and the rest of the poem could be understood as a huge extrapolation (or interpretation or reading) from the primal breathing word, the primal enunciation, 'go', signifying most immediately death, departure and separation. A slightly less sexual kind of separation is obvious in a poem such as Satire 1, 'Away, thou fondling motley humorist'. Here, the humorist (perhaps as an aspect of the speaker's divided personality, a representation or image of the persona) rushes from the poet in the street and away to his love, leaving the poet alone:

> At last his Love he in a windowe spies,
> And like light dew exhaled, he flings from mee
> Violently ravished to his lechery.

There is some evidence here to suggest that the poet and humorist are one, and that this is another Donnean 'dialogue of one', as he calls it in 'The Extasie'. For what the humorist sees in a window is, of course, his own image or representation, his own breath. But it is important to make this clear: it is not that there is a split personality in a conventionally understood sense, with two 'persons' somehow uneasily cohabiting in the presence of one body; rather, it is *two personae without one person* here, for the representation in the window is also generative of the 'representation' of the 'real' humorist. That is to say, the window offers the reflection of its own reflection, and we have two mirrors, two breaths, facing each other. The speaker, for instance, is described in precisely the terms of imprisonment in which we find the humorist in the body of the poem. They thus reflect their own images back on each other:

> Leave mee, and in this standing wooden chest,
> Consorted with these few bookes, let me lye
> In prison, and here be coffined, when I dye . . .

> . . .Now we are in the street; He first of all
> Improvidently proud, creepes to the wall,
> And so imprisoned, and hem'd in by mee
> Sells for a little state his libertie . . .

And, of course, they exchange positions in the movement of the poem, with the humorist ending up in the position of the speaker.

In other words, separation and dying as a characteristic of the activity of the breath need not be a 'real' separation between two different people; it can be, as in this text, the separation between a consciousness and the words uttered by that consciousness. This is, perhaps in greater cohesion with the contemporary theological philosophy of Donne's time, expressed in the poem in terms of the alienation of soul and body:

> At birth, and death, our bodies naked are;
> And till our Soules be unapparrelled
> Of bodies, they from blisse are banished.
> Mans first blest state was naked, when by sinne
> Hee lost that, yet hee was cloath'd but in beasts skin,
> And in this course attire, which I now weare,
> With God, and with the Muses I conferre.

Here even nakedness becomes understood in terms of clothing. For nakedness turns out to be no real nudity at all, but a clothing of the soul in bestial skin. The skin, then, as surface or material of the body is itself a representation or image of the soul. Further there occurs here a fundamental confusion of the notion of personal identity in these lines. This 'course attire' may be the clothing of the scholar, worn by the speaker; but it may also, now, be referring to the bestial skin of the soul of the speaker, the speaker's breath, which is to be revealed in instants of birth and death. To that extent it is, punningly, a *'corps' attire*, the body itself. Who, we might now ask, is wearing motley? For what the speaker wears, through the pun here, becomes itself the embodiment of motley changeability, as the dress of the scholar becomes the dress of the jester. Morever, this motley is itself characterized as a state of supposed nudity, the skin of the body. Now, scholar and jester are not representations of two different people or even guises; rather there is no person here at all, but only a series of personae. That is to say, motley is the condition of human existence here: we are all, in our most complete nakedness, still wearing motley, still mutable representations of a self which is nowhere present. Like the space between two reflecting mirrors (between the motley humorist and the lover/window), there is a vacancy, an absence, which describes the human condition. Any reality which can be generated from this absence depends upon motley, upon mutable *representation* only.

That is to say, there is always a gap or space between a persona and her or his words, her or his breath. This is the dislocation which used to be considered in terms of the essential soul and the material and relative body. Here, though, it is construed in such a manner that even the soul, the breath, is mediated not as essence but as representation, as transient and mutable image. In the fact of self-consciousness then, such as we have it in Satire 1, the breath or utterance or representation of the (now absent) self can be, indeed must be, *hypocritical*. Hypocrisis such as this (most basically, of course, in the ascription of personal evil under the alias of the motley humorist) is axiomatic to Donne's mode of representation in writing. Representation implies failure and loss, and these imply change and transformation: the represented 'entity' or 'somewhat' becomes more and more absent, as it were, more and more transformed through a series of representations, and representations of representations. In their turn then change and transformation seem to imply, for Donne, entropy, disease and death, or 'going' in time. In other words, even if we could find the much vaunted individual voice of Donne, we would discover it to be fundamentally split and double, even duplicitous; it would be a representation of itself, and a hypocritical representation at that. The voice is no longer carried on Donne's breath, as it were.

Donne's alchemical fascination with the elements insists upon the relation between air, as the medium of the human breath, and its embodiment in such representations as angels, apparitions, ghosts and so on. Underlying the poems which deal explicitly with this topic ('Aire and Angels', 'The Apparition', 'The Blossome', 'The Computation', 'Loves Deitie', and Satire 3 with its intertextual reference to *Hamlet* and 'thy father's spirit'), there is a fundamental concern with the air as a medium for the embodiment of the voice, with the materiality of words themselves. In this respect interpretation of the texts as material writing becomes more important than assertions about the supposed character of Donne; for, if the texts represent anything of Donne, they represent or indicate only his *absence*, not his material presence.

The first of Donne's poems to appear in the materiality of print was 'The Expiration', which appeared in 1609. His first publication then, or the first expression of his writing beyond the circle of friends who read or heard manuscripts being recited, was precisely an 'expiration', an exhalation of the breath (and perhaps also a death of sorts). In the activity of writing or transcribing this dying breath, this expiration, a transformation comes about; this is clearly not a 'faithful' recording of the breathy voice of Donne. The inevitability of this transformation is explicable in the terms of Satire 5, from which I take one epigraph to the present chapter where I have set some lines from this poem in apposition to Hopkins's lines from 'As kingfishers catch fire'. Hopkins's text, concerned with the *haecceitas* ('thisness') of the worldly objects of its descriptions, strives to present faithfully the elements of the world which the poetry celebrates. But this is 'achieved', if at all, only through gross distortions (*ostranenie*, making strange) of the world and especially of language and the speaking voice. Moreover, this very mode of linguistic description and distortion invites an *infidelity* to the *haecceitas* of the world and its elements. For Hopkins is always forced to confuse the object of his description with himself as phenomenological perceiver of the object; and, more importantly, his distorted language or 'style' *exceeds* its supposed object: 'I say more'.

Donne seems perhaps to have been already aware of this potential confusion or interference among the elements of the world. Each thing in the world is to be perceived, according to these lines in Donne, as a microcosmic model of the entire world which it articulates or 'represents':

> If all things be in all,
> As I thinke, since all, which were, and are, and shall
> Bee, be made of the same elements:
> Each thing, each thing implyes or represents.
> Then man is a world . . .

This is to say, representation, even in the form of the most perfect repetition, is never 'faithful'. The very repetitions in these lines stress this fact. 'Be' and 'each thing' are repeated in a very obvious manner, drawing attention to the fact of their repetition through the convoluted syntax. A paraphrase of the fourth line here cited, 'Each thing, each thing implyes or represents', would be 'Each thing represents each thing', or, putting it more algebraically and abstractly, 'X represents X'. However, even though the line uses such direct and perfect repetition, it stresses the *difference* between X and X, between 'each thing' and 'each thing'; it stresses the difference not only between each thing and its representation, but also between each thing and itself. Given that there are no presences, but only representations, then each thing differs from that representation of itself which it is. So that the sense of this line might be more like 'Each thing represents just about everything *except* itself, except that thing which it is'. This justifies logically the otherwise irrational proposition that 'man is a world'. In fact here the very elemental *haecceitas* of things is brought into question: now, for example, 'man' is not and cannot be identical with 'man' or with himself, but is here 'a world'.

In this instance Hopkins is following in the line of Duns Scotus, arguing for or giving credence to a principle of individuality, thisness, *haecceitas*. Donne, on the other hand, is more clearly in the Jesuitical line of Thomas Aquinas, denying the possibility of knowledge of individuals and remaining content with knowledge of form, of universals rather than 'accidents'. However, it is the universal formal *quidditas* of objects which is now being brought into question through extensive attention being drawn to meta-phorical language. These few lines stress the fundamental and intrinsic aspect of self-differentiation which is integral to the 'identity' of a concept, an object or an element. In articulating the *quidditas* of the universal concept, Donne establishes not its self-identity, but rather a principle of difference actually within the supposed integrity of the concept. In short, the elements, as in a metaphor, undergo a process of self-transformation: 'man' becomes 'a world', and such a metaphorical proposition becomes perfectly logical, acceptable, even normative.

'The Expiration' has one of the most fundamental transformations of this kind as one of its central organizational principles. The poem mutates between the opening duplication of the word 'so' towards its closing duplication of the word 'go'. It is, as it were, a movement between inspiration and expiration, between kissing and parting, between 'sucking' or inhaling (and perhaps 'so-ing'/'sowing') and 'bidding' or expiring ('go-ing'). The poem opens:

> So, so, breake off this last lamenting kisse,
>> Which sucks two soules, and vapors Both away,
> Turne thou ghost that way, and let mee turne this . . .

Here there is an equivalence between 'so' and the kiss; the enunciation or breathing which pronounces the word 'so' (and this is what an expiring or dying breath sounds like, a whispered 'so' through pursed lips) is, as it were, the sucking motion of inhalation, a motion which seems to fit the description of the poem's kiss. 'So' is repeated for the simple reason perhaps that there are two lovers involved, two kisses, and two extensions of this 'so', in the two 'souls'. Elaborating on the idea explored in my interpretation of 'A Feaver', the lovers, once they have stopped kissing, are but empty representational carcasses of each other, 'ghosts'. But there is, clearly, a pun involved here. 'Ghost' is itself a reiteration of 'goest', and the line means, among other things, 'thou goest that way'. Along

with this verbal turning, there is also the silent half-transfor-
mation of the word 'so' through 'soul' into 'ghost' (perhaps via a mute
'ghoul') and thus into 'go'. It is towards the enunciation or the
breathing of this word that the poem moves and develops. The text
is, after all, an 'expiration' and strives towards such an expiration
articulated in the verbal inflection 'go'. That word is again repeated
twice, despite the fact that the text asserts that it will not be said
at all:

> nor will we owe
> Any, so cheape a death, as saying, Goe;

> Goe; and if that word have not quite kill'd thee,
> Ease me with death, by bidding mee goe too ...

Not only is the word repeated twice, at the very instant in which the
speaker denies that it will be said; there is also a demand for its
further echoing in the second stanza. The text mutates from the
kiss (so) to the expiration or death (go). The difference between love
and death here would seem to be that slight, a simple verbal slip.
Moreover, since the poem mutates the word or verbal inflection 'so'
into 'go', there may be no real slip here at all: the notion of death may
indeed be, linguistically at least here, interwoven into the fact of
the breathy kiss, and vice versa.

 Moreover, the assumption that this poem is a poem dramatizing a
scene of separation between two distinct lovers is an unnecessary
one. Just as in Satire 1 the speaker is, in a sense, speaking to himself
or herself here, establishing or discovering a differential principle,
that is a difference, as the very condition of her or his 'identity'. S/he
realizes the paradox of the assertion: 'I will not say "Go" '. This
paradox entails the very expiration, enunciation or going which it
seems to want to deny. That is, the voice which utters the final
word of that phrase cannot be identified, by definition, with the 'I'
which proclaims that it will not utter the word. There is a difference
within this supposedly self-identical 'I'. Further, the first instance of
the word 'I' in the phrase is not itself identifiable with some
supposedly transcendent identity. The speaker here has to say 'go'
in order to deny that s/he will say it. This forces the Freudian slip of
the tongue which facilitates the enunciation 'go' as a replacement
or transmutation of 'so':

> Ease mee with death, by bidding mee goe too.
> Or, if it have, let my word worke on mee,
>   And a just office on a murderer doe . . .

The word, 'accidentally' uttered or exhaled, turns back upon its speaker; that is, it 're-turns' as a 'ghost', like the ghost of 'The Apparition' and haunts the speaker. Thus the speaker may indeed here be talking to her or himself. There need be no 'real' kiss and separation at all. The poem could rather be the merest dramatization of the acts of inspiration and expiration, the act of the breath which enunciates death as a very condition and determinant of its being, and difference as the condition of its identity: 'so . . . go'.

Such an expiration, such a mutation between 'so' and 'go' is repeated within the poem, in its final couplet:

> Except it be too late, to kill me so,
>   Being double dead, going, and bidding, goe.

This double death occurs because there are two breaths, two expirations in the formation of the poem: 'The Expiration' represents 'The Expiration', as it were, and thus doubles itself. These two expirations may indeed be characterized as the breaths of two lovers, but it is more cogent to consider them as the two breaths of a single (self-differential) speaker. In this case it is as if the second breath, a representation or echo of the first, comes more quickly (over the space of two lines), closer to death than the first one. The movement of expiration is itself doubled in this, either in the speaker's correspondent (ultimately, of course, the person who rehearses 'The Expiration', that person who 'inspires' it or breathily enunciates and materializes it, the reader), or alternatively, in the speaker her or himself, effecting the transformation of 'so' into 'go' with increasing rapidity as s/he 'expires' or dies.

Many of Donne's poems obey a similar sort of pattern. They are, in a sense, minimalist poems, in that they dramatize the most basic inflections of tongue and breath, making a poem from the difference between inhalation and exhalation, between the phonemes 'so' and 'go', for instance. More generally, what is going on in this kind of practice is a metaphysical incarnation or materialization of the breath or spirit in the form of the word. Such an aesthetic clearly has its roots in theological notions of incarnation. But in Donne's poetry there is a counterpart to the notion of incarnation, in the function of imagination, making imaginary or dematerializing the word in a sense. Another way of regarding this might be to consider a function in Donne's poetry which changes the status of the alphabetically written word: rather than considering this printed word as an object, or even as surrogate object (occupying the place of the 'real' object designated by the word), it might be more apposite to consider the word as *event*. Paradoxically, this dematerializing or imagination of the printed word renders it more historical, that is, more *real*. Ricoeur is appropriate at this point, in what he suggests concerning the effect of this upon the practice of reading generally:

> It is undoubtedly necessary to go still further: just as the world of the text is real only insofar as it is imaginary, so too it must be said that the subjectivity of the reader comes to itself only insofar as it is placed in suspense, unrealised, potentialised. In other words, if fiction is a fundamental dimension of the reference of the text, it is no less a fundamental dimension of the subjectivity of the reader. As reader, I find myself only by losing myself. Reading introduces me into the imaginative variations of the *ego*. The metamorphosis of the world in play is also the playful metamorphosis of the *ego*.[17]

This is to say, the self which is formed through the act of reading becomes fundamentally historical, engaged in the production of a series of differences from itself, projecting itself forward in desire into a constantly deferrable final position or identity. This self (and its desire) must, by definition, be fundamentally *hypocritical*. Hypocrisis can be understood here in some such sense as 'betrayal', 'infidelity', 'differentiation', 'lack of identity' or even 'lack of faith'. It is this aspect of hypocrisis which informs both the notions of transformational representation (the failure of mimesis, or the failure of 'true' presentation of a stable self) and also the notion of entropic adulteration of the writing as a condition of its reading. This requires further explication and examination.

Notes

1 Hans Blumenberg, *The Legitimacy of the Modern Age* (1966) (trans. Robert M. Wallace), Cambridge, Mass., MIT Press, 1983, 139.
2 T.S. Eliot, *Selected Essays*, 3rd edn, London, Faber, 1951, repr. 1980, 287–8.
3 John Milton, *Paradise Lost*, Book 8, lines 615–29.
4 Walter J. Ong, *Orality and Literacy*, London, Methuen, 1982, 91.

5 William Carlos Williams, 'This is just to say', reprinted in Michael Roberts (ed.), *The Faber Book of Modern Verse*, revised by Donald Hall, 3rd edn, Faber, 1965, 286.

6 William Shakespeare, *Hamlet*, II, i.

7 John Carey, *John Donne, Life, Mind and Art*, London, Faber, 1981, 9–10.

8 T.S. Eliot, op. cit., 286; F.R. Leavis, *Revaluation* (1936), reprinted Harmondsworth, Penguin, 1972, 18; R.G. Cox, 'The poems of John Donne' in Boris Ford (ed.), *Pelican Guide to English Literature 3: From Donne to Marvell* revised edn., Harmondsworth, Penguin, 1974, 101–2.

9 Donne, 293, 294, 295, 299.

10 Donne, 297.

11 Donne, 63–4.

12 Donne, 39–40.

13 See Charles Sanders Peirce, *Collected Papers* (ed. Charles Hartshorne, Paul Weiss and Arthur W. Burks in 8 vols), Cambridge, Mass., Harvard University Press, 1931–58; for a brief introduction to the concepts of *index*, *icon* and *symbol* in Peirce's semiotics, see Terence Hawkes, *Structuralism and Semiotics*, London, Methuen, 1977, 128–30.

14 William Shakespeare, *King Lear*, V, iii; and cf. A.C. Bradley, *Shakespearean Tragedy* (1904), reprinted London, Macmillan, 1974, 241, for the classic, but critically misguided, attempt to 'recuperate' Cordelia's death and to suggest that Lear dies in 'unbearable *joy*', convinced that Cordelia lives. The reading suggested in the present study should controvert Bradley's seeming trust in the absolute veracity of signs.

15 Geoffrey Hartman, *Saving the Text*, Baltimore, Johns Hopkins University Press, 1981, 26, 153–4.

16 Donne, 20.

17 Paul Ricoeur, *Hermeneutics and The Human Sciences* (trans. John B. Thompson), Cambridge, Cambridge University Press, 1981, 144; and cf. Ong, op. cit., *passim*, on the Hebrew term *dabar* which means both 'word' and 'event'; cf. also Kenneth Burke's work on the 'dramatistic' (for example in his *Language as Symbolic Action*, Berkeley and Los Angeles, University of California Press, 1966, *passim*), which also makes the poem less of a 'thing' and more of a historical action or event. Note also, in the lines quoted from Ricoeur here, the theological aspect of the 'loss of self' as a means of finding the self; a notion which is of relevance to Donne in specific terms.

INTERSTICE

4
Identity and difference:
individuality betrayed

Les questions de l'art, du style, de la vérité ne se laissent donc pas dissocier de la question de la femme. Mais la simple formation de cette problématique commune suspend la question 'qu'est-ce que la femme?' On ne peut plus chercher la femme ou la fémininité de la femme ou la sexualité féminine. Du moins ne peut-on les trouver selon un mode connu du concept ou du savoir, même si on ne peut s'empêcher de les chercher.

Il n'y a pas d'essence de la femme parce que la femme écarte et s'écarte d'elle-même. Elle engloutit, envoile par le fond, sans fin, sans fond, toute essentialité, toute identité, toute propriété... Il n'y a pas de vérité de la femme mais c'est parce que cet écart abyssal de la vérité, cette non-vérité est la 'vérité'. Femme est un nom de cette non-vérité de la vérité.

Il n'y a pas une femme, une vérité en soi de la femme en soi, cela du moins, il [Nietzsche] l'a dit.... Pour cette raison même, il n'y a pas une vérité de Nietzsche ou du texte de Nietzsche.

(The questions of art, of style, and of truth cannot be dissociated from the question of woman. But the mere formulation of their common problematic suspends the question 'what is woman?'. One can no longer pursue the woman or the femininity of woman or feminine sexuality. At least, one cannot find these by following recognized modes of thought or of knowledge; even if one cannot stop oneself from seeking them.

There is no essence of woman because woman diverts* and moves aside from herself. She swallows up and veils† endlessly

and without ever touching bottom all essentiality, all identity
and all propriety ... There is no truth of woman, but it is because
this abyssal swerve from the truth, this non-truth is the 'truth'.
Woman is a name for this non-truth of truth.

There is no such thing as woman, no truth in itself of woman in
herself; this much, at least, Nietzsche has said ... For this very
same reason, there is no such thing as the truth of Nietzsche or of
the text of Nietzsche.]

(Jacques Derrida, *Eperons*)

* *écarter* also means 'to spread the legs'
† *envoiler* hovers between 'veiling' and 'bending' as a sail

the Conceit of Dones transformation or μετεμψυχοσις was
that he sought the soule of that Aple which Eva pūlled, and
therafter made it the soule of a Bitch, then of a sheewolf & so of a
woman. his general pūrpose was to have brought jn all the bodies
of the Hereticks from ye soūle of Cain & at last left it jn ye body of
Calvin. of this he never wrotte but one sheet, & now since he was
made Doctor repenteth highlie & seeketh to destroy all his
poems.

(Ben Jonson, *Conversations* with
William Drummond of Hawthornden)

1

In late Renaissance England human identity was related to
questions of space and place. 'Place is identity' in a hierarchized
topology of the universe and society. The scheme, of hierarchized
hygienic propriety, subtends at least two major consequences.
Firstly, a principle of individuation comes to dominate notions of
personal identity: we each have our 'own', 'proper' place in the social
system. Secondly, this 'place' is itself determined in terms of capital,
private 'ownership', specifically of land. This, in turn, goes with
some theological notions, derived from Duns Scotus, concerned
with the supposedly fundamental individual thisness or *haecceitas*
of the objects of our perception. It is commonly thought that Donne
subscribed to such notions of individuality, if not to Scotist
philosophy; in fact, however, his writing challenges these notions of
individuation.

These notions of 'spatial' identity are supported further by
temporal consolidations of a principle of individuality in personal

identity. At roughly the same historical moment, the so-called 'nuclear' family becomes a dominant mode of social organization, regulating individual identities and social names. Stone acutely comments that 'It was the relation of the individual to his lineage which provided a man of the upper classes in a traditional society with his identity, without which he was a mere atom floating in a void of social space'.[1] Parents, especially fathers, 're-present' themselves precisely in the figure of their offspring, especially sons; and the 'identity' of father and son in this organization preserves the myth of sameness through historical time: that is, it preserves the myth of the individual essence of the identity (sameness) of a person, and more precisely of a personal 'proper' name.

The production of children, images of the self, is perhaps one fairly basic form of 'representation' available as a social fact. Many of Donne's poems deal in one way or another with such ideas of the generation or regeneration of himself. True identity is retained only if these representations are regulated according to an ethos of 'legitimacy': bastards threaten to disperse or displace the integrity of the familial name or identity. Identity has to be legitimated if the myth of individual essence is to be maintained. Donne ponders this issue in many poems, both sacred and secular. Satire 3, 'Kind pitty chokes my spleene', is an example which unites the sacred and the secular in this area of contentious debate. The poem is, among other things, about the discovery of an identity, that of the true church. This identity is aligned with personal human identity; the present is considered as a representation of an original fathering source of truth and authenticity or legitimacy. Looking for these identities, and specifically for that of the 'true church', Donne writes:

> unmoved thou
> Of force must one, and forc'd but one allow;
> And the right; aske thy father which is shee,
> Let him aske his; though truth and falshood bee
> Neare twins, yet truth a little elder is;
> Be busie to seeke her . . .[2]

This is the notion that verifiable identity, authentic individual essence, is maintained through the regulation of history in the form of faithful repetition or representation. The problem, however, is that such representation is impossible, as I argued above. Further, not only did Donne 'betray' the faith of his father and familial heritage, he also wrote a large number of poems which either argue that this kind of betrayal is fundamentally constitutive of fidelity to 'reality' or truth, or which demonstrate that faithful representation is saturated by *hypocrisis*, infidelities, betrayals or transformations of reality. Truth and identity are muddled thereby.

In fact, Donne most frequently substitutes 'interpretation' for 'truth'; unfaithful representation for individual essentiality. He replaces the notion of individuality with that of *ecclesia*, congregation and the identification of the self only through its relation to community, specifically the community of the church. Satire 3, with its early allusion to *Hamlet* ('shall thy fathers spirit/Meete blinde Philosophers in heaven') domesticates the issue of identity and truth. This allusion to *Hamlet*, moreover, refers us to a play in which there is a predominance of questions about domestic fidelity and sexual promiscuity. Against the lines from Satire 3 cited above, we can immediately place many contrary poems: 'The Curse' dramatizes the inheritance of betrayal itself; Elegies 1 and 4 both contain and seemingly validate scenes of domestic infidelity; and 'Confined Love' is a sustained argument against the 'naturalness' of monogamy, and in favour of promiscuity and community. Donne seems, even at this most basic level of content, to attend more obsessively to the dissolution of identity which results from an ethos of promiscuity than he does to the flattering myth of personal individuation.

Elegy 1, for instance, celebrates the discovery of the means of maintaining an adulterous relation outside the bounds of a domestic space or home, the locus of assured identity. Basic to the poem is the fact of the male's ownership of his 'properties': the other people in the house, the social space of the house, and the entire domestic personality or character, including the personal 'property' of the woman. The text argues, however, that though the jealous husband may control the private realm of this space, still betrayal can, indeed will, occur:

> Now I see many dangers; for that is
> His realme, his castle, and his diocesse.
> But if, as envious men, which would revile
> Their Prince, or coyne his gold, themselves exile
> Into another countrie, 'and doe it there,
> Wee play'in another house, what should we feare?

There we will scorne his houshold policies,
His seely plots, and pensionary spies,
As the inhabitants of Thames right side
Do Londons Major; or Germans, the Popes pride.[3]

Here the woman's proposed adultery threatens the identity, property and familial name or integrity of her husband; in short, she threatens to rupture the walls of the house, which equate with the walls of his individual essence. As such, she poses a threat to the individuality which is identified or fetishized in the domestic property, that of the male authority in the household. Further, although we normally consider these lines to be spoken by an adulterous lover, it is quite easy to imagine them as spoken by the *husband*. In the arrangement of the nuclear family, this husband would have threatened the integrity of the identity of the woman's father in precisely the same terms as an 'adulterous' lover threatens that of a husband. Fundamentally, then, the text helps show that 'betrayal' is a basic constituent of 'fidelity'. Betrayal in these terms is positively obsessive in Donne's poetry.

There is an important corollary to this. Donne may intend the most faithful representation of himself or of his consciousness in his poems, but the public reading of the texts threatens them with dissemination or with an 'adulteration' of any such fidelity. The poems, as the fetishistic location of Donne's 'individuality' (as his property, 'signed' and 'owned' by him) undergo transformation or contamination in their representation or reproduction. As the reader 'animates' them, breathes through them, the texts fundamentally change. Any picture we might construct of Donne, then, is but a *hypocrisis* of Donne, a hypocrisis upon a hypocritical 'representation' of Donne. There is, simply, no pure identity of Donne which is accessible to us through the writing. His much vaunted 'individuality' is based upon an evasion of the theoretical problems which the texts themselves raise for the notions of individuality and personal identity.

Elegy 5, 'His Picture', would be an obvious case in point here. The poem is explicitly about representation, and shows that in Donne, fidelity to historical realities is grounded necessarily upon infidelity to, difference from and transformation of, those realities. Such transformation, of course, further corroborates the notion that this writing is itself historical activity. These poems are not, and cannot be, the 'verbal icons' of a New Criticism; they are rather historical *action*, activities of writing in the historical realm of symbolicity. This is to say that, in describing reality, reality is of necessity displaced and transformed; the individuality of objects or persons, their specific *haecceitas*, even if it were to be considered as really existent in some way, must remain unknown to us and inaccessible to language. Donne writes:

> Here take my Picture; though I bid farewell,
> Thine, in my heart, where my soule dwels, shall dwell.
> 'Tis like me now, but I dead, 'twill be more
> When wee are shadowes both, then 'twas before.[4]

He then goes on to give a portrait or representation of himself on his return from battle. There are then at least two portraits in question here: there is the picture given to the lover (which we do not 'see' or have in any represented detail in the poem), and there is also the picture which the *text* gives, fulfilling its titular promise, an image of Donne as battle-worn, wounded and (and this is the single most substantial point here) *changed*. This is a moving picture show. The poem is set at a moment of crisis, the moment of departure; and the picture offered by the poet (not the poem) is supposed to be a kind of preservative of this temporal instant. However, there is no identity between the picture given to the lover who is left behind and the picture which the text *hypocritically* represents. The moment of crisis becomes one of hypocrisis. Donne gives one picture and, in the act of representation itself, betrays that picture, giving another entirely dissimilar portrait. To repeat: there are (at least) two pictures or representations here (not including the images of the lover which are implied but never represented). There is one of the fair and delicate Donne (as he 'presently' is, in the critical moment of departure); and there is the one which the text actually proffers (the representation, a hypocritical image of Donne) of a wounded, foul coarse man: fair is foul. In other words, in the very poem in which we might expect the most 'faithful' representation of Donne, we have, once more, a hypocritical betrayal of that image, and its transformation into something else. Donne, quite genuinely, is 'wounded' in the poem, even 'killed'; for the supposed identifiable individual Donne becomes a series of representational hypocrises, a series of disintegrating figures or masks, as it were. 'His Picture' moves, changes and becomes, finally, unnameable, unidentifiable.

It should be noted that there is a distinction being made here between what the *poet* gives and what the *poem* gives, in terms of representations. Such a distinction is common in hermeneutics, offering two different modes of interpretive practice. Ricoeur, in his examinations of Schleiermacher and Dilthey, calls these two modes 'Romantic' and 'critical'. Basically the Romantic mode, as favoured by Schleiermacher, concerns itself not with what a text says, but rather with who says it: that is, with the specific identity of an authorial source or consciousness which informs it with meaning. This is problematized somewhat after Dilthey (who nonetheless remains himself within the Romantic mode to an extent). Dilthey examined more closely the historical determinants of interpretation and knowledge: 'What there is in human nature is revealed by the great turning-points of history. For history alone shows what man is'.[5] According to this, we have to come to some interpretive understanding of the 'text' of history before we can arrive at any knowledge of specific human individuals. According to Ricoeur, it is Heidegger who finally takes the Diltheian insight to its logical limit, in a shift which bases hermeneutics on the philosophy of Hegel rather than that of Kant. Understanding is grounded then not upon 'being-with' an other who would duplicate and guarantee our subjectivity, not concerned with understanding another 'psychology' (or not upon the supposed 'Romantic' communication between two consciousnesses); rather understanding is grounded in terms of our 'being-in' the world, in the wider sphere of historical determinations. 'The question of the *world* takes the place of the question of the other. In thereby making understanding *worldly*, Heidegger *de-psychologises* it,' writes Ricoeur.[6]

This is relevant to the problem of representation, and specifically to that of self-representation in Donne. Romantic hermeneutics bears some similarity to the conceptual base of the philosophy of Duns Scotus, a contemporary and rival of Thomas Aquinas. Scotus organized much of his thought around a principle of individuation, *haecceitas*; Aquinas, on the other hand, thought that the real object of human knowledge was not individuals, but *forms*, and specifically what he called *substantial form*. Kenny describes the Thomist situation thus: 'The intellect can grasp what makes Socrates a man, but not what makes him Socrates'.[7]

The examination of Donne's 'His Picture' demonstrated that for Donne there is no possibility of establishing identity in an individual; if we accept that the two (or more) representations subtended by the poem have the same referent, then we must also concede that there is some element of difference which actually forms this referent and is constitutive of it. That is, the hope of identity is destroyed by the fact of Donne's fundamental difference from himself. But although it may be impossible to represent the individual, 'Donne', in all his integrated specificity and uniqueness, still there is some kind of substantial form being represented here. There is no 'uniqueness' or identifiable individuality to Donne or his consciousness here; but there is the substantial form of the *historical*, secular changing human, a 'moving picture'.

Any attempt to discover the uniqueness of Donne then, the specific or individual 'structure of his imagination', or the identity of his 'real, speaking voice' and so on, seems to be basically misguided. Any individual imagination or unique identity which may be constructed is itself determined by the wider 'text' of history and is conditioned by historical differentiation from itself. Donne's view of historical knowledge, in so far as it can be constructed from these poems, seems to have been 'de-psychologized' and anti-individual, in fact. That is to say, from the texts themselves, we can discover a Thomist substantial form of Donne, a 'universal' form which reveals itself through Donne's texts; but we cannot find any Scotist *haecceitas* or identifiable individual, 'John Donne'. This Thomist manner of thought, moreover, seems to be entirely appropriate to interpreting Donne, since he seems to have thought and written in such a way himself. In the well-known exchange between Donne and Ben Jonson on 'The First Anniversary' in commemoration of Elizabeth Drury, Donne coincides more or less precisely with this mode of thought. William Drummond of Hawthornden reports Jonson as saying:

> that Dones Anniversarie was profane and full of Blasphemies that he told Mr Donne, if it had been written of ye Virgin Marie it had been something to which he answered that he described the Idea of a Woman and not as she was.[8]

Representation of individualities seems to have been irrelevant to Donne; the substantial form or 'Idea' of his referent was more apposite. Individuality should also now be revealed to be inappropriate to our criticism of Donne's texts, in which representation, even of the most fully integrated identity, always discovers a lack of self-identity, a fundamental element of differentiation, as the constituent base of any such 'individuality'. In representation in writing, any such identifiable individuality (even supposing it existed as a historical possibility) is vitiated, adulterated, transformed or 'betrayed'.

In refusing to treat the poems of Donne as the expressions of a unique individual, validated by the specificity of that individual, I am following the critical and theoretical precepts regarding the possibilities of interpretations of representations and the production of historical knowledge which organize the texts themselves. The anti-individualist line of this criticism is fully corroborated by the cultural premises which determines the shape of the texts themselves as historical entities. But Donne's anti-individualist notions of history do not lead necessarily to the notion of Donne as proto-collectivist. Rather his leanings towards Thomist theology lead him to theologize historical eventuality. Rather than a class-collectivist notion of history, the texts are more likely to subtend an ecclesiastical view of the construction of history, with the collective as congregation or *ecclesia*. The human body then is realized or represented in the poems in terms of the church, as the 'Body of Christ' on earth. This fundamental misrepresentation is extremely important in Donne's poems.

2

The 'adulteration' of individuals was an issue of some interest to Donne. It is one aspect of what he saw as 'betrayal', a secular, most frequently sexual, counterpart to his own fundamental act of infidelity, his religious apostasy. Such a turning away or 'revolution' in Donne's life, from Rome towards England, is a revolutionary moment which is itself conditioned by notions of betrayal, infidelity or adulteration. Neither human historical relations, then, nor individual identity, can ever be 'pure': there is always some element of 'impurity' in identity, some element of differentiation which threatens the suppositious integrity of the human individual. More importantly, any such construction of individuality is seen to be dependent upon the logical priority or anteriority of the wider promiscuity of bodies which make up either the mass of the body politic or the 'mass' of the ecclesia in the Body of Christ. Such a 'Body', however, is an abstraction which requires some kind of 'incarnation' or material realization in the poetry. This area, of the incarnation of an imagination, the realization of a representation, is one which seems to be obsessive in the poems.

In 'The Expiration' it might be apposite to turn to the vexing question of identity. What is the identity, for example, of the 'ghost' in the third line: 'Turne thou ghost that way, and let mee turne this'? This ghost appears at a moment of 'go'-ing, a moment of turning away the face. Could this be some spiritual ghost in a theological sense, as well as being the materiality of the breath in going: a union, then, of the motions of 'incarnating' the word (uttering and articulating a breath or spirit), and of 'imagining' the real (converting the material word into an immaterial spirit)? If so, there is some allusion to the turning of the face away from this 'reality' of a holy or spiritual ghost; and this turn is a 'revolution' which occupies Donne very much in the Divine Meditations.

One simple example of this is Divine Meditation 1, 'Thou hast made me', in which:

> I dare not move my dimme eyes any way,
> Despaire behind, and death before doth cast
> Such terrour, and my feeble flesh doth waste
> By sinne in it, which it t'wards hell doth weigh;
> Onely thou art above, and when towards thee
> By thy leave I can looke, I rise againe . . .⁹

The speaker here is contracted to a tiny, paralysed space, as in the 'Lecture', 'The Sunne Rising' and many other poems: this is a critical revolutionary moment. Here the turn in the crisis focuses on whether Donne can return to God, can turn the face to the God who has 'gone', in a sense (being above), and who exists now as one who 'goest', as a ghost. But there is a silent echo of this kind of thing in the so-called secular or libertine poetry as well. The clearest manifestation, indeed, of Donne's fears concerning infidelity or religious betrayal occurs in the secular realm of sexual relations. The poems are full of worries about inconstancy, about the possibility or even the necessity of infidelity. In fact, one might go so far as to suggest that human love for Donne, whether love of another human (or of the reflection of the self in an other), or love of God, is always the love of a 'ghost': the object of desire has always 'gone'. As such, this love is necessarily and predominantly charac-terized by loss and infidelity. It is only through the infidelities of inconstancy that a lover can re-new, re-begin or re-present the contractual commitment to love. Revolution and discontinuity are of paramount importance here. One must 'turn the face away' in order to be able to turn the face towards and recognize the lover, always as if for the first time. That is, the love of a repeated representation (an image of the loved object) has to be replaced by a repeated act of cognition of that other: the 'ghostly' representation has to be made 'present', at least in the imaginary act of cognition. This is one of the senses of the lines from 'A Lecture': 'Love is a growing, or full constant light;/And his first minute, after noone, is night'.[10] Love, or indeed any genuine historically realized relation, must constantly be 're-presented', with all the inherent difficulties, hypocrises and infidelities that representation entails.

The relation concerned with this historical reproduction which interested Donne most was undoubtedly the sexual. The failure of mimesis, the failure to 'capture' the loved object, could be explored as a theme in writing of sexual relations; and further, the relation between word and object becomes here a basic concern. The 'reproduction' which constitutes historical action can be understood as a secularization of the theological, a realization of the articulated word, or (and here the sexual element is clearly invited) an 'incarnation' of the word or imagination. It is perhaps not too surprising, in view of this, that the relation of the human to God is mediated almost exclusively in sexual terminology.

The revolution or turning which informed Donne's relation to God was that of the resurrection, essentially, a dying to be reborn, to re-new the commitment to life, to re-produce historical life; and this is a change from one mode of existence to another, secular to sacred. In fact, it is best characterized as a change in ontological status; but, as the lines from 'Thou hast made me' already cited indicate, such a notion is immediately translated into sexual terms, terms of carnality. 'Thou hast made me', among other things, is about the construction of a cross. Like many poems discussed earlier in this study, it organizes itself around a 'crossing' or trafficking-point; but where that crossing was commercial, a market forum, in those poems, here it becomes a theological cross. The poem organizes itself around the relations between horizontality and verticality. Such a 'cross' is seen, further, as constitutive of the critical and revolutionary 'difference' which characterizes the 'individual' (an individual who is now to be described precisely as 'divided'). Firstly, there is an entropic decay of the speaker's horizons, and the space behind and before narrows down into the space of the eye itself. This recapitulates the entropic reduction of the 'I' to which the opening line of the poem alludes. But, as in those other poems which toy with perspective, there is a turning-point to be awaited. Specifically the turn here effects a revolution which converts the horizontal into the vertical, thus generating the cross which informs both the poem and the 'identity' of its speaker. The poem turns at the instant of greatest waste:

> Despaire behind, and death before doth cast
> Such terrour, and my feeble flesh doth waste
> By sinne in it, which it t'wards hell doth weigh;
> Onely thou art above, and when towards thee
> By thy leave I can looke, I rise againe . . .

Horizontality (before, behind) is translated into verticality (up and down) at this point. The poem begins to make the human body or the organization of human space a embodiment of the cross itself: 'crossing' or 'difference' becomes constitutive of this body or material existence. Such an organization is central, of course, to another poem, 'The Crosse', in which the poet discovers crosses everywhere as the fundamental arrangement of space in which the human is discovered:

> Since Christ embrac'd the Crosse it selfe, dare I
> His image, th'image of his Crosse deny?
> . . .
>   the losse
> Of this Crosse, were to mee another Crosse;
> Better were worse, for, no affliction,
> No Crosse is so extreme, as to have none.
> Who can blot out the Crosse . . .
> . . .
> Who can deny mee power, and liberty
> To stretch mine armes, and mine owne Crosse to be?
> Swimme, and at every stroake, thou art thy Crosse;
> The Mast and yard make one, where seas do tosse;
> Looke downe, thou spiest out Crosses in small things;
> Looke up, thou seest birds rais'd on crossed wings;
> All the Globes frame, and spheares, is nothing else
> But the Meridians crossing Parallels.[11]

In 'Thou hast made me' it is also at the crux of the text that we discover the relation between human and divine love. Donne complains of 'my feeble flesh'. Interestingly, this is usually explicitly sexual: the 'flesh' usually refers to the genitals. In the poem this is made more clear. The flesh weighs towards hell (which, apart from its theological meaning, was also a contemporay euphemism for the vagina); that is to say, Donne is incapable of manifesting desire in the form of an erection, and his phallus points downwards, weighed towards the devil. But when given leave to look at God, to 're-cognize' God, 'I rise againe'. This clearly is now not only a resolution of the crucifix which the poem constructs, in the form of the resurrection; it is also a kind of *res*-erection, as Donne's fleshy part stands upright once more, and as the material 'thing' is ontologically raised to a different level of existence.

This casts a new light on contemporary understandings of the incarnation and transubstantiation (another kind of hypocrisis, of course). The Word made flesh becomes, in some sense, construed in sexual terms; and in this particular poem this primal word is identified with the male phallus. Donne's use of this hidden conceit is not entirely idiosyncratic, however. Cowley was to write the poem 'Coldnesse', whose basic joke is the fact that it boasts of a perpetual erection sustained by the poet, and compares this erect phallus with the rising figure of Christ:

> You may in *Vulgar Loves* find always this;
> But my *Substantial Love*
> Of a more firm, and perfect *Nature* is;
> No weathers can it move:
> Though *Heat* dissolve the *Ice again*,
> The *Chrystal* solid does remain.[12]

Here '*Substantial Love*', with its verbal hint of transubstantiation, directs attention towards the parameters of religious love. This orientation is corroborated by the pun on 'Chrystal' as 'Christ-like'. This flesh, now solid as a rock, as to speak, transubstantiates the genital flesh into the permanently erect flesh of the poet. Christ jokingly becomes a solid, unchanging love; or, as the poem has it, a kind of guaranteed perpetual erection, a *res*-erection rather than a resurrection. The Word or language in this case becomes entirely phallogocentric. The confusion of *res*-erection with resurrection is precisely what is at work also in Donne's text of 'Thou hast made me', and also in many other religious poems.

Donne's activity as a writer thus frequently comprises a basic idea that in writing, in this 'incarnation of imagination', he is performing a fundamental act of theological representation, an *imitatio Christi*. I indicated earlier, for instance, how he contrives to locate himself in the place of the sun/Son in 'The Sunne Rising', a rhetorical gesture which is tantamount to a poetic reincarnation of the figure of Christ in the figure of Donne or poet. The theological incarnation and the *imitatio Christi*, of course, are themselves both kinds of representation, the manifestation of Christ or the Son through the figure or vehicle of Donne. The question is whether this kind of representation can even be 'faithful'.

The most glaring example of such a manoeuvre, perhaps, is in Divine Meditation 11, 'Spit in my face you Jewes', in which there is a clear and avowed impersonation of Christ on the part of the poet. The poem is a demand of Donne to replace the Son, for Donne to be crucified (and subsequently glorified) in place of Christ. As in Divine Meditation 1, 'Thou hast made me', there is a kind of crucifixion or rhetorical crossing of the poet going on in the poem. Donne's brave impersonation fails, remains literally unsatisfactory as his failure, paradoxically, constitutes precisely the 'crossing' of Donne or of his intention:

> But by my death can not be satisfied
> My sinnes, which passe the Jewes impiety:
> They kill'd once an inglorious man, but I
> Crucifie him daily, being now glorified.[13]

Here, the sins spoken of may include the presumption of rehearsing God's text, repeating the words of Christ. At the point of 'communion', when Donne is, as Dean of Paul's, being his most faithful in rehearsing the words of his Christ-figure, the impersonation *fails* or miscarries, and infidelity, in the form of sinful presumptuousness, sullies the impersonation. Donne is thus 'crossed' in his aim to imitate Christ satisfactorily; but this crossing, in its paradoxical turn, turns out to substantiate precisely the *imitatio Christi*, at least at the level in which Donne is crossed figuratively, rhetorically. From *Biathanatos*, it should be recalled that Donne, in sophistries, demonstrated that Christ was a prime model for the suicide, and that Christ also 'crossed' or crucified himself. When Donne writes that 'I/Crucifie him daily, being now glorified', there is a more stringent confusion of Donne with Christ. This is no longer Donne transposing himself into the place ascribed to the Jews as killers of Christ after all; rather it is Donne in the position of Christ, 'crossing' himself, and thus being glorified. This glorification could be that of Christ on the cross; but it could equally refer to Donne's own secular glorification in his position as 're-presentative' of Christ, in his role as Dean of Paul's. This is followed by a futile attempt at humility in the final comparisons:

> God cloth'd himself in vile mans flesh, that so
> Hee might be weake enough to suffer woe.

The notion of incarnation in these lines becomes one of God taking on some kind of flesh, but flesh as a form of 'covering'. An internal comparison with Jacob is made:

> And *Jacob* came cloth'd in vile harsh attire
> But to supplant, and with gainful intent . . .

whereas God's incarnation, though itself equally a kind of disguise or covering or assumption of animal flesh, is supposedly not informed with the same kind of intent as that of Jacob. That is to say, incarnation here comes to be mediated not as a 'dis-covery' or faithful revelation of God, but rather as a tacit 're-covery', the re-covering of God under another duplicitous disguise or representation. The poem offers the reading of Donne as that very representation or *imitatio Christi*. Once more, however, this incarnation is adulterated in the factor of disguise: it is not a *pure* representation of God. While admitting thereby that Donne is not God, not the ghostly presence but merely a representation, the text still suggests that Donne is a manifestation (however impure) of God. Perhaps more importantly for a general understanding of this poetry, there is the suggestion implicit throughout that the Word, language, is based on a specific kind of 'flesh' or incarnation: the Word becoming flesh allows the construction of a phallogocentric ideology of language. Donne, in Divine Meditation 11, is conforming fairly clearly with the admonitions of Thomas à Kempis in his complaints that:

> JESUS hath now many lovers of His heavenly kingdom, but few bearers of His Cross . . .

Many follow JESUS unto the breaking of bread; but few to the
drinking of the cup of His Passion.
Many reverence His miracles, few follow the ignominy of His
Cross.[14]

But the point of the Donne text is that only an infidel can be
'crossed': the bearing of the cross requires the adoption of a position
of infidelity (the failed *imitatio Christi*) from which the infidel can
turn or deviate in order to come to a recognition of God in her or
himself.

In some of the poems the equation of Donne with Christ is
slightly more muted. Agreeing with the sentiment expressed in
Satire 5, that 'man is a world', Divine Meditation 5, 'I am a little world
made cunningly', looks for a re-elementation of Donne or a kind of
re-incarnation of Donne, in the figure of Christ. But the equation of
Christ and Donne remains less explicit here. Realising that 'black
sinne' has destroyed the world which Donne 'is' or 'represents', he
demands a new world and new elements. The poem proceeds
through the discovery of such new elements (especially water and
fire) and uses them to 'incarnate' the new world, a world understood
in terms of writing and generated through the text itself. What is
asked for, fundamentally, is a series of new writings, new maps as it
were, which constitute new geographies and new configurations,
and, since 'I am a little world', a new 'I', new people. This new world
is also established in terms of its internal difference from itself, the
non-identity of 'I' and 'I'.

The poem is a subdued version of a poem of rebirth, like those
other poems set at revolutionary or critical moments. The fire
which Donne requests turns out to be therapeutic rather than
corrupting, for it is 'a fiery zeale/Of thee and thy house, which doth
in eating heale'. At this point, the theme of re-elementation which
has been integral to the poem *turns* and becomes a kind of 're-
alimentation': Donne wants the fire, but wants to be eaten by it.
This digestive metaphor recalls the eucharistic idea of rebirth,
purification and incarnation which has been submerged through
the poem. Most importantly, it places Donne, as the aliment/
element to be eaten, in the position of the digested eucharistic body
of Christ. The poem makes of Donne a 'new I', as it were, a 'crossed I'
(self-differential) in the configuration, metaphorically attained, of
Christ.

This *imitatio Christi* informed by hypocrisis, as a construction of (displaced) identity for Donne, becomes more obviously a typical device in Divine Meditation 2, 'As due by many titles'. This poem takes the conventional domestication of religion quite seriously. Addressing God, Donne writes:

> I am thy sonne, made with thy selfe to shine,
> Thy servant, whose paines thou hast still repaid,
> Thy sheepe, thine Image, and, till I betray'd
> My selfe, a temple of thy Spirit divine . . .[15]

Here Donne explicitly refers to himself (in what is fundamentally an orthodox manner, after all) as 'image' or representation of God and uses metaphors which clarify this relation, especially 'thy sonne'. The omnipresent pun on sun/Son is here; but this time the idea of Donne as Son of God is the dominant aspect in the reading of the pun. The poem is about resignation: that is, about some kind of 're-signing'. The tenor of the argument is that the poem requires repetition and a re-signature. This re-signing is not to be done in the name of Donne, but in that of God: 'As due by many titles I resigne/My selfe to thee, O God'. The repetitions of 'I' and 'thee' in close consort in the first few lines begin to collapse the separation of 'I' and 'thee', and the resultant confusion of identity corroborates the re-signature in the name of 'Donne/God', as it were. This confusion between 'I' and 'thee', between Donne and God or Son and Father, becomes more crucial when Donne writes:

> and when I was decay'd
> Thy blood bought that, the which before was thine;
> I am thy sonne . . .

Whose blood is whose here; whose body the 'property' or identity of whom? The confusion of identity is made shockingly explicit in the identification of Donne as other than himself, as the Son or representational incarnate figure or image of the 'Father' or God. In so far as Donne is also a temple of the Spirit (a repository of the breath/spirit, perhaps, or medium through which the spirit articulates itself in history), he becomes the Holy Ghost, and its manifestation as ecclesia, as temple or church itself. This is consonant with some extreme forms of Protestantism and constitutes Donne's apostasy or 'betrayal' of Rome (and, paradoxically, his betrayal of the faith of his real historical father and parentage). The important point, however, is Donne's acknowledgement that betrayal is constitutive of this fidelity: he was a temple 'till I betray'd/My selfe'. Following the same kind of sophistry that we find in *Biathanatos*, it might be apposite to suggest that Donne found in Christ not only a model for suicidal self-crossing, but also a model for apostasy and for the betrayal of a historical lineage: Christ, after all, 'betrayed' Judaism. Betrayal thus becomes a fundamental attitude of ecclesia; and apostasy is the very constitution of Christianity.

The comment on his act of betrayal, however, could equally well be applied to Donne's *regret* at the abandonment of Rome. But this ambiguity is productive: it involves the reader in making some kind of decision. That is, it invites the reader to partake of or negate the same kind of infidelity which constitutes the poem's crisis. The poem is a rhetorical act, symbolic action as Burke would call it, radically involving us, historically, in its own critical stance. Hypocrisy, infidelity, betrayal, apostasy: these are all more or less suitable titles for the concept which dominates this and other poems. They cross the reader, forcing him or her to choose which way to 'turn' when faced with the poem's own crisis or crossing of itself.

The paradox is made more explicit in Divine Meditation 8, 'If faithfull soules be alike glorifi'd', which locates the problem of accessible, clear truth *versus* the vagaries of unreliable interpretation, or reality and its representation, within the domestic sphere of Donne's own betrayal of his father and of his father's religion. In the poem, there are two competing hypotheses: (a) if faithful souls are glorified like angels, then they perceive truth immediately, and so Donne's father could see 'That valiantly I hels wide mouth o'rstride',[16] thus making the poem redundant and assuming the propriety of his father's religion; (b) if, on the other hand, these souls have to interpret from duplicitous signs, how can they be assured of truth? There are, after all, many deceitful signs such as that of the idolatrous lover, the blaspheming conjuror or the pharisee dissembling devotion; and generally there is the factor of hypocrisis. The problem becomes one of the validation of interpretation: how to tell true from false (thus recapitulating the fall from Eden, of course), or 'How shall my mindes white truth by them be try'd?' There are two ways out. Either the first hypothesis above is the case (and the text becomes redundant and answers its own queries); or alternatively the pensive interpreting soul should turn to God, using God as a transcendent source of authoritative or legitimate interpretation.

It is this second avenue which the poem seems to open. But such an interpretation is based upon faith, itself the second word of the poem (qualified by the scepticism of 'If'). The original two hypotheses thus collapse and resolve themselves into the advocated activity of 'faithful' interpretation. Fidelity is crucial to the poem and its reading then; but the poem exists at all partly because of Donne's own infidelity, his nonconformity with the religion of his father. The poem thus becomes a blind against Donne's own infidelity, his own misinterpretations, even his own bad writings (bearing in mind that the poem is about inter-pretation). The poem also strives to protect Donne from mis-interpretation, in this sense: it is an attempt to preserve his theological safety.

But there is a problem with this. Hell is a gaping mouth in the poem, waiting to devour Donne; or, perhaps, waiting to rehearse his words in a misinterpretation which will damn Donne's soul. There is a suggestion that the poem is itself just such a demonic mouth, open to interpretation, and an opening which Donne's faith is supposed to close or 'o'rstride'. If this is the case, then 'unfaithful' interpretation, unfaithful representation on the part of a son to a father becomes crucial to the poem. If the poem is to be 'closed' or to be traversed in the security of faith, it might indeed be a text suggesting its own illegibility or illegitimacy: like the 'Lecture', it is not to be read if we and Donne are to be saved from the dangers of unfaithful, mistaken interpretation. It might thus suggest that Donne, despite outward appearances or signs, despite represen-tations such as this one, has in fact retained the faith of Rome, and exists as a faithful representation of a father or God. In short, the poem admits what it pretends to avoid: it does have to be read; but in this reading, representation or incarnation imply some kind of hypocrisis or infidelity.

The clearest address to this issue comes in Divine Meditation 19, 'Oh, to vex me, contraryes meet in one'. The poem is another 'crossing' poem, seemingly about the paradox that fidelity to God depends upon betrayal or infidelity, promiscuity or ecclesia. The final three lines of the poem compress and illustrate the paradox:

> So my devout fitts come and go away
> Like a fantastique Ague: save that here
> Those are my best dayes, when I shake with feare.[17]

The poem complains of Donne's 'inconstancies', primarily with respect to religious faith, but also in relation to other infidelities which, he claims, have informed the present wavering. But these 'devout fitts', though in appearance like a disease, turn out to be therapeutic: disease and instability are a condition of health, of Donne's 'best dayes'. The paradox arises because the genuinely felt faith is one which demands constant renewal and restatement or reiteration. Like the secular love, it has always to be on the point of beginning. This is validated most succinctly in 'Lovers infinitenesse':

> Yet I would not have all yet,
> Hee that hath all can have no more,
> And since my love doth every day admit
> New growth, thou shouldst have new rewards in store . . .[18]

Repetition or constant renewal ('re-nowal', to coin a neologism) of the confirmational contract or scene of recognition between Donne and lover (woman, self or God) is required for the love to be authenticated, considered as a legitimate love at all. Love itself, in these terms, exists in the mode of crisis, of making the decision, commitment or turning to love 'now' and 'now again' and so on. This, in fact, is the substance of the contrariety which Divine Meditation 19 welcomes, rather than laments. Once more Donne assumes the cross, contradiction, contrariety or difference for himself in the manner suggested by Thomas à Kempis. The point is that this fidelity is itself dependent on infidelity: faith is constituted by hypocrisis. Representation or incarnation of the father in the image of the son, of the word in flesh (or vice versa) is always conditioned by betrayal.

'The Dreame' from *Songs and Sonets* corroborates these proposi-tions that incarnation, understood as carnal representation or materialization of a spirit, image or idea, is in fact tantamount to infidelity; and further, that personal representation (the hypothesis that the poems are an expression or representation of an identifiable individual) is always fundamentally vitiated by hypocrisis, the difference which confounds the identity of an 'individuated' consciousness. The dreamer dreams of a partner and, at the critical turning point of awakening, the dream is actualized as reality, the partner 'incarnated'. But this 'reality' is itself immediately confused, in terms of its ontological status, becoming a dream or ghostly representation itself. Historical fact is confused with fable, fiction and lie:

> My Dreame thou brok'st not, but continued'st it,
> Thou art so truth, that thoughts of thee suffice,
> To make dreames truths; and fables histories ...[19]

Further the partner is confused firstly with angels (an inaccurate representation, to say the least) and then becomes anonymous: 'rising makes me doubt, that now,/Thou art not thou'. 'Thou' are not 'thou': difference is the condition of this fabular identity of the dreamed or hallucinated partner. The incarnation of the partner turns out to be different from the partner: that is to say, the material individual 'identity' of the partner is fundamentally duplicitous, different from itself, a misrepresentation or betrayal of itself. The person dreamed of turns out to be other than this material representation. This, of course, suggests once more that the incarnation or even verbal articulation of a spiritual entity or imaginary word is tantamount to the loss of that entity or word, its misrepresentation. Infidelity is the determinant of identity. It suggests further that the poem itself and its speaker, poem and poet, are formulated in a mode of hypocrisis: text and speaker are fundamentally hypocritical, infidel, treacherous, differing from themselves.

The problem of failed representation, linked as it is to failed expression or revelation of an individuated identity, raises the issue of nomination in the poems. It is to this that I now turn.

Notes

1 Lawrence Stone, *The Family, Sex and Marriage in England 1500–1800* abridged edn, Penguin, Harmondsworth, 1979, 29.
2 Donne, 136ff.
3 Donne, 71–2.
4 Donne, 77–8.
5 Wilhelm Dilthey, 'The great poetry of the imagination', reprinted in Wilhelm Dilthey, *Selected Writings* (ed. H.P. Rickman), Cambridge, Cambridge University Press, 1976, 84.
6 Paul Ricoeur, *Hermeneutics and The Human Sciences* (trans. John B. Thompson), Cambridge, Cambridge University Press, 1981, 56.

7 Anthony Kenny, *Aquinas*, Oxford, Oxford University Press, 1980, 73.
8 *Ben Jonson*, vol. 1 (ed. C.H. Herford and Percy Simpson), Oxford, Clarendon Press, 1925, 133; cf. Anthony Kenny on Aquinas, op.cit., 10, 36.
9 Donne, 293.
10 Donne, 63–4.
11 Donne, 302–4.
12 Abraham Cowley, *Poems* (ed. A.R. Waller), Cambridge, Cambridge University Press, 1905, 113–14.
13 Donne, 298.
14 Thomas à Kempis, *Of the Imitation of Christ*, Grant Richards, 1903, 68.
15 Donne, 293.
16 Donne, 296.
17 Donne, 302.
18 Donne, 16.
19 Donne, 33–4.

SECTION II

Therapies and (ir)resolutions

5

Play, poetry, prayer:
the 'vocation' of 'Donne'

... usual seventeenth-century practice in elegiac poems was not to mention the person's name in the poem, though a fanciful name might be used (e.g. 'Lycidas')

(Earl Miner)

Honour as reward for virtue, as a motive for action, is taken for granted. So is our concern for self-perpetuation in futurity: it is to this that our procreation of children, our anxiety to continue our names, our practice of adoption, inscriptions on monuments, panegyrics, all testify – so Cicero says. It is the name that endures. ... Naming is within the family and the community: it asserts individuality through relationships.

(D.J. Gordon)

John Donne made many travels abroad. In this respect he was a real traveller, as well as being an 'exile' in the more metaphysical senses of the post-Copernican human discussed above. Sometime around 1589–91 he was probably touring Europe; in 1596 he took part in Essex's expedition to storm Cadiz; and following that, he sailed with the Islands Expedition. After these 'adventures', his next major travel took him to France and the Netherlands in the company of Sir Robert Drury; and this journey lasted for almost a full year away, from November 1611 to September 1612. In 1619, after having sought an appointment as ambassador in Venice, he went to Germany as chaplain to an ambassadorial party. Such travel, especially in his more mature years, nearly always tied in with possible social advancement. But the fact that Donne seems positively to have sought out the possibility of travel on so many occasions implies some kind of attraction to Europe, and even perhaps to exile, for its own sake. The facts of Donne's career-minded ambition and his need for gainful employment or patronage after his marriage to Ann More must not be forgotten here. But it is also of importance to suggest that in terms of culture and ideology, Donne was a 'European' of sorts.

Donne's attitude to Europe offers some parallels with that of his admirer, T.S. Eliot. In 'Tradition and the Individual Talent', Eliot argued that poets must acquire a 'historical sense', which 'compels a man to write not merely with his own generation in his bones, but with a feeling that the whole of the literature of Europe from Homer and within it the whole of the literature of his own country has a simultaneous existence and composes a simultaneous order'.[1] If this was important for Eliot in 1919, an American in England after the Great War, then it was also equally of importance for Donne, writing at a time of great turmoil in the very concept of the 'historical', and the threat of war and dissent, especially of a religious nature, always in the air in England as in the rest of Europe.

Donne was a 'European' in another sense: the merest glance at *Biathanatos* betrays an enthusiastic eclecticism in Donne's reading. In his travels he must have been exposed to the literatures of Spain and Italy, France and the Netherlands. Without necessarily considering the dubious questions of influence or imitation, it remains useful to see Donne's writing in a European, not simply an English context. He was a product of the culture of Europe as much as of the English and Catholic background which gave birth to him. It is within such a context that I shall consider Donne here, with especial reference to his use of one of the most startling rhetorical manoeuvres in sixteenth- and seventeenth-century European poetry, *antonomasia*.

I have already 'produced' Donne's own proper name in the examination of 'The Anagram' above. The present chapter will address this rhetorical gesture more theoretically. In a note commenting on Surrey's poem, 'Yf he that erst the fourme so lively drewe', Emrys Jones chooses the first two lines as an illustration of antonomasia:

> Yf he that erst the fourme so lively drewe
> Of Venus faas . . .

and he remarks that 'This allusive and circuitous way of referring to

Apelles without naming him directly is a rhetorical figure called *antonomasia*; it was much favoured by humanist poets'.[2] This is both a huge understatement and also slightly misleading. Many poets of this period in Europe were obsessed with this figure (among other similar rhetorical tropes); and some writers who can be seen to be of an anti-humanist cast, also made use of the figure. Here I shall show that it is but one aspect of a wider cultural or poetic phenomenon, which I shall loosely term 'euphemism'.

'Euphemism', as a means of communicating that which cannot be voiced or written directly, comes to some clear definition in Shakespeare's Polonius, a character who prefigures in many ways the dilemma of the contemporary Eliotic Prufrock. These characters struggle to make portentous announcements, but never come to any direct enunciation. They stutter and stammer, never managing to head directly towards whatever it is they might want to say. Their struggle is not only to find a voice, of course, but also to find words of significance which that voice can pronounce: they strive after intention or will, so to speak. As such, they provide poetic euphemisms, which might be thought of as not so much texts in themselves, but rather as 'pre-texts' for a vocalized interpretation, an elucidation of the meaning which the euphemism avoids.

Euphemism is in some senses the very condition of poetry and, for the late Renaissance, it serves to distinguish poetry as an art from historiography. This is one of the senses of Sidney's apology for poetry. Poetry, fairly literally, provides an exemplum of nature, but in the euphemistic 'language of flowers':

> Nature never set forth the earth in so rich tapestry as divers poets have done – neither with pleasant rivers, fruitful trees, sweet-smelling flowers, nor whatsoever else may make the too-much loved earth more lovely. Her world is brazen, the poets only deliver a golden.[3]

That is to say, poets provide euphemisms which make the earth or reality more bearable for the human. Euphemism, in the failure to call a pretty boy a pretty boy, for example, writing instead of 'beauty's rose', as Shakespeare does in the first of his *Sonnets*, becomes an element of primary importance to poetry, even becomes constitutive of poetry. This affects our conception of Donne's writing. The best starting-point for a consideration of this is in the fundamental rhetorical aspect of euphemism, antonomasia, the disguise or suppression of proper names.

1

Donne's ambition, in material worldly terms, was quite literally to 'make a name for himself', to create his own name or to name himself. Closely allied to this was a cosmic ambition or theological ambition, to see or have that name canonized. Many of Donne's European contemporaries, in this age of burgeoning, if problematic, individualism, shared at least the first of these ambitions; but they, like Donne himself, understood the activity of 'making a name for oneself' in a very specific way.

The proper name seems to be closely linked with the question of individual human identity in a straightforward way. It is supposed generally to demarcate or indeed to give an identity to a person across time. There are problems with this, however, some of which were laid out by Plato in his *Cratylus*. At one point in this dialogue, the 'propriety' or aptness of a proper name is considered. On one theory, that of Cratylus, proper names have to be 'significant' in the sense that they work as linguistic 'descriptors' of their bearers. Thus, for instance, the name 'Dionysus' is a 'proper' name because, etyomologically understood, it can be shown to derive from *didous oinon*, or 'giver of wine', and perhaps can be derived finally from the words for 'god of wine'. Since this is an essential description of the character of Dionysus, the name is deemed by Cratylus to be 'proper' or germane to Dionysus.

But there is a difficulty here, outlined in Plato's irony. One of the correspondents here is Hermogenes, whose name 'means', if we trace its etymology or genealogy, 'of the race of Hermes, god of riches'. The problem is that Hermogenes is poor. For Cratylus then 'Hermogenes' is not and cannot be the 'proper' name of this character, no matter how many people may address him by it. Here the name is being treated as a word, and there is false assumption that a word has some necessary and indissoluble link to its referent: it is assumed that there is something about a tree, say, which makes the word 'tree' the proper or consonant word to describe the object.

Even without the sophisticated linguistics of Saussure or the thoughts on nomination of theorists since A.H. Gardner in the present century, we can see that the mere fact of the babel of languages works against this kind of proposition: 'tree' is not the 'proper' word for a tree to a French or Greek speaker. But if we negate the Cratylian argument completely, then we may perhaps tread in equally dangerous waters: we may lose, for instance, the link between name and person, between wage and earner, between human and society. In a certain sense the proper name, or at least its stability, works as a guarantee of identity, of some kind of continuity of the person in history.

Consider, for example, the two sentences placed in express juxtaposition: 'John Donne was a Roman Catholic. John Donne was an Anglican.' These sentences contain some basic similarities in terms of structure and organization, and also some similarities in the content of that structure; but there is a fundamental discrepancy between them, at least in terms of content. They are both organized according to the formula: subject + verb + complement. In both cases, the subject and verb are precisely the same, while the complements are different. We make sense of these two sentences, and more precisely of their juxtaposition, by establishing a coherent link between them. Although they might seem logically to be descriptions of two persons, both called by the same proper name 'John Donne', their juxtaposition asks that we construe them both together. The same person or identity could not be described as both 'Roman Catholic' and as 'Anglican' simultaneously. But even in this extreme case, we can make a sense of the two senses. The weight of the direct repetition of the proper names almost demands that we construe them both together and *establish* the identity between them which is, at best, latent. We make this identity, or this single, self-identical proper name, by constructing a *narrative* between the two sentences: 'John Donne was born into a Roman Catholic family, but later he converted to Anglicanism'. Hartman has suggested, in fact, that all narrative can finally be reduced to an act of nomination; I will expand this below. Ong indicates that the construction of a narrative is one useful way of remembering lists of names in an oral culture:

> In the text of the Torah, which set down in writing thought forms still basically oral, the equivalent of geography (establishing the relation of one place to another) is put into a formulary action narrative (Numbers 33:16 ff.) 'Setting out from the desert of Sinai, they camped at Kibroth-hattaavah. Setting out from Kibroth-hattaavah, they camped at Hazeroth. Setting out from Hazeroth,

they camped at Rithmah . . .', and so on for many more verses. Even genealogies out of such orally framed tradition are in effect commonly narrative. Instead of a recitation of names, we find a sequence of 'begats', of statements of what someone did: 'Irad begat Mahajael, Mehajael [*sic*] begat Methusael, Methusael begat Lamech' (Genesis 4:18).[4]

The important point here, in Ong, which may seem to be missing in the more basic formulation of Hartman, is that these acts of nomination are actually constitutive of historical (or geographical) *relations* between or among the named entities. The act of nomination is itself part of what might be called a 'scene of recognition', in which 'proper' names can be repeated, and persons can thereby be 're-cognized'. It is this which happens in the two sentences about 'John Donne' above. The narrative is a construction of historical relations which are themselves constitutive of what we normally think of as the recognizable identity of Donne, his 'personality' or 'what he was perceived to be like'.

This construction of a narrative identity requires a position which transcends the two statements and can unite them at a higher or more sophisticated level of juxtaposition. The construction of an identity for Donne allows for the construction of another identity, that of the critic who constructs the narrative. That is to say, in the act of recognizing Donne, there is fundamental activity of self-recognition, or self-nomination (at least at the level of self-identification), going on in the activity of the critic. The relation between the scene of recognition and the act of (self-)nomination can be explored and explained in some detail by a consideration of the European poets of the late Renaissance.

Making a name for oneself, or making oneself a name, implies a construction of the self as an original of some kind, a 'primary source' which can be imitated or recognized. Some post-Modern abstract art works on precisely this principle; a painter may repeat the same configuration endlessly, thus generating a recognizable style. In looking at such a series of paintings we pass directly from the canvas to a name: vertical lines with irregular oblongs between them are 'Robert Motherwells', for instance. Fiedler once suggested that this was true of all abstract art:

> The abstract painter, for instance, does not, as he sometimes claims, really 'paint paint,' but signs his name. So-called abstract art is the ultimate expression of personality.[5]

Repetition and recognizability are crucial to identity. Imitation thus works as a guarantee of identity, but more importantly it posits the notion of an *original*, an authorial source (or nameable identity) from which the recognized repetition is derived. This basically is one Derridean understanding of originality. Culler has most economically explained this:

> Imitation is not an accident that befalls an original but its condition of possibility. There is such a thing as an original Hemingway style only if it can be cited, imitated, and parodied. For there to be such a style there must be recognizable features that characterize it and produce its distinctive effects; for features to be recognizable one must be able to isolate them as elements that could be repeated, and thus the iterability manifested in the inauthentic, the derivative, the imitative, the parodic, is what makes possible the original and the authentic.[6]

This is one way of expressing the state of affairs which I have applied to Donne in terms of hypocrisis: it is the inauthentic or hypocritical which conditions the very possibility of isolating and identifying the 'authentic' and 'critical'.

Abstract art simply makes manifest what is implicit in many other, if not all, works of art, in relation to the question of discovering or constructing the authority of the artist as a nameable, recognizable identity. The question of authority, in this respect, linked to the question of making a name for oneself, is intimately related to questions of formal style, rather than of some supposedly isolable 'content' or message. 'Donne' or the name of 'the Donnean' is characterized not by what Donne 'said', but rather by matters of 'significant style', the formal elements of writing which are always in excess of the 'message' as such. Further, it is precisely the singular name or identity of the author which this elaboration of style produces. As Ricoeur has it:

> Since style is labour which individuates, that is, which produces an individual [or what I have referred to above as an 'original'], so it designates retroactively its author. Thus the word 'author' belongs to stylistics. Author says more than speaker: the author is the artisan of a work of language. But the category of author is equally a category of interpretation, in the sense that it is contemporaneous with the meaning of the work as a whole. The

singular configuration of the work and the singular configuration of the author are strictly correlative. Man individuates himself in producing individual works. The signature is the mark of this relation.[7]

What I want to retain from this formulation is the notion of style as transformational practical labour, and a work which produces the signature or proper name of an individual. Style, which some theory may want to see as the merest of ornamentation, is actually significant here; it produces the precise sign of a proper name.

One clear example of this is the construction of 'the Petrarchan' or indeed of 'Petrarch' himself, as the 'original' of a certain type of lyric poem, the sonnet. The sonnets and songs of Petrarch are, among other things, an elaborate method of establishing an identity for Petrarch through a series of fantasized 'scenes of recognition' between himself and Laura. In 1326, Petrarch, then aged 22, went to Avignon where, in the church of Saint Clare on 6 April 1327, he set eyes on Laura de Norves who had been at that moment married for two years to Ugo de Sade. This became the primary material which was to constitute the organizational principle behind all the poems of the *Canzoniere*. As Piero Cudini puts it in his introduction to the *Canzoniere*:

> Laura diviene così l'occasione della poesia, intendendo per occasione lo spunto immediato e insieme la possibilità di un distacco, di una mediazione che nella mente del poeta si compie tra la figura concreta, l'effetto da essa suscitato su di lui e, estrema risoluzione, la realizzazione poetica.[8]

[Laura thus becomes the 'occasion' of the poetry, meaning the immediate cue for its beginning together with the possibility of a parting, of a bartering which, in the mind of the poet, is performed between the concrete figure and the effect that it rouses in him, and, in the extreme resolution of this mediating, the poetic realization.]

Turning to the poetry itself, it becomes clear that some qualification of this is necessary. In many instances it is not so much Laura herself, real or mythologized, who is the occasion of the poetry; rather this role is frequently taken by the *name* of Laura. The possibility or otherwise of expressing such a name, that is, the possibility of Petrarch calling both vocatively 'Laura', and datively to Laura, in an act of nomination and recognition, forms the condition of organization for much of the verse. A number of the poems make this extremely clear. For the most part, there is no explicit nomination of Laura within the texts; most frequently Petrarch makes conventional use of the figure of antonomasia. He substitutes an adjectival phrase, say, for the name of Laura, thus referring us to Laura without actually pronouncing her name: 'She, whose eyes dart . . .', 'She, whose beautiful hair . . .', or whatever. On a significant number of occasions, however, this play is complicated. One of the most striking examples of such complication comes in the sonetto 'Quando io movo i sospiri a chiamar voi'. Here the name becomes the clear mainspring of the text; it both conceals and reveals the name 'Laura' at the core of the verses themselves:

> Quando io movo i sospiri a chiamar voi,
> e 'l nome che nel cor mi scrisse Amore,
> LAUdando s'incomincia udir di fore
> il suon de' primi dolci accenti suoi;
>
> vostro stato REal, ch'encontro poi,
> raddoppia a l'alta impresa il mio valore;
> ma: TACi, grida il fin, ché farle onore
> è d'altri omeri soma, che da' tuoi.
>
> Così LAUdare e REverire insegna
> la voce stessa, pur ch'altri vi chiami,
> o d'ogni reverenza e d'onor degna:
>
> se non che forse Apollo si disdegna
> ch'a parlar de' suoi sempre verdi rami
> lingua morTAl presuntuosa vegna.[9]
>
> (When I summon my sighs to call for you,
> With that name Love inscribed upon my heart,
> in 'LAUdable' the sound at the beginning
> of the sweet accents of that word come forth.
>
> Your 'REgal' state which I encounter next
> doubles my strength for the high enterprise;
> but 'TACitly' the end cries, 'for her honour
> needs better shoulders for support than yours.'

And so, to 'LAUd' and to 'REvere' the word
itself instructs whenever someone calls you,
O lady worthy of all praise and honour,

unless, perhaps, Apollo be incensed
that 'morTAl' tongue be so presumptuous
to speak of his eternally green boughs.)

(from Petrarch, *Selections from the Canzoniere
and other works*, trans. Mark Musa, Oxford,
Oxford University Press, 1985)

Here, the text reveals the name 'Laureta' which the poet will not expressly pronounce; the 'body' (literally) of the text reveals the sacred or taboo name at its 'heart'.

This may be thought to be an extreme example of antonomasia and euphemism. But the *Canzoniere* are riddled with examples of more or less complex and more or less explicit games, all being elaborated upon the name of Laura. The relation of the name of Laura to the breath which is made explicit in 'Quando io movo i sospiri a chiamar voi' is a prevalent theme in the poems. Many begin, for example, with the word/name 'L'aura', a nicely ambivalent word which hovers between meaning 'breeze' or 'air' on the one hand and in a more specific usage on the other, 'l'aura poetica' as poetic evocation or inspiration. Less obvious are sonnets in which the name is slightly more disguised. The sonnet 'Amor fra l'erbe una leggiadra rete' refers us in its third line to 'l'arbor sempre verde ch' i' tant' amo'; and another sonnet opens 'Quando dal proprio sito si rimove/l'arbor ch'amò già Febo in corpo umano'. In both references to trees here, the referent is the laurel, 'il lauro'; this in itself is a kind of concealed pun on the name. There is both an evasion of the enunciation of the name and also its disguise under another 'euphemistic' term: but the name 'informs' or shapes the verse nonetheless. Even a reference to gold, 'l'oro', begins to become suspicious in these terms.

I suggested earlier that there is link between the act of nomination and the construction of narrative. This can now be clarified in more detail. Narrative appears as a result not so much of nomination, but from the evasion in euphemistic terms of the direct evocation of proper names. As such, it enacts a situation in which a historical scene of recognition can be enunciated in the absence of the characters or persons who are (indirectly) named. That is to say, in the case of Petrarch, it allows the recognition in narrative between Petrarch and Laura, despite the historical impossibility of Petrarch's ever being able to call out the name 'Laura' directly in a historical meeting between them.

The texts then as 'embodiments' or 'stylizations' of the name of Laura are also 'narrativizations' of the scene of recognition between Laura and the other unnamed character in the texts, the 'I' of Petrarch. For as embodiments not of Laura but of her name, the poems suggest a notion that this name or word is the inscription not upon the body of Laura but in the heart of Petrarch. As such then, the poems are 'embodiments' of Petrarch, stylizations of that name under the guise of the name of Laura, just as much as they are embodiments of Laura. The texts are thus the narratives of the locus or scene in which a fantasized meeting of these two names and by extension two persons is enacted. The texts are extremely elaborate euphemisms for such a scene or act of recognition and nomination.

Antonomasia is not simply a harmless pleasant ornamental device indulged in playful innocence; it is a stylistic gesture of historical significance. In the writing of the Pléiade poets, it assumes a further dimension which is of relevance to Donne's work. Donne was in France in 1611 and probably earlier, when the popularity of Ronsard was being seriously threatened for only the first time since his death in 1585. It was really only later in the seventeenth century, when the writings of the Pléiade came under attack from Malherbe and Boileau, that the monumental reputation of this group of poets seemed for a time to fade. In 1611 then Donne was entering a culture dominated by the aesthetic of the Pléiade poets. An interesting book which had some popularity in France at this time was the *Bigarrures du Seigneur des Accords*, written by Étienne Tabourot in 1583. This and Du Bellay's *Deffence et illustration de la langue françoyse* are illustrative of the cultural and linguistic ideas with which Donne would have come into contact during his séjour in France and the Netherlands with Robert Drury.

Tabourot's treatise takes over where Plato left off in the *Cratylus*. He wonders at the invention of the alphabet and at the origins or provenance of language (and specifically 'poetic' language) itself. The letters of the alphabet, according to one theory which Tabourot explains, come from the shape of the mouth in their enunciation. Some people have said that:

A estoit large au dessoubs, pour ce que le prononceant on elargissoit la bouche. O, tout rond pour ce que le nommant, on le mettoit quasi de ceste facon. Q, pource qu'il ressemble au cul duquel sort de l'ordure[10]

(A was broad at the bottom because, in pronouncing it, you broaden your mouth. O is round because in saying it, you make that shape. Q is the shape it is because it resembles the arse from which the crap comes*)

(* the letter 'Q' is pronounced, in French, like the word 'cul', meaning 'arse')

Tabourot is explaining this idea in order to mock it, and he comments tartly that he will leave the reader to imagine what grimaces are necessary to discover the origin of the rest of the letters. The 'explication' then is highly contrived and suspicious; the provenance of writing remains mysterious to Tabourot. But in the revoked explication, the grounds of the Platonic debate in the *Cratylus* have shifted somewhat. In the suggestion of some link between the letters and the shape of the mouth which pronounces them or with the human body in some of its basic biological functions, Tabourot's text brings the area of debate on writing to focus on the connection not between word and world, but between the name and the body which speaks it.

His attention is taken up in several chapters of the treatise by a consideration of some Greek rhetorical manoeuvres, which might appear to us to be mere play in language, pleasurable or indeed comic games, but which seem to have been of substantial importance for all that in the cultural understanding of the crafts of poetry and rhetoric in Europe at the time of Donne's writing. Tabourot examines 'contrepeteries' which look like Spoonerisms and finds some examples in Rabelais. A 'contrepeterie' involves the transposition or 'displacement' of the initial letters of words in a given sequence. For example, Pantagruel comments that 'Femme folle à la messe est volontiers molle à la fesse', in which 'folle' and 'messe' transpose to give 'molle' and 'fesse', 'soft buttock'. Clearly the letters thus transposed convert a seemingly acceptable phrase into a more or less prurient one. This becomes more sophisticated when the 'taboo' phrase is tacitly conveyed or suggested entirely through the enunciation of its 'purer' counterpart. In a certain situation

Tabourot suggests that the phrase 'Goutez cette farce' must be understood as 'really saying' 'Foutez cette garce'. This becomes enshrined, according to Tabourot, as a recognized courtly rhetorical manoeuvre; and interestingly he characterizes it as a mode of speech which is particularly suitable to women. Once more, then, there may be some cultural or ideological equation of duplicity, euphemism, ambivalence and 'woman' here. If so, there is perhaps an equation between 'woman' and poetry in some sense; and indeed in the later seventeenth century, Rapin in France, as well as many writers in England, complains about what is seen as the 'effeminization' of culture.

But there is more to this euphemistic mode of writing than may meet the eye. Tabourot may have got some of his material here from his consideration of the writings of Ronsard and Du Bellay, especially in the *Deffence*.[11] In sonnet 14 of *Les Regrets*, Du Bellay offers one rationale for the use of such rhetorical devices, writing there that 'Les vers chantent pour moy ce que dire je n'ose' ('Verse sings for me things which I don't dare say'). Tricks such as the 'contrepeterie' might allow a writer to 'say the unsayable' or a reader to 'think the unthinkable'; that is to say, these tropes might suggest a possible means of circumventing censorship and a dominant ideology. If this is 'comic', then it is comedy used to extremely serious ends: linguistic 'play' or style as a means of making historical statements and actions, and of getting such statements past the censoring authorities, political, ecclesiastical, ideological and psychological.

In Du Bellay's case there seems to have been a conscious manipulation of his poems in order to 'make a name for himself' in and through them. As has been indicated before in criticism of Du Bellay, the sequences *Olive* and *Les Antiquités de Rome* focus, even in their titles, on proper names. But it is in *Les Regrets* that the most significant examples of antonomasia occur. There are many comparisons of the nameless or anonymous poet, Du Bellay, with other, more successful 'big names', especially Ronsard and Jean-Antoine de Baïf in the poems of *Les Regrets*. In sonnet 8, Du Bellay mentions himself by name for seemingly the first time:

> Ne t'esbahis Ronsard, la moitié de mon ame,
> Si de ton Dubellay France ne lit plus rien.[12]

> (Do not be astonished, Ronsard, you who are

half my soul, if France no more reads your Du Bellay)

Du Bellay as proper name is compared here with the 'really' 'proper'
name of Ronsard. But the first line contains a pun which serves to
merge the two names, prompting actual nomination of Du Bellay in
the second line. The 'moitié de mon ame' is not entirely unlike the
'moitié de mon nom'; and the names, seemingly contrasted, thus
become to some degree interdependent: 'Ronsard' is half Du Bellay's
name.

Once alerted to this, the name of Du Bellay crops up in many
euphemistic disguises all over the poems. It has, for example,
appeared even before sonnet 8 where we have its first explicit
enunciation. In sonnet 7 there is a movement from the name of
Marguerite, sister of the king of France, to that of Du Bellay himself,
submerged under comic play on the name:

> Ce pendant que la court mes ouvrages lisoit,
> Et que la soeur du Roy, l'unique Marguerite,
> Me faisant plus d'honneur que n'estoit mon merite,
> De son bel oeil divin mes vers favorisait . . .[13]

> (At a time when the court read my works, and the
> unequalled Margaret, sister to the King, did me
> more honour than was my due, casting her divine
> and beautiful eye over my lines)

The bright divine eye of Marguerite here becomes not only the eye
which reads and judges favourably the text of Du Bellay; it is also
the location of the name of Du Bellay. The words 'bel oeil' pun on
'Bellay'; thus the name of the poet is made, and 'recognition' is had,
in the eyes of the woman, Marguerite. This woman's name, derived
from the word for a pearl, is the French word for a specific kind of
flower, the ox-eye daisy, whose Latinate name (established much
later, of course) coincidentally is *Bellis perennis*: Bellay is 'forever'
recognized in the pearly eye of Marguerite, gaining his name
literally in perpetuity here.

Another kind of example makes the name a more integral part of
the words of the poem. Sonnet 9 makes France the mother of the
poet, suggesting not only the rebirth of the vernacular languages,
but also, in the covert antonomasia which informs the poem the
'adulterate' or bastardized form of that vernacular:

France mere des arts, des armes, & des loix,
Tu m'as nourry long temps au laict de ta mamelle:
Ores, comme un aigneau qui sa nourrice appelle,
Je remplis de ton nom les antres & les bois.[14]

(France, mother of arts, arms and laws, you have
fed me long from the milk of your breast; now, like
a lamb calling out to be suckled, I fill with your
name the caves and the woods)

Here is Du Bellay compared with a lamb. But this lamb bleats out
the name of France, the vernacular language which now becomes
dependent for its existence and articulation upon that lamb. The
French word for the verb 'to bleat' is 'bêler' (Bellay); and the word for a
'ram' is 'le bélier'. In this sonnet then Du Bellay makes his appearance
as a lamb, a kind of adulterated or emasculated version of his proper
name; but this lamb is going to grow in the poetry into the form of
the ram: that is to say, it is going to grow into the name *du bélier*, Du
Bellay. Once more, even at the level of words which may seem to
have no real status as proper names, the poet works to 'make a name
for himself' in a fantasization of a scene of his own recognition.

A clearer case of the use of these rhetorical devices for saying the
unsayable or taboo, and one which some might think of as being
closer to the case of Donne, is in Sidney's *Astrophil and Stella*
sequence. 'Stella' is a euphemistic nomination of Penelope Devereux,
the daughter of the Earl of Essex, who was married, unhappily, to
Lord Rich in 1581. The fundamental antonomasia in the entire
sequence here, the naming of Sidney and Devereux as Astrophil and
Stella respectively, serves to mythologize both persons. The scene
of recognition can safely take place in the realm of fiction, myth,
the starry heavens, whereas it is not so easy to realize such a scene
historically. As 'starry names', these myth-characters are already in
a situation of mutual recognition; Astrophil is part of the 'con-
stella-tion' with Stella and is also the position from which this
constellation, these stars, *Stella* is figured. The sequence becomes a
sublimation of some historically desired meeting between two real
names, Sidney and Devereux, or 'Philip' and his 'Pen'(elope).

One obvious use of the proper name in these poems is the
reference to Lord Rich or to Stella in her 'guise' as Lady Rich, in
terms of the use of the word, 'rich', used as adjective rather than
proper name. But even in this use of antonomasia, there were cases

in which 'saying the unsayable' could not be circumvented. This was the case with sonnet 37, 'My mouth doth water, and my breast doth swell', in which the allusions to Lord Rich were so bitter, and so transparent, that the poem was not printed until 1598, in the folio *Arcadia* of that year. Much more subtle is sonnet 24, 'Rich fools there be, whose base and filthy heart'. This poem effects a transmutation of its opening words, 'Rich fools', into the closing words of 'folly rich', through an antonomasia in the middle of the poem which works as a strophic turning-point (a 'revolutionary moment', as it were) and allows the suggestion that Rich is a fool:

> But that rich fool, who by blind fortune's lot
> The richest gem of love and life enjoys,
> And can with foul abuse such beauties blot . . .[15]

This is a conventional antonomasia; but as the description is elaborated it becomes clear that the poet is not writing so much of 'that rich fool', as of 'that fool Rich'. It is through this strophic turn, in which the antonomasia reveals the name of Rich, that the poem effects the transformation from its opening phrase 'Rich fools' to the close, 'folly rich'; and, in line with this transformation, there is the fundamental strophic turn, from 'that rich fool' to the subtext of 'that fool Rich'. Here Sidney quite legitimately manages to suggest, if not, at some level, directly 'say', the unsayable.

In the introduction to her edition of *Selected Poems* of Sidney, Katherine Duncan-Jones comments of the *Astrophil and Stella* sequence that 'What reality lay behind the sequence – whether a courtly game, a pretext for writing poetry, an intense personal experience, or some mixture of all three – we shall never know'.[16] Such historical facts may indeed remain obscure; but from the texts themselves, especially when placed in this wider European context of rhetorical tradition, we can begin to discover some of the cultural beliefs which informed the writing. Most significantly, there is the equation of woman with the source of poetry; and this is of significant interest, of course, in Donne's writings.

Sidney's first sonnet in *Astrophil and Stella* has provoked much debate on the question of artistic sincerity, focused on the conventionality, or spontaneity, of the closing line: ' "Fool," said my muse to me; "look in thy heart and write." '. But this has diverted attention from some other cruces in the poem. One of the things which the poem is about is 'invention'. In sixteenth-century poetics, invention was opposed to 'imitation' (of other authors). From sonnet 3, in which Sidney compares himself with such Pléiadic imitators, it seems that invention is favoured; this invention might include the imitation of nature, not imitation of other authors. But in order to invent, Sidney finds himself, in the first sonnet, examining the writings of other poets. The question of the origin or source of poetry becomes central. I have suggested from examining the text of the *Bigarrures* of Tabourot that this source of poetry is somehow thought of as being close to the biological fact of the human body or mouth. This becomes all the more clear in this Sidneian sonnet, where the notion of the origin of poetry mutates into that of the 'birth' of poetry. Invention or novelty is seen as stemming from the natural self, or body, independently of education and nurture or the learning of method. But this 'natural' body seems to be specifically female in some way:

> Thus great with child to speak, and helpless in my throes,
> Biting my truant pen, beating myself for spite,
> 'Fool,' said my muse to me; 'look in thy heart, and write'[17]

The penultimate line here is extremely important in the development of the notion of the male writer as somehow inspired by a female source of poetry, authority or identity. Firstly, the poet is in labour, not merely stylistically but also historically; like the mute *infant*, he looks for an articulate voice or style. The attempt to produce this 'child' is an attempt to produce the poem; but also to produce through the poem the historical meeting with or vocation to Devereux. Such a vocation comes in the penultimate line, in which he bites 'my truant pen'. Here the name of Penelope appears, despite her own truancy or absence in historical terms. But this physical attack upon the 'pen' or Penelope turns out to be also an attack on the poet himself, as he is simultaneously 'beating myself for spite'. The confusion of the identity, and gender, of Sidney and Devereux, Astrophil and Stella, is compounded further when the poet looks into his heart to discover not himself there but the trace of his 'pen', the image of Stella. That which 'inspires' or writes through the breathing, labouring body of Sidney turns out here to be at some level of sophistry and rhetoric, specifically female.

In sonnet 3, Sidney claims that other poets are the merest imitators of appearance, while he regards nature as it is in itself. This 'real nature' is found, he argues there, by consulting the naked face of Stella; this notion follows logically from the idea of 'natural writing' in the first sonnet. But then Stella's face becomes itself a text, an already written artifact:

> In Stella's face I read
> What love and beauty be; then all my deed
> But copying is, what in her nature writes.[18]

Sidney, following the dictates of his heart, finds that these coalesce with the text or face of Stella, as the inspirational source of the poetry which he then merely copies out. However, the text which constitutes Stella (as opposed to the historical realities of Devereux) is none other than the text which Sidney has already written or is about to write. When he looks into his heart, not only does he find the text of Stella, but he also finds the image or copy of his own writing; that is to say, he sees both himself and Stella in the same text, or heart. The heart has become a mirror; and the mirror here reflects Astrophil and Stella simultaneously, thus becoming the scene of their recognition. In such a scene there is a confusion in the poet's identity. As I showed to be the case in Donne, the origin of identity here is not sameness but difference: who is who, between Astrophil and Stella?

Sidney then 'bites' the 'truant pen', that is to say, he 'wounds' the name of Penelope (and the antonomasia is precisely such a 'wounding'), and in this wounding of the now female pen (Penelope) he discovers the source of the writing; he discovers, in the flow of blood, the 'ink' which enables the production of his own authority. In sonnet 2, 'Not at first sight, nor with a dribbed shot', there is a ramification of these issues. The love which spurs this poetry came by degrees, like that between Celia and Oliver in *As You Like It* (V, ii). There is an equation of the breath itself here with the 'bleeding' or 'wounding' which results from the arrival and presence of love: 'Love gave the wound which while I breathe will bleed'. It is conventional enough to write of the wound from the arrow of Cupid; but the wound here seems to have struck not at the heart but somewhere closer to the mouth or lungs, the organs of respiration of perhaps inspiration. The degrees of love are then charted:

> I saw, and liked; I liked, but loved not;
> I loved, but straight did not what love decreed:
> At length to love's decrees I, forced, agreed . . .[19]

One interesting fact about these lines is that the punctuation invites the very breath which is described in the poem. But with this breath, of course, there must come, according to the poem, a parallel series of bleedings, a flow of blood. The breathlessness induced in the enunciation of the lines equates with the wound of love itself; which is as much as to say that the punctuation and grammar effect the love-act which, the lines finally concede, has occurred. The bleeding element in such an act, however, is traditonally not so much the male heart as the female genitals. Who then is the 'I' who speaks the poem? Having begun as Astrophil, this 'I' begins to assume the posture, perhaps through its location in the heart/mirror scene of recognition, of Stella in a fantasized violent sex-act: 'At length to love's decrees I, *forced,* agreed' (italics mine). Sidney may look within, like a kind of Renaissance Virginia Woolf, but what he finds inside himself as it were is not himself as male individual; rather he discovers a scene of recognition where what he recognizes essentially is the anteriority of the woman who acts as the source of inspiration, as 'apology' for the poetry. In so far as he finds himself as male, moreover, he is the male who is defined in terms of a fantasized 'forcing' of the female body; he 'wounds' that body in order to establish himself as male 'love'-poet.

The culmination of this kind of approach to poetry can be found in some lines in sonnet 16, 'In nature apt to like, when I did see', and in sonnet 50, 'Stella, the fullness of my thoughts of thee'. In sonnet 16 Sidney draws explicit attention to the moment of a visual recognition:

> But while I thus with this young lion played,
> Mine eyes (shall I say cursed or blessed?) beheld
> Stella: now she is named, need more be said?[20]

Here it is as if the discovery of a name, the enactment of a nomination, means the end of poetry: once the person has been 'recognized' in the name, need anything more be said or done? At one level, no more need be said; and it would seem that Sidney wrote no more poetry after this sequence. But that sequence itself requires to be written, as a substitute for or transformation of the material and historical desire for a real scene of recognition not between Astrophil and Stella but between Sidney and Devereux. Sonnet 50 clarifies this some more. It depends entirely upon the primacy of the name of Stella, and the text as a whole is a euphemism of a euphemism: it elaborates a circumlocution around the antonomastic name, 'Stella':

> Stella, the fullness of my thoughts of thee
> Cannot be stayed within my panting breast,
> But they do swell and struggle forth of me,
> Till that in words thy figure be expressed.[21]

The poem is yet another failed attempt to contain, comprise or comprehend the figure of Stella: the person (Devereux) cannot be embodied or revealed through these veiling words (Stella). That is to say, in more general terms, Sidney cannot call out explicitly or vocatively to Devereux; there is no scene of recognition in historical terms. The text of the poem, however, is an elaborate euphemism for the raw material of its opening word, the vocative 'Stella'; and this antonomastic name keeps the poem in existence, even as a 'failure'; for as Sidney considers the destruction of the verses, this sacred name 'contains' him, stops him from destroying the poem, for it works as a talisman protecting not only the name of Stella, but also the person of Devereux.

There are at least three points of importance for a consideration of Donne in this wider European context:

1 There is the question of a confusion of identity. To some extent, for example, Astrophil *is* Stella (which is one reason why his name need not appear). This confusion of identity in the heart/mirror scene of recognition subtends at least two corollaries. In the first place the poet, regarding what is now essentially himself in the mirror of his own heart, could be said to be writing in a Narcissistic manner, addressing these poems of love to himself; thus the real 'hidden name' would be Astrophil, his identity protected by never being explicitly named. Secondly, in so far as this poet turns out to be inspired by some vaguely female principle, Narcissus has become Echo, and her womanly voice becomes not only the source of the poetry in a sense, but also the voice which guarantees or conditions the male voice of Narcissus/Astrophil.

2 The act of nomination is seen to depend upon 'impersonality' or, better, 'impersonation'. Sidney has to adopt the personae of Astrophil and Stella in order to establish some kind of fantasized contact, and some mythic scene of recognition, between Sidney himself and Penelope Devereux.

3 Following on from one of the corollaries of point 1, the poetry

itself becomes mutable, dialogic. Echo's words are *different* from those of Narcissus; they are a kind of 'critical edition' or transformation of the words. Thus a notion of 'self-differentiation' becomes the very condition of identity in these texts. The poet speaks, as it were, both in her or his own voice and also in that of a personified character. Poems such as these can be said to be largely exercises in self-understanding, or in self-construction through the activity of 'hearing-oneself-speak'. That is to say, they are attempts to stabilize historical relations through the discovery of Cratylian 'proper names' for poet and addressee; but the singularity of such a 'proper name' is vitiated because the selves involved in these scenes of nomination or of recognition are always, fundamentally, involved in Echoing dialogues with themselves. Individuality is fractured at the very moment when the name seems to guarantee its integrity.

These three points are of especial importance in the writings of Donne.

2

Donne, I suggested, wanted to 'make a name for himself' and to 'canonize' that name. The great name, the unspeakable, even unidentifiable, name which he wanted to 'appropriate' (make his own 'proper' name) was none other than that of God. This may seem startling; it becomes more acceptable if we locate the identity of God in another speakable name, which Donne could try in quite legitimate theological terms, to impersonate or live through: the name of Christ. Given that this is an age which I have characterized as the entry of the human into existential history, there is perhaps another authority for this suggestion in the Sartrean notion, examined in *Being and Nothingness*, that 'man is the being whose project is to be God ... man fundamentally is the desire to be God'.[22] Donne himself seems on many occasions to have been fairly clear on the ambition of the project.

A useful place to open a consideration of this argument is in the collocation which I revealed earlier between the utterance of the 'primal word', 'go', and the activity of respiration and inspiration. 'To go' is a minimally breathed text, a minimal inspiration or breath, which undergoes transformation in order to generate the full text of the narrative or poetic situation; thus 'to go' mutates into a debate on the difference between life and death, as it is transformed into the divergent texts 'now' and 'no' in 'A Valediction: forbidding mourning'. On a similar principle, we can consider the aspiration in Satire 4, 'Well; I may now receive, and die', in which the poet whispers or breathes out the word 'God'.

In the European tradition that I have briefly outlined, this poem contains a lengthy example of antonomasia and seems, in its opening section at least, to be overtly concerned with nomination. The poet finds it impossible to name the anonymous creature who comes to plague him, for it is 'A thing, which would have pos'd Adam to name'.[23] In Genesis Adam is given his 'proper' name (through the transformations of translation: 'Adam' is derived from *ādām* the Hebrew word for 'man') precisely at the moment (2:19) when he gives names to all the animals. He names Eve at their moment of banishment (3:20–4) which is the moment when Adam and the (anonymous) Eve have tried to 're-name' themselves as God (3:22: 'And the Lord God said, Behold, the man is become as one of us, to know good and evil'). The project of these two, then, is rather like that of Donne, as I am characterizing it here. After the circuitous antonomasia which skirts the name of the poet's correspondent in Satire 4, the stranger in fact performs the act of nomination upon the poet (like Adam upon Eve perhaps): 'He names mee and comes to mee; I whisper, 'God!/How have I sinn'd, that thy wraths furious rod,/This fellow chuseth me?" '. It is indeed interesting to imagine this as Eve's thought as Adam approaches to 'know' and 'name' her in Genesis.

But there is more to this. This purgatorial visitation by the unnamed stranger is, according to the poem, for the sin of going to Court. But the language in which this is expressed ties in thematically with many of the concerns of this study. The poet begins with an acknowledgement of the fact that he went to Court in a manner similar to an inattentive jester who goes to a Mass for fun. This makes the court-visit 'sinful', and the line expresses it perfectly as such: 'Guilty of my sin of going' is the parenthesis in which there is some kind of confession of guilt. This self-enclosed parenthesis makes the guilt precisely the guilt at 'going'. Since 'going' is some kind of frequent equivalent of the activity of breathing, this might suggest a Manichaean or radical Calvinist notion of the implicit sinfulness of existence itself; life, as that which is in creation 'different' from God becomes evil by definition, the location of 'not-God', as it were. Less radically, human existence can be seen here as an entropic deviation from the paradisical state of unnameable Godhood.

Further into the poem, we can witness a particular instance of this 'sin of going'. At the moment of nomination, when the poet is addressed, he whispers, or breathes out, the minimal word, 'go'. It occurs in the line already quoted and is immediately transformed into its extended form, as 'God': 'He names mee, and comes to mee; I whisper "*God*!" ' (italics mine).

Suddenly, now, all the many poems of departure, poems of coming and going, of separation and meeting, naming and differentiating, can be seen as a kind of muted version of this line. 'I whisper go' becomes 'I whisper "God" ' on precisely the same principle as the word 'go' itself mutates into the breathily differentiated 'now' and 'no' in the valediction poem. The whisperings or breathings of 'going' can now be understood as a form of muted invocation, or nomination, of God. In Satire 4 this nomination occurs at the moment when the stranger names the poet, a moment in which I have already shown a similarity to the nomination of Adam and Eve at the moment when they enact their project to become God, 'one of us'. At the moment of the poet's nomination, there is the enunciation of the sacred name, that of God. The comparison with which the poem opens, between poet and jester, takes on further significance. The opening comparison strengthens the reading that this whisper is a blasphemous one; but the poem itself mutes the blasphemy to some extent. For in its own context the uttering of the sacred name is precisely a vocative, and one might even suggest not simply an invocation of God, but a *vocation* to God. What threatens to make it most blasphemous, of course, is the suggestion that the name or identity of the poet is 'God'.

Complaining of the vices of the Court, the poet meets with the reply that it is sweet to talk of kings. In fact, the only talk of kings which goes on in the poem is that which is done, playfully, by the poet who suddenly saturates the speech with the word 'king'. The tomb-keeper at Westminster 'From King to King and all their kin can walke:/Your eares shall heare naught, but Kings; your eyes meet/Kings only; The way to it, is Kingstreet', he says, but if there is a real 'king' or kin of kings in the poem, however, it is the poet himself. After some time, the stranger or beggar asks for money, and finally goes:

> thankes to his needy want,
> And the prerogative of my Crowne

This pun, on 'crown', makes of Donne the unnamed, untitled (and perhaps now uncrowned) king in the poem.

This 'king' is further transformed. The intervention of the beggarly visitor provokes much in the way of playful dialogue. But this is most frequently comic in the poem because the speakers are at cross-purposes. On the part of the poet this is deliberate, with the aim of preventing further discussion, but:

> as Itch
> Scratch'd into smart, and as blunt iron ground
> Into an edge, hurts worse: So, I (foole) found,
> Crossing hurt mee

As the poem continues, the beggar himself becomes a kind of cross which the poet has, purgatorially, to bear. The 'hurt' of the crossing is also the cross as burden:

> since I am in,
> I must pay mine, and my forefathers sinne
> To the last farthing; Therefore to my power
> Toughly and stubbornly I beare this crosse but the' houre
> Of mercy was now come

The wearing of the crown reduces to the pain of the last farthing here. More importantly, there is an explicit revelation of the real comparison in the poem, which is that between the poet and the unnamed king who bore the hurt of the cross, Christ. This is not meant to deny the playful humour of the satire; it rather deepens it in the comic revelation of a serious theological impulse behind the aesthetic play.

The unnamed king in the poem, then, is none other than the poet himself, now identifiable as Christ. The text then becomes an elaborate euphemism for the moment of vocation, the rejection of courtly life in favour of another kind of king; and it is an expansion of the kernel phrase, the basic and minimalist text of 'I whisper "God!" '. By not expressly identifying himself as the real caller here, as God, Donne manages to speak even more clearly in the name of the Christ who was about to bear the agony and death as described in John's Gospel. For it is not Donne himself, but the reader, almost

as a Pilate-figure, who has given Donne the kingly title, the INRI. As
John has it:

> Then Pilate entered into the judgment hall again, and called
> Jesus, and said unto him, Art thou the King of the Jews? . . . Jesus
> answered, My kingdom is not of this world: if my kingdom were
> of this world, then would my servants fight, that I should not be
> delivered to the Jews: but now is my kingdom not from hence.
> Pilate therefore said unto him, Art thou a king then? Jesus
> answered, Thou sayest that I am a king . . .[24]

The parallel here to my explication of the Donne text is clear. This
is the basic strategy of Donnean antonomasia: it leaves unsaid, but
supposedly tacitly understood, the sacred name which Donne
wants to work as an informing principle of the writing and
guarantee of its authenticity. Donne, in this poem at least, performs
a contrived *imitatio Christi*, by which he manages to suggest that
he is in a position analogous to, if not more strictly identified as,
Christ.

Read in this light, the opening and closing lines of the poem
become doubly charged. The opening could, quite conceivably, be a
translation of Christ's moment of resignation, a moment which is
itself a kind of scene of recognition or of vocation in Gethsemane,
when Christ resigns himself to the title of sacrificial king and
recognizes God in the phrase 'thy will be done'. In Donne's breezy
'free translation', this becomes a more material kind of resignation,
put to euphemistic purpose; 'Well, I may now receive, and die'.
There is a serious element in the humorous suggestion that life
itself has been a purgatorial trial in this way. If the speaker of the
poem is identified as this Donnean Christ-figure, then, as this
Christ becomes sacrificial king and hence identified as God, the
poem becomes itself a canonized or sacred text: Scripture. This is
indeed how the poem closes, establishing its own, if not the poet's
canonization:

> Although I yet
> With *Macchabees* modestie, the knowne merit
> Of my worke lessen: yet some wise man shall,
> I hope, esteeme my writs Canonicall.

Writing after the Copernican displacements, Donne found
himself in a period when the truth which was simultaneously

veiled and revealed by allegory ceded place to the necessity for persuasive rhetoric. Bunyan's later allegory, *The Pilgrim's Progress*, comes at an opposite pole to the writings of Donne. In Bunyan, as in the Cartesian philosophy in France, there is a restabilization of truth, located in the figure of the human subject; by allegorizing all sorts of mental states as personifications, 'characters', Bunyan locates truth and stabilizes it, in the reactions of the central figure, Christian, to other 'characters'. Christ/ian provides the locus of truth in the allegory, largely because everything that threatens to displace that truth is seen or allegorized as a state of Christian's mind in the progress; everything gets its meaning from its relation to Christian. For the earlier Donne such a restabilization of the stable centre of truth in the human subject was not available; rather, he had to write in a manner not strictly allegorical, but amidst all the vagaries of uncertain rhetoric. His writing may or may not resemble closely the work of other European schools such as *marinismo* or *Gongorism*, but one thing is sure: like those involved in those 'movements', he had to adopt and adapt rhetoric in an argumentative poetry which struggled to locate a truth identified in himself, as the antonomastic figure of God.

The merest glance through Donne's poetry is sufficient to demonstrate his liking for antonomasia and euphemism (a mode of writing which perhaps owes much to the vogue of Lyly's *Euphues* of 1578[25]). A poem like 'The Indifferent', for instance, becomes more than a particular gripe about some inconstant relation between a specific woman and man; through its extensive use of antonomasia it begins to enter the dimension of serious philosophical comment and argument. The generalizing tenor of this rhetorical figure leads the poem to take on the air of philosophical discussion or treatise:

> I can love both faire and browne,
> Her whom abundance melts, and her whom want betraies,
> Her who loves lonenesse best, and her who maskes and plaies,
> Her whom the country form'd, and whom the town,
> Her who beleeves, and her who tries,
> Her who still weepes with spungie eyes,
> And her who is dry corke, and never cries[26]

There is not only a categorization of discrete entities going on here ('the kind of woman who'), there is also an establishment of taxonomical parameters between opposites worked into a dialectical form of argument. This is the case with the organization of a number of these poem-arguments, like 'The Blossome', 'The broken heart', 'Communitie', 'Loves Alchymie', 'Loves Deitie' and many more. Further, the suppression of the proper and individuating names in Donne's antonomasia, with the resultant transposition of particular poem or statement into general proposition, frequently lends a mythic status to the characters in the poems and, by extension, to the unnameable mythic name of their poet. Such is the case in lines like 'Who ever comes to shroud me' ('The Funerall'), or 'Who ever guesses, thinks, or dreames he knowes/Who is my mistris, wither by this curse' ('The Curse').

In the example of 'The Curse' there is a double antonomasia, the suppression of identities of both the mythic 'Whoever' and of the 'mistress'. Such a double antonomasia is frequent, and important. Usually the two names involved will be those of the lovers in the poem. This leads to some interesting postures on Donne's part, seen most pertinently here in a text such as 'The Canonization'. This poem enacts a scene of recognition in the discovery or canonization of the two lovers as mythic emblems (almost acquiring the status of allegory) of love itself. It might appear that the suppressed name might be that of Cupid or Venus or Eros or something like this, names which sometimes figure in other love-poems by Donne. But here this is not the case. As in Satire 4, the speaker renounces responsibility for the act of (self-)nomination, forcing others to complete or articulate an implied name: like the Christ-figure in Satire 4, the speaker here says 'Call us what you will'. This, it should by now be clear, is a guise under which the real titles of poem and speakers are hidden. As the poem progresses, it becomes obvious that the scene of recognition is not one between writer and reader, but between the two characters or lovers in the text; it is they who acknowledge each other in the discovery that they are in some respect the same person or *persona* (as in the poems I have discussed previously). Their mutual nomination or recognition is tantamount to a self-blessing, a self-nomination:

> The Phoenix ridle hath more wit
> By us, we two being one, are it.[27]

Naming themselves here, they coalesce in the one object, the phoenix, into which they have merged from separation as eagle and dove. But this allows for a further mutation of the identity of the lovers, for, as phoenix, they become the locus of a resurrection: 'We dye and rise the same, and prove/Mysterious by this love'. That is to say, once more, the lovers, in their moment of recognition, find themselves (literally) in a position analogous to that of Christ in the resurrection. The hidden name becomes not 'Venus', but rather the unspoken identification of Christ as a locus of this love-scene. The poem, in terms of its rhetorical propositionality, can be grouped profitably with others such as 'The Sunne Rising', 'Break of day', 'The good-morrow', and so on, all of which depend upon a similar identification of the body of Christ as scene of love. Such love, of course, is always being seen from an exclusively male point of view; the central element in the identification is the notion of rising, of erection. But the identification of Christ as a central name in the poem serves its main purpose of self-canonization, and of the mythologization or canonization of its characters in the legion of saints.

Now, in so far as the unspoken name of the text is revealed as Christ-in-resurrection, a further scene of recognition or, more precisely, of vocation, is called for; the reader is tacitly to reconsider the poem and read it as an address to or from Christ. That is to say, the poem invites its own repetition, its own canonization (in literary terms), and invites a scene of recognition or vocation between (unnamed) reader and (unnamed) Christ. It is this secondary part of the double antonomasia which is of particular importance. Further, this makes of the 'recognition' between writer and reader (both now of uncertain identity) a moment of the suppression of personal names, personal identities, and their mutual identification in the text, or with the text, now understood as an embodiment of Christ; that is, there is a eucharistic moment of meeting in the 'body of Christ', in the ecclesia, that small but potentially infinite (catholic, universal) church established by the poem between writer and all readers of this now safely 'canonical' text.

The most fundamental example of this rhetorical play in 'the Donne canon' is in 'The Relique'. This theological title already orients us to a specific kind of reading of the poem, in terms of the ecclesia. The grave which is to be broken up seems at first to be the grave of a singular person, for it is to be opened 'Some second ghest to entertaine'.[28] But almost immediately it is clear that the grave itself is a scene in which two people have already met in some sense. The famous 'bracelet of bright haire about the bone' invites the suggestion that this is a grave in which two lovers lie, intertwined. In fact, there is but one body, although it is a body already constituted by at least two identities organized around the bone and hair. The single identity of the body in the grave is thus questioned. The ring made of hair around the bone becomes a symbolic metaphor of 'carnival' (carne-vale; farewell to the flesh, and also suggestive of comedy), of a carnivalesque love-scene similar to that which operates in 'The Canonization', making of the grave a scene of recognition. In fact, of course, according to the Cratylian precepts, it would be exactly at such a moment of death and not of birth that one could attain one's 'proper' name; it is only at the moment of death that nothing more can happen to an individual to affect her or his identity. The grave becomes the carnivalesque scene of nomination *par excellence*.

The two identities then come closer to explicit nomination. One of them is in fact named, as 'a Mary Magdalen'; but significantly the other name remains suppressed, as 'A something else'. The obvious 'translation' of this hesitant antonomasia, 'A something else', is into the phrase 'A Jesus Christ', which is metrically equivalent to 'a something else', as Ricks has remarked. But even in this translation there remains something indefinite about this Donnean Christ-figure; there are, as it were, some ghostly edges around this 'identity'. This line, of course, explicitly states that Donne will be something indefinite, inarticulate, '*a* something else'; but more fundamentally the indefinition is present due to the fact that he is an indefinite article. The one word which remains unchanged in the translation which I have suggested is the opening and capitalized word, 'A', the indefinite article, the 'inarticulate', itself.

Empson has commented on this line in such a way as to suggest that this unchanging 'A' (a word which is, by definition, supposedly changing, mutable, indefinite, but which here be-comes the sole sign of definition) is the most important word. In his article, 'Donne the space man', Empson commented on Redpath's edition of the *Songs and Sonets* and noted with pleasure that Redpath acknowledged this euphemism for 'A Jesus Christ'. But the important point in that article is not the blasphemous suggestion that Donne is Christ; rather it is that Donne is 'a' Christ. The retention of the indefinite article makes it clear, suggests Empson, that the figure of Christ is iterable. There may be, indeed must be in the age of the Copernican revolution, more than one

Christ in order to redeem life elsewhere in the universe.²⁹ Strictly
speaking, however, it does not follow from the multiplicity of
worlds that the person of Christ must be iterable for the Christian;
rather the implication is simply that the figure, or perhaps name, of
Christ be so repeatable. The name or 'figure' (rhetorically understood) of 'Christ' becomes the very locus of the indefinite article, of
indefinition, lack of identity and certainty, even an infantile
inarticulacy.

This, of course, is a common theological motif, at least since
Augustine. The notion that '*the* Word' is realized in fleshly terms as
an *infans* (non-speaker) was a paradox that pleased Augustine, and
would probably be of interest to Donne as well. The argument
might then be that it is not in direct vocation to God, that is, in
direct invocation of God's name, that prayer should be conducted.
On the contrary, antonomasia becomes fundamental to prayer. In
this poem the 'inarticulacy' of 'a' Jesus Christ is the single most
important verbal point in the text: here, as it were, is the poet
becoming 'infantile', conforming to the Christian precept as recorded
by Mark:

> Suffer the little children to come unto me, and forbid them not:
> for of such is the kingdom of God.
> Verily I say unto you, Whosoever shall not receive the kingdom
> of God as a little child, he shall not enter therein. (Mark, 10:14-15)

These 'infants' are precisely those whose verbal mode of existence
is a kind of silence or, better, inarticulacy. The child as 'player'
becomes the sainted adult as 'prayer' here. Moreover, in this
movement into inarticulacy, there is a kind of rejection of poetry as
such in a certain sense: Donne rejects the poetic metaphor for the
mundanity of the euphemistic antonomasia 'a something else', as if
language fails him at this point. In this light the poem itself, 'this
paper', might be precisely the relic mentioned in the title; it is the
'remains' of Donne as poet, and the instigation of a characterization
of Donne as inarticulate prayerful infant of indeterminate identity.

But it must be objected that at some level there is a nomination of
Donne here, in the figure of 'a Jesus Christ'. This name, however, is
now indeterminate: it is a kind of empty space awaiting phenomenological occupation, as it were, by anyone else, by anyone who
comes to perform the *imitatio Christi* which seems to be the subject
of the poem. The name then becomes an empty space awaiting

(silent, infantile, playful/prayerful) nomination in a scene of recognition. The kind of recognition which is most easily theologized for Donne is that between two or more carnal lovers, as here. This facilitates the 'identification' of the name 'Christ' as the embodiment of love or, more clearly, of this kind of tryst in the form of a communion. In the communion here, individual distinction disappears, as all names and identities are subsumed in the one totalizing (because indefinite) name, as an embodiment of the name of Christ. To express this more briefly, the carnal lovers become not an 'embodiment' so much as the Body of Christ: that is, 'The Relique' (both the bone and hair, and the paper or text itself) produces the church, or ecclesia. To this extent the poetry becomes prayer, through a muted invocation to an unnamable 'God'.

The name of 'Christ', according to this, becomes for Donne a 'scene' or phenomenological space in which all personal individuated identity is lost, as the self is identified with a number of other selves, 'something else', in a corporate or carnal union of sorts. For Donne, the name 'Christ' becomes the location of writing itself, especially if we understand writing in the manner of Barthes, say:

> writing is the destruction of every voice [and thus 'infantile'?], of every point of origin [like the determinate 'I']. Writing is that neutral [and neuter?], composite, oblique space where our subject slips away, where all identity is lost, starting with the very identity of the body writing.[30]

The name of Christ is, almost by definition in Donne, that which cannot explicitly be articulated; and its very suppression is what allows the poems to come into writing at all. The texts themselves can be understood, in many cases, as elaborate euphemisms referring us to Christ, inviting a 'recognition' of a relation between ourselves and Christ, without ever blasphemously mentioning the name, usually understood as sacred or taboo, itself. Euphemism such as this is an extremely complex manoeuvre, especially when carried out in these theological interests.

The point of euphemism in many texts of Donne is frequently to dissolve the very notion of individuality which most critics have vaunted as the essential distinguishing fact about Donne. Its point is to make the name 'John Donne' into a kind of 'trembling name', a name poised to be fragmented, shattered, shivered, into pieces. In fact, of course, this itself is a legitimate *imitatio Christi*, for according to the theology, Christ's body or identity is blessed and broken not only in crucifixion but also in communion, in that construction of *ecclesia* which incorporates many fleshes in the 'Body of Christ'. What is being imitated then in these poems, whose mimesis consists in an *imitatio Christi*, is fundamentally non-individual: this 'Christ' is plural, iterable. The notion of coming to inhabit this name implies for Donne a multiplication of personality, which is paradoxically, as in Eliot, the escape from individual personality and the construction of an ecclesia or personae, a community, always found first and foremost within the one flesh.

The poet's name does explicitly 'tremble' in 'A Valediction: of my name, in the window'. But whose name is this? We should perhaps be alerted right from the first lines of the poem, when some emphasis is placed on the word 'graved' in its form as 'engrav'd':

> My name engrav'd herein,
> Doth contribute my firmnesse to this glasse,
> Which, ever since that charme, hath beene
> As hard, as that which grav'd it, was[31]

Aside from the notion of imprinting, the verb 'to engrave' contains the idea, made explicit in the poem itself, of being 'graved' or buried. The name, then, is some kind of buried name; that is, it is hidden in the text, a name under the words of the text, and is also perhaps a reference to some dead and buried entity. The tenor of the poem suggests, further, that this person, even in an extended absence, is 'firm' and constant, not really dead at all. Proof of this continued existence lies in the fact that the name remains as a talisman fixed on the glass of the window; it is kept 'alive' if only the listener or reader will keep an eye turned towards the glass, rather than looking through it, darkly. As the poet puts it, giving incidentally another hint towards the name in question (if we have not already seen it by turning our gaze upon this glassy text, these at least semi-transparent letters in stained glass):

> Thine eye will give it price enough, to mock
> The diamonds of either rock.

These diamonds (a word derived from the Greek *adamas*, adamant, thus establishing a link to the final line of Divine Meditation 1, 'Thou hast made me') may be the substance, engraved in rock and then 'extracted' from it to make cut glass, and thus may refer to the window itself. Alternatively, they may refer us to the diamond which has been used (according to the title of the poem in many manuscript versions 'Upon the engraving of his name with a diamond in his mistress' window when he was to travel') in order to do the actual engraving of the name. In both cases, whether the diamonds are engraved or engraving, whether as object or subject, they are identified (even 'named') as diamonds of 'rock'. The 'rock', of course, refers us as euphemism to another kind of rock, closely associated with engraving or burying and 'de-graving' or digging out the buried body again. The rock refers us then to the rock at the entrance to Christ's tomb and, by conventional extension, to that other 'Rock', Christ,[32] who is frequently referred to, in euphemism, as 'the Rock'.

We return to the opening question: whose name is this in the window/text? Even if it appears to be that of 'John Donne', the lover on the point of departure, this name is intercepted by another unspoken name, that of Christ. When the poet asks for the intervention of the name in the window between the eye of the lover/reader and the name of another lover, it is now indeed more acceptable to suggest that what is being demanded is the inter-position of the silent name of Christ between the lover/reader and Donne. This, once more, would 'canonize' the poem, if we take it that the real speaker of this stanza becomes none other than Christ:

> And when thy melted maid,
> Corrupted by thy lover's gold, and page,
> His letter at thy pillow' hath laid,
> Disputed it, and tam'd thy rage,
> And thou begin'st to thaw towards him, for this
> May my name step in, and hide his.

Here, it is as if the poet tries to suggest that the name in the window, now being that of Christ, is the name which should interpose between the letter of a lover (i.e., this poem) and its reader. Further, the name at the bottom of this poem/letter is itself to be 'graved' or hidden under the name of the real author, that of Christ as transcendent lover.

Any response to this poem, any writing in response to it, is thus further to be converted to the status of some kind of prayer, an invocation to the name of Christ, as the following stanza makes clear:

> And if this treason goe
> To an overt act, and that thou write againe;
> In superscribing, this name flow
> Into thy fancy, from the pane.
> So, in forgetting thou remembrest right,
> And unaware to mee shalt write.

This reflects back on the poem which Donne has written here, of course; for this poem is itself a response, in writing, to another anterior writing, the writing of the name in the window. The poem becomes an invocation to God, and the response to it, this criticism which is the poem itself, is supposed to be a parallel kind of invocational prayer. Whether we know it or not, and whether Donne is conscious of it or not, the poem, according to this reading, is nothing more or less than a scene of ecclesiastic recognition, nomination and invocation, not of the names of two separate lovers, but of the act of loving itself, 'crystal'-ized in the rock or diamond Crystal, and punningly or euphemistically in Christ. It is the suppression of Christ's name in the text which permits or conditions the poem's generation of such a kind of 'communion' in the act of reading.

That scene of mutual recognition or nomination is also made fairly clear in the poem's second stanza which focuses on the important theoretical issue of the transparency or substantiality of the glassy text or window. In one way the glass is transparent, as are the words of the text, permitting us to discern or discover the sacred, buried or 'engraved' name. In another way, however, this discovery of this name is actually a discovery or 'remembering right' of the forgotten presence of this name within the perceiver; the glass thus becomes precisely analogous to the mirror/heart which we have looked into before, in Sidney. It and the text become scenes of recognition, like looking into a self-reflection in a mirror; but the person that we recognize in that mirror is no longer the self we knew, but someone other, 'a something else'. The surface of the mirror or text is the location of the silent name of Christ, and that name, according to the poem is itself the meeting-place of 'I' and 'thee':

> 'Tis much that Glasse should be
> As all confessing, and through-shine as I,
> 'Tis more, that it shewes thee to thee,

> And cleare reflects thee to thine eye.
> But all such rules, love's magique can undoe,
> Here you see mee, and I am you.

At the moment of recognition, the name clearly becomes a 'trembling name', and this is so even before the throwing open of the sepulchral rock of the crystal casement: these lovers no longer have separate identity. This confusion of 'I' and 'thee' is foreshadowed in the pun of the first stanza, at the moment of perception of the 'rock', when 'Thine eye will give it price enough to mock'; this 'eye' becomes itself the location of the 'I'. Thus, what has happened is that the location of the buried name has shifted ground, from the window as such to the window of the lover's eye. That is to say, what is in the eye of the lover (at present the text of the poem) itself becomes identifiable as the scene of recognition, and is the location of the buried name of Christ. The text then enacts what is a literal moment of revelation. In some respects, the poem is a response to another Christian parable, in which Christ challenged his disciples with the charge, appropriately enough in this context, of hypocrisy:

> And why beholdest thou the mote that is in thy brother's eye, but perceivest not the beam that is in thine own eye?
> Either how canst thou say to thy brother, Brother, let me pull out the mote that is in thine eye, when thou thyself beholdest not the beam that is in thine own eye? Thou hypocrite, cast out first the beam out of thine own eye, and then thou shalt see clearly to pull out the mote that is in thy brother's eye (Luke, 6:41–2)

The poem has, in fact, taken up on the reiteration of the words 'thine eye' which organizes most of this parable, and makes a response to the charges laid by Christ. The primary charge here is one which, as I have argued, Donne was, like his readers, extremely open to: hypocrisy. The poem is an attempt to escape from the mode of hypocrisy which conditions Donne's writing. The means of escape is the enactment of the advice in this parable: the removal of the beam from 'thine eye' in order not only to be able to see, but also to give such vision or revelation to one's sisters and brothers.

It is small wonder then that the name should be called a 'trembling name'. Not only does it literally tremble as the window is thrown open (allowing us to see clearly without the interposition of our own reflection, personality or shadow in the form of a named identity); it also trembles with a lack of fixity. It is not clear any more that the person identified by this name (a name which the text itself never reveals, but always works to cover or 'grave') is one single and stable identity; rather the name becomes a locus of identification of the self with an Other. That is to say, the function of the rhetorical trope of antonomasia is more than mere fashionable ornament: it serves the theological purpose of creating an illusion of ecclesia for Donne.

Such an ecclesia revokes the notion of propriety, of the 'proper' name itself. As the name trembles, there is also a corporal trembling in a religious, almost Quakerly, manner, to be made more explicit in Divine Meditation 19, 'Oh, to vex me', in which 'Those are my best dayes, when I shake with feare'.[33] One reason for such fear lies in the enormity of the rhetorical enterprise of antonomasia here, at the very moment when infantile play mutates into adult prayer, through poetry. For the name, of course, which Donne assumes in his bid to be as a little child, in his bid to evade hypocrisy, is none other than that of Jesus Christ. In this impersonation the escape from hypocrisy simply involves Donne in a much more fearful adoption of a hypocritical stance, as he 'pretends' or aspires to be God.

The 'incorporation' of the body of Christ in this rhetorical series of manoeuvres owes much to the Christian 'last supper' and first communion. In John, chapters 16 and 17, there are many analogues for the poetic procedures carried out by Donne. Concerning the notion of revelation which I have outlined in Donne's 'communion-text', there is the passage in which Christ 'explains' his euphemistic words, 'A little while, and ye shall not see me; and again, a little while, and ye shall see me', which is a kind of proverb to match Donne's poems:

> Now Jesus knew that they were desirous to ask him, and said unto them, Do ye enquire among yourselves of that I said, A little while, and ye shall not see me: and again, a little while, and ye shall see me? . . .
>
> ye now . . . have sorrow: but I will see you again, and your heart shall rejoice, and your joy no man taketh from you.
>
> And in that day ye shall ask me nothing. Verily, verily, I say unto you, Whatsoever ye shall ask the Father in my name, he will give *it* you.

Hitherto have ye asked nothing in my name: ask, and ye shall receive, that your joy may be full.

These things have I spoken unto you in proverbs: but the time cometh, when I shall no more speak unto you in proverbs, but I shall shew you plainly of the Father.

At that day ye shall ask in my name (John, 16: 16–26)

Here, the working through of the 'proverb' or poem leads to the discovery of the Father/God-figure in a moment of revelation, or prayer uttered 'in my name'. At that moment there is a promised end to euphemistic words, to proverbs, and their replacement with history itself, with 'the real thing', as it were, shown 'plainly'. Clearly Donne owes much to this in his own 'relics' or remains. Further, the notion of communion as elaborated by Donne, especially in the 'Valediction: of my name, in the window', owes much again to John, and to Christ's prayer in Gethsemane:

I have manifested thy name unto the men which thou gavest me out of the world [a 'fit audience, though few', perhaps]: thine they were, and thou gavest them me; and they have kept thy word ... I pray for them: I pray not for the world, but for them which thou hast given me; for they are thine.

And all mine are thine, and thine are mine ...

Keep through thine own name those whom thou hast given me, that they may be one, as we *are*. (John, 17: 6–11)

The elaboration, in euphemism, parallels the parabolic words of Christ in the Authorised Version of the Bible. The confusion of 'thine' and 'mine', of 'thee' and 'I', even of 'I' and 'I', all stem in some way from biblical example. Moreover, the source of such confusion of identities, of such a communion which produces ecclesia, is to be found in the tacit name which Donne strives to reveal and cover simultaneously in his poems, the name of God.

By the rhetorical devices available to him, Donne contrives two major effects. In the first place his texts elaborate at a metaphysical level the ecclesia as such: that is to say, they are 'incarnations' or articulations of the theological 'infantile' and playful Word, constructing or realizing at that same theological level the Church as Body of Christ. And secondly Donne contrives to locate himself in the identity of the name of Christ, thus becoming himself an articulation of the inarticulate, a realization of the fundamental non-identity or anti-individualist stance of a reiterable Christ: in neo-Platonic terms, he strives to fulfil the name of Christ and to be a material realization of that formal Idea. But the idea as such has no specific identity: the name, 'Christ', quite simply means for Donne the space of writing, of prayer, that space where 'all identity is lost, starting with the very identity of the body writing'. Donne's Christian church is precisely the sphere of an anti-dogmatic theology, always 'decentred' (rather than focused) upon an always absent or mutable notion of the unutterable name of 'God'.

In making himself out to be God, or at least Christ, in this way, Donne makes all of his poems prayerful vocations: poems of departure and of 'new days' (revolutionary moments, as I have called them) all become poems which phatically address or call out to readers. Both 'The good-morrow' and all poems of 'farewell' or valediction, become euphemisms of the fundamental theological phrase, 'God be with you'. 'Good-bye', of course, is a derivation from the fuller phrase 'God be with ye', and 'good-morrowing' becomes a plea to let 'God' (i.e. Donne) remain with whatever lover/reader he addresses. Donne's poetry plays itself out as vocational prayer in this sense.

One final example on this head should clarify a debt to the Bible in the ways outlined here, and perhaps more also in terms of cadence or poetic organization of these carefully chiselled words. In 'The good-morrow', a phrase such as 'My face in thine eye, thine in mine appeares', which in terms of rhythm and balanced (even paradoxical) organization is extremely typical, has a root in the biblical phrases already cited even in the present chapter, and perhaps most clearly in another line from John (17: 23): 'I in them, and thou in me, that they may be perfect in one'.

It is in sources such as this that the impetus in Donne, striving towards Godhead in untrammelled ambition, becomes more problematical as an individualist exercise; Donne's paradoxical 'mirroring' relations, in which there are eyebeams crossed and propagations of one's own reflection, work fairly consistently not to render the importance of individuality so much as to rend individuality itself. The result is what Donne seems most frequently to characterize as an 'ecstasy', an ecstatic dissolution of indivi- duality, producing one (specific, namable) body (that of Christ); but this is a body which, when carnally realized, speaks a 'dialogue of one', speaks with a playful or prayerful forked tongue.

The final paradox in this attempted elaboration of Donne's identity in the name of 'Christ' is that it leads to a situation where he speaks like the serpent, with the forked tongue of duplicitous hypocrisy. Hence the need for more prayer, for more poetry, for a greater and more 'faithful' imitation of Christ. When Donne reaches the point of saying 'Deigne at my hands this crown of prayer and praise' (in the *La Corona* sonnets), all he has done is manage to reach a point at which the crown, the prayer, and the poetry must all begin once more. In Eliot's re-working of the whole schema here:

> With the drawing of this Love and the voice of this Calling
>
> We shall not cease from exploration
> And the end of all our exploring
> Will be to arrive where we started
> And know the place for the first time[34]

Donne's similar search is for a tongue in which to call, to make a 'vocation', and in that calling of prayer, to enable a scene of recognition, not between himself and a lover, but between himself and God.

Notes

1 T.S. Eliot, *The Sacred Wood*, London, Methuen, 1920, 49.
2 Henry Howard, Earl of Surrey, *Poems* (ed. Emrys Jones), Oxford, Clarendon Press, 1964, 10, 115.
3 Philip Sidney, 'Apology for poetry', reprinted in Edmund D. Jones (ed.), *English Critical Essays XVI–XVIII Centuries*, Oxford, Oxford University Press, 1975, 7.
4 Walter J. Ong, *Orality and Literacy*, London, Methuen, 1982, 99.
5 Leslie A. Fiedler, 'Archetype and signature: a study of the relationship between biography and poetry', *Sewanee Review*, 60 (1952), 263.
6 Jonathan Culler, *On Deconstruction*, London, Routledge & Kegan Paul, 1983, 120.
7 Paul Ricoeur, *Hermeneutics and the Human Sciences* (trans. John B. Thompson), Cambridge, Cambridge University Press, 1981, 138.
8 Piero Cudini, 'Introduzione' (unpaginated) to Francesco Petrarca, *Canzoniere*, Milan, Garzanti, 1974.
9 Petrarca, op. cit., 5.
10 Étienne Tabourot, *Les Bigarrures du Seigneur des Accords*, Paris, Jehan Richer, 1583, 3.
11 See Joachim du Bellay, *La Deffence et Illustration de la Langue Françoyse* (1549) (ed. Henri Chamard), Paris, Marcel Didier, 1970, 153–5, and cf. Tabourot, op. cit., 91, for two precisely similar examples; and cf. P. Delaudun d'Aigaliers, *L'Art Poétique* (1597), bk 3, ch. 9–10, for others. Cf. also Floyd Gray, *La poétique de Du*

Bellay, Paris, Nizet, 1978, for a fuller discussion of nomination in Du Bellay.

12 Joachim du Bellay, *Les Regrets et autres Oeuvres Poëtiques* (ed. J. Jolliffe), Geneva, Librairie Droz, 1974, 65.

13 ibid., 64.

14 ibid., 66.

15 Philip Sidney, *Selected Poems* (ed. Katherine Duncan-Jones), Oxford, Clarendon Press, 1973, 128.

16 ibid., xiv.

17 ibid., 117.

18 ibid., 118.

19 ibid., 117.

20 ibid., 124.

21 ibid., 141.

22 Jean-Paul Sartre, *Being and Nothingness* (trans. Hazel E. Barnes), New York, Philosophical Library, 1956, 566.

23 Donne, 141ff.

24 John, 18: 33–7.

25 'Euphuism' is not the same as 'euphemism'; but both rhetorical practices produce similar tropes.

26 Donne, 12.

27 Donne, 14.

28 Donne, 55–6.

29 William Empson, 'Donne the space man', *Kenyon Review*, 19(1957), 337–99.

30 Roland Barthes, 'The death of the author', in Roland Barthes, *Image-Music-Text* (trans. Stephen Heath), Glasgow, Fontana/Collins, 1977, 142.

31 Donne, 23.

32 The church, then, is built not upon the specificity of the Word, but rather upon the euphemistic ambiguity of the pun: rock=peter.

33 Donne, 302.

34 T.S. Eliot, 'Four Quartets', in *Complete Poems and Plays of T.S. Eliot*, London, Faber, 1969, 197.

6
Donne's praise of folly

Mutato nomine de te fabula narratur
         (Horace, *Satires*, Book 1, Satire 1,
         cited by Karl Marx in *Capital*, vol. 1,
         ch. 10, sect. 5, 'The struggle for a
         normal working day')

         On a huge hill,
Cragged, and steep, Truth stands, and hee that will
Reach her, about must, and about must goe;
And what the hills suddennes resists, winne so;
Yet strive so, that before age, deaths twilight,
Thy Soule rest, for none can worke in that night.
To will, implyes delay, therefore now doe:
Hard deeds, the bodies paines; hard knowledge too
The mindes indeavours reach, and mysteries
Are like the Sunne, dazling, yet plaine to all eyes.
         (John Donne, Satire 3, 'Kinde pitty
         chokes my spleene')

This is a disadvantage I am powerless to overcome,
unless it be by forewarning and forearming those
readers who zealously seek the truth. There is no
royal road to science, and only those who do not
dread the fatiguing climb of its steep paths have
a chance of gaining its luminous summits.
         (Karl Marx, letter to Maurice La
         Chatre, cited in Althusser and
         Balibar, *Reading Capital*)

1

In 1873 Arnold established a distinction between 'scientific' and 'literary' language which had been latent in theoretical thought for centuries. He posed the distinction in his preface to *Literature and Dogma*, where he suggested that 'To understand that the language of the Bible is fluid, passing, and literary, not rigid, fixed, and scientific, is the first step towards a right understanding of the Bible'.[1] This problematic of exegesis focuses on the conflict between truth and interpretation. It is a problem which the English church had faced before, most clearly at the moment of its institutionalization in the Reformation. When Henry VIII divorced England from Rome, he inadvertently inaugurated a problem or conflict of 'many authorities', and a relativization of truth in scriptural exegesis. The publication of an *Authorized (King James) Version* in 1611 did little to alleviate the problem. A *version* (from *vertere*, to turn) is a translation, a turning or *trope* (from *tropos*, a turn); this version then comes dangerously close to a rendering from a specific point of view, and thus a variant or interpretation. The *Authorized Version*, in fact, contributed to the outbreak of a Civil War in which one party questioned precisely the 'authorizations' of the king. The king's 'good name', interposing itself as the mediator of the truth in this version/interpretation, had been 'wounded' or doubted; and the exegetical problems remained.

For Augustine biblical exegesis depended upon an initial act of faith, a *credo* which framed the act of reading. Once 'inside' this frame of faith, truth could be rendered directly to the heart of the reader, without the intervention of a sceptical, critical consciousness. But this faith, in ridding us of interested intermediaries, also rids us of our own consciousness. Our voices are silenced, *our* readings unheard: we are supposed simply to *hear* the words of scripture, as if they emanated from within, and to make no critical or even conscious response. Such 'faithful reading' depends on a notion that the source of the scripture and its guarantee of truth is within us: this Bible preaches to the *converted*, for it depends upon our *turning*, in complete faith, towards it, with it, and away from our own thought.

This strangely self-satisfying strategy was taken over to some extent by Renaissance humanists; but among some of these there was concern about the interposition of their own mediating consciousness or identity (their name) between the truth of the text and its interpretation or reading. Cave points out that Erasmus tried to circumvent this by the adoption of a quasi-phenomenological approach:

> Erasmus constructs the model of a dynamic imitation or reproduction of Scripture. The text is to be wholly absorbed by the reader and located in the *pectus*, that intuitive focus of the self which is presumed to guarantee profound understanding and *living* expression. In other words, the scriptural text is made consubstantial with the reader and is then re-uttered in a speech-act grounded in the living presence of the speaker, a process which achieves its end in that vivid penetration of the listener's mind which is in itself a mark of authenticity.[2]

The reader here is afflicated by glottophagia, swallowing her or his tongue as s/he digests the material of the text; the material thus absorbed is then re-produced, but transformed, spoken not in the tongue of the reader but in the tongue of God as ultimate authority. The experience of the listener is not a mark of authenticity in fact, but is rather a mark of ideology; for this reading-process pretends to eradicate the transforming labour, activity, or medium of the reader's name in the reading-production of the text. The reader, in mediating the word of God, 'identifies' her or his voice with that of God; and it is this voice which is supposed to guarantee and authorize the ideology. Such a reader performs two related 'impersonations': firstly, an *imitatio Christi* in the conventional sense; and secondly, an *imitatio Mariae*, impersonating the virginal mother in her innocent and 'immaculate conception' of the word of God, which she transforms, in her labour, into lived and living flesh. The dangerous mediating identity of the reader now meshes with the incarnation of God in the *pectus*: God, as it were, now inhabits the heart, spirit or personal identity (that is, individuated proper name) of the reader, and there is a mutual recognition (an acknowledgment of truth) in this consubstantiality of the two identities of God and reader.

The self-presence of the reader, this 'intuitive focus of the self' is actually informed then as a 'scene of recognition' by an 'impersonal' self; the *pectus* then is like the *name* as a scene of recognition discussed above. This kind of reading-activity came to determine secular writing as well. Erasmus prefigures the position adopted by

Montaigne whose essayistic attempt at self-portraiture (or self-nomination fundamentally) becomes one which involves structural change and a form of 'impersonality'. The portrait constructed in the *Essais* is always grounded in the response to previous writings, including previous *essais*; a degree of sceptical self-criticism is the result. In the *Essais* the self portrayed changes with the writing or production of the text as such, as each new essay adds to and, significantly, makes a critical response to, previous accumulations of details. Cave detects a similarity in Erasmus: 'The name or pseudonym of Erasmus (Desiderius, the loved one) figures in many of his writings – the *Praise of Folly*, the *Ichthyophagia* – as an ironically paraded self, a special instance of that mirror-image which, according to the theory of *oratio* as *speculum animi*, is to be composed by the text'. But this involves Erasmus, or that euphemistic pseudonym, Desiderius, in a process of impersonation, and hence in a kind of inauthenticity:

> Erasmus purports to write as an evangelical humanist; but the compulsion endlessly to extend his writing reveals, with increasing evidence, the desire to recognize himself (see his face in the mirror) and be recognized. He must become an alien surface in order to constitute himself as an identity, an *apparent* nature, grafted (perhaps) only on the culture of discourse. The Erasmian *sensus* or *sententia*, issuing supposedly from a unique identity, translates itself into words, and thus inevitably betrays itself.[3]

This translation, or *version*, of the self and its name produces not the Augustinian 'faithful reading', but rather, precisely the contrary, an act of 'betrayal' or *infidelity*. To put this more simply, the self, as an ideological construction in this cultural and historical milieu in and through which Donne lived, always finds itself in a state of differential, structural change; the name of the self is always to be found in its 'betrayal' or identification with the name of an Other.

The principle of change, which is constitutive of the construction of a historical selfhood, can perhaps better be described as a principle of exchange; and the fundamental locus of that exchange can be identified as the 'proper' name or word (now, clearly, no longer strictly 'proper') or individual essential identity. That is to say that at the very moment of constructing a 'pure' essential identity the impurities of a mutability or exchangeability appear. In terms of reading and writing, the effect of this is to replace the notion of an essential or grounding truth in a text by a conflict of mutable, critical interpretations; such interpretation is a properly historicized act of reading, a 'reading' now always mediated by an 'impure' reader who guarantees that there can be no possibility of hygienic 'sanity', no sanitization, of the text or of its reading. The name, identity or consciousness of a reader of the Bible or of a poem, say, enters to vitiate the purity or immediacy of truth in the text's reading, giving in its place a 'maculate' mediation or critical interpretation of the text. As a corollary, the proper name itself is but another *version* or trope. It is the purpose of this chapter not to lay bare the 'true name' of Donne (for such a final ground in truth is denied), but rather to reveal some important other versions or tropes of the name of Donne.[4]

2

Erasmus makes some play with proper names, though not specifically in the terms described above, in the Dedication of his *Praise of Folly*. The work is prefaced by its Greek title, *Morias Enkomion*, in its dedication to Erasmus's friend, Thomas More. The text becomes instantly ambiguous as Erasmus plays on the name of More and its near homonym, the Greek *morias*, and the title of the text is ironized:

> let me be hanged if I have enjoyed anyone more in my life! Therefore, since I thought that something should be done about it and the time seemed little fit for serious thinking, I decided to have some fun with a praise of folly.
> 'How did the goddess Pallas put that into my head?' you ask. First of all, there was your family name of More, which is as close to the Greek word for folly as you are from the meaning of the word. . . . and besides, you are a sort of Democritus amid the common run of mortals.[5]

More's name then is a kernel of the work by Erasmus; and further this 'praise of folly' becomes an oblique or ironic praise of the name of More/morias, in whose house Erasmus stayed, recovering from illness, while writing the text.

Folly enters directly to disrupt the stability of truth; the *pectus*, or scene of recognition between the name of More and the word for folly, far from being a locus of truth and authenticity, becomes tainted by the impurities of ideology, hypocrisy, madness or unhygienic insanity. Foucault has made the correlation between madness and truth in a suggestion that 'La folie commence là où se trouble et s'obscurcit le rapport de l'homme à la vérité'.[6] Further, madness is linked to the comedy of *quiproquo*, that principle of exchange which mediates between More and morias:

> La folie, c'est la forme la plus pure, la plus totale du *quiproquo*: elle prend le faux pour le vrai, la mort pour la vie, l'homme pour la femme, l'amoureuse pour l'Erynnie et la victime pour Minos.[7]

> (Folly is the purest, most complete form of *quiproquo*: it takes the false for the true, death for life, man for woman, the lover for the Fury and the victim for Minos.)

This, in fact, is one fundamental value of a comedy based upon the punning quiproquo: it suggests that things may be arranged differently from what they seem and allows for, or even encourages, the possibility of change, of the provisional triumph of one version or trope over other interpretations of the world. A quest for epistemological veracity, on the other hand, is inherently more tragic. The quiproquo of Sophocles's *Oedipus Rex* or of Racine's *Iphigénie en Aulide* turns towards tragedy when an essentially 'true' identity is revealed or discovered: quiproquo resolves into mono-logue or 'mono-logicity'. On the other hand, a drama such as Shakespeare's *Comedy of Errors* endorses a comic attitude in which impure identities can be tolerated or modified to suit the 'mad' but pragmatic pursuit of pleasure (however ideological that pleasure may be) rather than the dogmatic and nostalgic pursuit of a transcendent, monological version of an Absolute Knowing.[8]

Wilbur Samuel Howell has drawn attention to an opposition in the Renaissance between logic and rhetoric, an opposition which was typically reproduced symbolically:

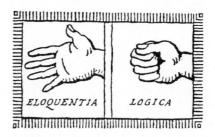

ELOQUENTIA   LOGICA

He writes in explanation of this metaphor of the open and closed hand that:

> Over and over again in logical and rhetorical treatises of the English Renaissance, logic is compared to the closed fist and rhetoric to the open hand, this metaphor being borrowed from Zeno through Cicero and Quintilian to explain the preoccupation of logic with the tight discourses of the philosopher, and the preoccupation of rhetoric with the more open discourses of orator and popularizer.[9]

Logic and rhetoric were regarded as two different, but complementary, modes of communication, according to Howell; and poetry was considered to be a third mode, one which was simultaneously closed and open:

> poetry was thought to be a form of communication which, because it habitually used the medium of story and characterization, spoke two simultaneous languages.[10]

This is a little misleading in its simplification. The separation of the two hands, for a start, is a falsification, for logic is always intertwined with rhetoric, philosophy always mediated stylistically.[11] That is to say, poetry as such is the ground of both rhetoric and logic, and the principle of exchange, of *dialogicity*, is the ground of poetry. Poetry may itself affirm nothing, but it forms the condition of whatever propositions may be made; it may *say* nothing, but it conditions what may be *done*, or at least what may be thought.

Dialogicity is integral and fundamental to Lyly's *Euphues*, a text which was immensely popular in the final decades of the sixteenth century, and which spawned many imitations of its style. The single most insistent device of Lyly's text is antithesis and antithetical chiasmus; and other devices, including rhyme and pun, the radical of antithesis and chiasmus, follow from this. Both rhyme and pun invite the possibility of potentially comic linguistic exchange, quiproquo and folly. Appropriately, Lyly's text closes on an act of intertwining of hands, in a formal handshake which operates as a clear symbol of the commerce of exchange, of the interchange of positions on the part of speaker and listener, and of the organization of a certain kind of friendship or social relation which is one of the major organizational principles in the text. This friendship is constituted precisely on a ground of exchangeability. The relation between Euphues and Philautus is disturbed only by the intrusion of the woman, Lucilla, who threatens, by the merest fact of her sexual difference from these characters, to displace their association. More immediately pertinent here, however, is the description of the establishment of friendship offered by Euphues:

> I have red ... and well I beleeve it, that a friend is in prosperitie a pleasure, a solace in adversitie, in griefe a comfort, in joy a merrye companion, at all other times an other I, in all places the expresse Image of mine owne person[12]

This is precisely in line with the Donnean and Montaignean realization of identity. The self is always a part of a social relation; that is, it is constituted by social dialogue and not through a monologue derived from that social relation with the Other. The self, then, derives from an anterior community; and the moment of discovery of self-awareness or of self-nomination is also the moment at which the self discovers her or his exchangeability, mutability and mutuality.

This is one aspect of Euphuism which Donne takes over to some extent; but in his hands, it becomes more clearly a kind of dialogical *euphemism*,[13] in which sacred or taboo words and names are 'heard' without being explicitly said. One extremely important such dialogical pun is, aptly enough, on the word 'mutually' in Elegy 7, a poem in which Donne writes of, and in, the 'language of flowers' or euphemism:

> I had not taught thee then, the Alphabet
> Of flowers, how they devisefully being set
> And bound up, might with speechlesse secrecie
> Deliver errands mutely, and mutually[14]

This is nothing less than an 'apology for poesy' and a kind of advertisement for the language of flowers. The play between 'mutely' and 'mutually', in which they come together as homonyms, and thus as euphemisms for each other, makes of these lines an apology for the dialogical handshake of poetic communication, and suggests that it is basic or fundamental to any other mode of communication. Further, this poesy substitutes itself for the historical 'posy', the wedding ring or circle into which Donne wants to break in the poem. The language of flowers, in Donne as in

Shakespeare,[15] allows secret messages to be understood; more pertinently here, the 'posy/poesy' establishes a parabolic riddle which is understood by an 'elect', those within the hermeneutic circle or 'ring'. This is essentially modelled on Christian parabolic teaching. As Kermode has it:

> To divine the true, the latent sense, you need to be of the elect, of the institution. Outsiders may content themselves with the manifest, and pay a supreme penalty for doing so. Only those who already know the mysteries – what the stories really mean – can discover what the stories really mean.[16]

The Donnean poetic riddling language is slightly different, inasmuch as it has conceded any notion of privileged access to the true. The 'latent sense' in Kermode's definition here is no more 'true' for Donne than any other sense. In this poem, what is at stake is simply the exchange of one 'posy' for another little ring; the exchange of the historical wedding-posy for the posy/poesy which establishes a ring or circle including Donne and his co-elect, the woman who now understands his language of flowers.

Although the text has given up the notion of making truth-propositions here, history has not been lost.[17] There is a movement from the play of signifiers, from the poesy (language of flowers) towards the establishment of historical action, in the formation of the posy. This posy, proposed in the act of reading the poem, establishes a ring or circle which demarcates an ecclesia of sorts around the poem. But, given the fact that the readers of this poem constitute a numerous group (the poem is not simply a letter to one historical individual woman), the shape and formation of this posy/ecclesia is indeterminate, open. That is to say, the movement from poesy to posy does not simply establish one specific 'adulterous' or unfaithful situation in the alignment of Donne and one woman and their consanguinity symbolized in the new posy; rather this potentially univocal and 'private' sense is opened out to a community of elect readers. It is this elect who make the poem legible and who legitimate or authorize its ecclesiastic community. Thus the text is inherently dialogical, if not multilogical.[18]

In the lines cited, this possibility of mutuality or relational identity (the establishment of open posies) arises from the interchange of 'mutely' and 'mutually'; but this is done in a specific way – 'with speechless secrecy'. What is 'mutely' communicated is important in this mutual relation or mutual consciousness; for it is this 'mute' aspect of the act of understanding which turns linguistic play into historical action. An example of relevance occurs in Satire 2, where we have:

> One would move Love by rimes; but witchcrafts charms
> Bring not now their old feares, nor their old harmes:
> Rammes, and slings now are seely battery,
> Pistolets are the best Artillerie.[19]

There is a manuscript variant which gives greater clarity to the concealed pun; there is justification to emend 'slings' to 'songs'. This makes more apparent the pun on 'ram/rhyme', giving what may in fact appear to be more coherent: 'Rams [rhymes] and songs now are silly battery,/Pistolets are the best artillery'. This makes doubly significant the pun on the word 'rhyme' itself, suggesting a reading or version in which the power of rhyme does, despite the first two lines quoted, have the historically real power of the 'ram'. 'Rhymes' can be, and are, more than mere rhetorical efflorescence and can have logical, scientific or, more generally, historical applicability and efficacy.

The 'mutism' of such linguistic exchanges is important when the poet wants to write 'indecorous' or controversial things, without actually saying them. The pun allows words to be 'heard' without their being said. A pertinent example is in 'Aire˜and Angels' where we hear of the poet who:

> Whilst thus to ballast love, I thought,
> And so more steadily to have gone,
> With wares which would sink admiration,
> I saw, I had loves pinnace overfraught[20]

The word 'pinnace' is odd in this context: a ship of fools may be one thing, but a ship of love or of lovers is another, even if Shakespeare may have aligned 'the lunatic, the lover and the poet' in terms of imagination in *A Midsummer-Night's Dream* (V, i). Drawing attention to itself the word 'pinnace' invites the obvious exchange with 'penis'. This silent reading makes explicit sexual sense of the lines, in which there appears now a revelation of the otherwise unspeakable enormity of Donne's erection, and a notion that it attracts such admiration as to make rival 'pinnaces' sink, fall downwards or become detumescent. The euphemistic language of rhetorical flowers is useful as a means of allowing a reader to 'hear' texts or voices other than that presented to her or his eyes and ears. It opens the poem to the intrusion of 'alien' impurities, ghostly verbal visitations which haunt the reader with the possibility of producing multiple meaning, 'dialogical sense', so to speak, of the poetry. The example cited here reveals the operation of euphemism in sexual matters; but precisely the same principle applies in poems (by Donne and many of his censored contemporaries) which make audible the politically unspeakable. The multiplicity of meaning produced in these instances offers the reader, in the now dialectical process of reading, a series of historical and political choices in terms of how s/he will understand and construe the poem, and thus opens up the possibility of historical action and political change.

Fundamental to this is the principle of exchange, through the 'friendly' intertwining of logical and rhetorical hands; but in Donne this seems more readily understood in terms of the clasping of these hands in an attitude of prayer. This enables the possibility of 'mute/mutual' relation between reader and writer, or rather among a community of interpreters, around the focal mirror of the text. The text itself, then, becomes a scene of mutual recognition, the producer of ecclesia. In the ideal, dialogical or poetic reading of poetry, namable personal identity is lost: the reader discovers or 'hears' herself or himself in the voice of the Other, and a corporate identity is produced, in a condition in which a kind of monastic silence allows the voice of a ghostly spirit to be heard. The theological idea is that through this economic ideology of the principle of bartering exchange in language, the reader has a chance to discover her or his own 'vocation' in hearing her or his name called out and identified in the ecclesia (where the reader comes to recognize herself or himself). In the hearing of silent puns, the reader is actually hearing/understanding herself or himself speak, 'mutely'; and such mutism is precisely the locus, in this theology, of mutuality and ecclesia. The body of the reader becomes the body of the church; but only through the 'madness' of mediation, of interpreting these punning exchanges seriously, and through the hearing or understanding of ghostly voices and spirits which haunt the reader in the act of comprehension'.[21]

3

The area between two stable certainties, which is precisely the area occupied by the exchange-pun in language, is characterized by Foucault as the locus of folly. Writing of the mad person on the 'ship of fools', Foucault suggests:

> Et la terre sur laquelle il abordera, on ne la connaît pas, tout comme on ne sait pas, quand il prend pied, de quelle terre il vient. Il n'a sa vérité et sa patrie que dans cette étendue inféconde *entre deux terres* qui ne peuvent lui appartenir.[22]

It is the very quality of alterity and the fact of alienation which constitutes Folly as such; the mad person is always an Other, alien to herself or himself. Moreover, another way of expressing the italicized phrase here, *entre deux terres*, is in a classical formulation as *in medias res*: that is, it is 'in the middest' or in the act of mediation (interpretation, hearing or reading) that such alterity is discovered, in hearing or even in understanding that folly or madness lies.

Might it be the case, then, that Donne is writing his own version, a comic version or revision of a *Praise of Folly* in his rhetorical poesy? It is apposite at this point to recall two things. Firstly, there is the theological information of the Reformation and of Ramist logic, in which Protestantism becomes instrumental in raising the voices of individual readers in a quasi-democratic babel of confusion and historical conflict, when conviction means simply the strident and stubborn proclamation of a monological discourse, deaf to all other voices in the babel. Secondly, there is the more particular principle of exchange which makes Erasmus's *Praise of Folly* fundamentally ironic and ambiguous: the 'hearing' of More's name in its Greek title, *Morias Enkomion*. In the light of these points, might it also be apposite to suggest that Donne is writing a concealed 'praise of More', and, by the slightest of anagrammatical shifts which is startlingly appropriate to the name of More, a praise of *Rome*, or of Roman Catholicism?

It has rightly been stressed that Donne was descended from the family of Thomas More, who was the uncle of Donne's maternal grandmother, Joan Rastell Heywood. If it were indeed the case that Donne was writing a 'praise of Folly/More' then he would clearly have to adopt the euphemistic mode of writing described here.

Given his historical situation, with the persecution of Roman Catholics and his own subsequent career in the Anglican church, he would have to tread warily if he wanted to produce a 'catholic' (universal, though some might say 'totalitarian') mode of prayer through his playful 'comic' verse. It may, of course, equally be the case that he simply could not erase all traces of his own personal theological history, and that he could not 'purge' himself of various Roman Catholic predilections. The ghost of More, as it were, echoes in many 'more-more-ings' or murmurings in the verse, alerting critics such as Paul M. Ochojski to the 'impurities' which reveal such residual Roman Catholicism in Donne's verse.[23]

More Mores than Thomas More, however, played an important part in the personal history of Donne. Not the least of these was his wife, Ann More, and her father, Sir George More. After Donne's hasty clandestine marriage to Ann, George More was instrumental in removing Donne from the service of Sir Thomas Egerton, thus leaving him without patronage and without a source of income, and he finally pursued Donne until he managed to have him imprisoned. From such circumscription, another 'posy' of sorts, Donne contrived to discover some comic 'poesy', in the linguistic play on his name: 'John Donne/Ann Donne/Undone'. The covert 'praise of (Thomas) More' and of a theological imperative might well be intertwined also with a 'praise of (Ann) More' and an imperative which has a greater bearing on sexual and marital matters in the writing.

In the Protestant ideology of Reformation England, questions of spiritual truth and of biblical exegetical interpretation begin to tie in with questions of a more 'privatized' domestic nature. In Satire 3, 'Kinde pitty chokes my spleene', Donne ponders the search for one true religion and finds an interesting way of discerning the true from the heretical:

> unmoved thou
> Of force must one, and forc'd but one allow;
> And the right; aske thy father which is shee,
> Let him aske his; though truth and falshood bee
> Neare twins, yet truth a little elder is[24]

To find the truth, Donne advises some degree of conformity to past or traditional models; more correctly, he suggests that we can learn something of the truth from our familial heritage. This is of special interest in Donne's own case, for it is precisely such a heritage, that of the family of the (Thomas) Mores, which he betrayed in his apostasy.

The argument advanced bears a similarity to the ideological imperatives of primogeniture, which had been a central political issue in Henry VIII's 'great matter' in 1527 and after, when Thomas More had questioned Henry's actions, at great cost. Given the law of primogeniture, there is an assumption that truth, essence or veracity, like familial or more precisely patriarchal blood, flows in the veins of the faithful sons of fathers. In the marital arrangement which this produces, women are explicitly variable 'counters' or mutable vehicles through whom truth is mediated and represented (as son echoes or represents father). By extension, their names become extremely mutable (as they change the name of a father for that of a husband in marriage), and with this mutability of nomination goes an exchangeability of identity, according to the ideology.

The name of the woman, then, is in some ways analogous to the very springs of poetry based upon the principles of exchange. Women, Ann More among them, become the unnamable mobile counters who derive their identity from appropriative men in this arrangement. But it is through women, and more pertinently through the mobility of their names, that the stability of a masculinist epistemology which claims access to the truth is assured. Male lovers look into the mirror of their lover's eye, or womb, and see the reflection of themselves (or of their sons, as representations of themselves), thus supposedly guaranteeing a stable, transhistorical male identity; and such eternal 'sameness', identity, slips into 'truth'.

Yet there is a contradiction here, and one which reveals the logical priority ascribed to woman in the lines from Satire 3 cited above, in which the *father* becomes the vehicle upon an anterior *female* church: 'aske thy father which is shee'. It is, in fact, from the name of the woman, understood as the location of a scene in which an act of mute/mutual recognition can occur, that the poetry can be written at all. The exchangeability of the woman's name becomes paradigmatic of the organization of the rhetoric of poetry as such. Woman, or her name, is thus logically prior to the poetic creation (of both the written text, and of a poet's masculinity) and is tantamount to the very condition of the poem's possibility. In Donne's case the search for the name and stability of truth (in religious terms, equated here with the name of his Roman Catholic heritage in Thomas More) is satisfied with a name that 'puns' or exchanges with it, that of Ann More. Most importantly, such an exchange reinstates the priority of the woman's name over the demands of the masculinist epistemology which reposes in primogeniture.

The marriage between Donne and Ann More also betrays a father, and it refuses George More the degree of patriarchal control of his family and especially of his primogenitive history, which was the societal and ideological norm. This betrayal, or 'infidelity', threatens the stability or control of the family name and identity (really the Name of the Father) and thus also, as a corollary in this arrangement, dissolves transcendent truth into historical interpretation. The writerly equivalent of this 'Name of the Woman', which can be identified as the principle of linguistic or rhetorical exchange, similarly threatens the truth-propositionality of any text. If the language of a text is rigidly controlled, in ways which strive to combat the principle of rhetorical mutability and to reinstate the myth of a monological discourse, then the poem approaches the condition which not only stabilizes a (male) identity for the poet, but also establishes a masculinist epistemology.

If, on the other hand, a 'promiscuity' of linguistic play is indulged the opposite happens: there is a seeming madness or folly in the language which frequently allows two contradictory things to be heard simultaneously, and the individual identity of a voice which makes such poetic statements is threatened. The reader/hearer of such a text is forced to mediate, as a historical activity, and to produce historical meaning. The Name of the Woman, then, which in Satire 3 is identified as the true religion or true church, is that which allows the poet to *escape* from individuated personality; for he here betrays a patriarchal filiation in some way and replaces the stability of an eternizing truth with the mutable and historical or secular discourse of Folly.

Donne's writing is done in the name of more/More; that is to say, it is a writing which, like that of Erasmus or Montaigne, produces or demands 'more' writing, more mediation, more interpretation; and this 'more' or supplementary excess of writing is 'done' and 'undone' in the now ambiguous 'identity' (really a non-identity) of More (Roman Catholic Thomas, and female Ann). After the model of punning Erasmus, Donne can write his own 'praise of Folly'; and it is this folly which allows the interweaving of a metaphysical quest (for truth in theology) with a physical one (for material meaning in secular affairs, or ideology). It also generates the link between the praise of Thomas More (and thus of 'true' religion) and that of Ann More (who, with Donne, enacts that religion in an act of betrayal of dogmatic 'truth', and an act which threatens the promiscuous dissemination of the name of More). To write in this now dissolute or impure 'name of More/more' suggests precisely the 'undoing' of the name of Donne in the seemingly incidental joke: 'John Donne/Ann Donne/Undone'. When George More had Donne imprisoned and held his own daughter until April 1602, there was an attempt being made to 'undo' the name of Donne and to challenge its power to appropriate Ann More. Four months after the marriage, however, the suit between Donne and Ann More was declared legally binding, 'legitimate'. The attempt to control his familial history, on the part of George More, was fundamentally an attempt to 'cross' or undo the name of Donne, as Donne himself saw.

4

I have commented already on the extensive use of chiasmus in the Euphuistic manner of writing which dominated English culture in Donne's early years. The fundamental chiasmus performed in 'undoing' Donne's name is of especial interest. The word, *chiasmus*, derives from the Greek letter *chi*, X, the symbol, for us at least, of a cross; and rhetorically chiasmus is a 'trope of crossing' or mirroring. In 'crossing' himself, a movement akin to blessing himself, Donne's name is reversed and becomes precisely the caricatural figure which George More had applied to Donne the libertine: 'Don Juan'. This 'crossing' or crucifixion, in the undoing of Donne, makes him the 'lord' or 'don' after his Spanish travels; and it also replaces the patriarchal familial name with the perhaps more aribitrary first or given name, John/Juan.

This legend of Don Juan is more than a fortuitous play on names; the legend is important in Donne's 'moorish/More-ish' writing. The first literary transcription of the Don Juan legend is usually considered to be Tirso de Molina's *El burlador de Sevilla y Convidado de Piedra*, written some time after Donne had been in Spain. But the legend had existed in many other forms before Tirso or Calderon (in *Tan largo me lo fiáis*) created stage versions of it, and it was of some prominence in Spain. In one form the myth is simply that of the libertine of masculinist sexual ideology, clear enough as an ostensible influence on Donne's verse. But the other part of the legend, the address to or from a dead person or statue (often in the form of a skull or skeleton of sorts) is of even more pertinence to Donne. Shakespeare takes the motif over wholesale in *Hamlet's* gravedigger scene; Donne contrives addresses to relics and bones which no longer claim any singular shape or identity. Shakespeare takes on the idea of the living statue in *The Winter's Tale*; Donne puns on the idea of the 'living stone' and theologizes it. The church or 'true religion', and even truth itself for Donne, is not built upon the stability of a rock or even of the theological Word. 'Where the word was, the pun shall be', as Hartman writes in another context.[25] The church of More is built not upon a rock, but upon a pun, operating between the word for 'rock' and the proper name 'Peter'.

Donne's folly then, his existence as a mad figure *entre deux terres* in Foucault's formulation, between (Thomas) More and (Ann) More, between spirit and body, between tradition and independence, between 'upright' John Donne and 'crossed' Don Juan, is axiomatic to his writing. The 'one true church' is precisely the church which is 'crossed', bifurcated, undone. It is in the undoing of the patriarchal name, and the undoing of the illusion of truth in that Name of the Father, that ecclesia can be historically found or constructed. That is to say, the act of sexual and social infidelity and promiscuity which is basic to Donne's 'self-undoing' in his marriage to Ann More is precisely what constitutes religious fidelity, or faith, legitimacy, authenticity and 'right reading'. The one true church here is no dogmatic institution but is rather, as in Donne's own version of the Don Juan legend, a 'living rock' or Christian sepulchre around which ecclesia or community is to be produced.[26] Donne's praise of divinity is also then a praise of morias/folly; and paradox (itself a term with specific theological connotation) or 'madness' is at the root of the writing in this particular sense: faith (as a historical act replacing a transcendent truth) lies in 'crossing' oneself, in 'infidelities' (paradoxes, heterodoxes) which threaten the sense of personal transcendent individuality.

Folly becomes the medium through which the divinity is revealed or 'betrayed'. One of Erasmus's ironic presentations of rhetorical exegesis clarifies this and offers one rationale for the

kind of rhetorical criticism which I proffer here. Folly speaks of a
fool/scholar who meditated on the name of Jesus, akin to my
concentrations on nominations here, and shows that through an
adulteration of the name of 'Jesus' lies the 'pure' meaning of that
figure; through a kind of bastardization of the name lies legitimacy
and right reading:

> The name Jesus was equally divided into two parts with an s left
> in the middle. He then proceeded to point out that this lone letter
> was ש in the Hebrew language and was pronounced Schin, or Sin,
> and that furthermore this Hebrew letter was a word in the
> Scottish dialect that means *peccatum* (Latin for sin). From the
> above premises he declared to his audience that this connection
> showed that Jesus takes away the sins of the world. . . . when did
> the Greek Demosthenes or Roman Cicero ever cook up such a
> rhetorical in*sin*uation as that?[27]

The rhetoric may be mad, but there is method in it, and it is
productive of an orthodox truth or belief of the church. Folly may
mock the procedure, but it does produce the 'sane' proposition that
'Jesus takes away the sins of the world'. What is of consequence here
for Erasmus is 'right reading', a hermeneutic productive of faith; and
this hermeneutic is also therapeutic, a hygienic 'sanitizing' mode of
exegesis. But orthodoxy can be discovered only through paradox,
and the way to therapeutic sanity, for an exegetical manner based
on Folly, is through an 'insane' adulteration of the text with
meaning.

Donne argues precisely this in 'The triple Foole', whose title is
suggestive, as are all 'threes in one' in Donne, of the theological
Trinity. The point of this poem is to validate the proposition that,
although love and grief can be 'fettered' in verse or poesy, the
reading of that verse works to release or reactivate such feelings
historically. Donne begins by being already 'duplicitous', a 'double
fool':

> I am two fooles, I know,
> For loving, and for saying so
> In whining Poëtry[28]

But he immediately sets out to justify his lines by suggesting that
poetry can be cathartic, therapeutic:

> I thought, if I could draw my paines,
> Through Rimes vexation, I should them allay,
> Griefe brought to numbers cannot be so fierce,
> For, he tames it, that fetters it in verse.

The paradoxical problem, however, is that this simply produces more folly, in publication of the original two follies or in the reading of this 'binding' verse:

> But when I have done so,
> Some man, his art and voice to show,
> Doth Set and sing my paine,
> And, by delighting many, frees againe
> Griefe, which verse did restraine.

And so, in the very act of reading this poem, there is a multiplication of folly, and no recovery: 'And I, which was two fooles, do so grow three'. The problem is that the reading of this poem produces folly; but we must read it in order to be able to make the very proposition which the poem seems to be thus making. It is not an apotropaic warding-off of folly at all, not a balm for the grief of love or the posy-ring, but is actually precisely the construction of folly, and the multiplication of this 'insanity'. Such production, further, is exponential: duplicitous folly becomes triple folly; this triple folly is itself doubled and tripled on subsequent reading of the poem, and so on, potentially indefinitely.

This paradox fuels a greater paradox. The production of the triple fool, which is also the rehearsal or production of the text of the poem, 'The triple Foole', depends upon a reading of the poem, carried out *before* the poem can be written. Folly is very much the condition of these lines: the writing of the poem, the production of the triple fool, is itself dependent upon the reading of the poem, paradoxically before it has been written at all (for it is the reading which produces 'The triple Foole').

The text we have, then, is but a *version* of 'The triple Foole'. This 'insane' proposition, that reading is prior to writing, is in fact the one sound proposal to come from the text. Contrary to what it seems to suggest, that writing fetters grief, it demonstrates that writing, poesy, produces the 'insanity' or impurity of historical emotion, the historical fact of the posy-ring which causes the problem in the first place. In these terms, the exponential production of folly, of 'more' insane writing, becomes inevitable: the greater one's emotional 'insanity', the 'more/More/morias/madder' one has to write in order to counter the folly and find health; but such a fettering of the folly of the posy (love) is itself merely productive of even more 'insanity' or, one might say, 'comedy', in the activities of reading and writing.

Folly is aligned not only with love, both sacred and secular, but also with poetry itself. Donne writes in the name of More/Folly and finds himself in a situation which prefigures a comic Shandean state of affairs. The search for the production, in writing, of 'sanity' or health finds itself instrumental in the production of, or even search for, precisely that which in fact 'wounds' such health. Some of these writings, done under the mute pseudonym of 'more', are also contrived meditations on the fundamental 'folly' of another act of self-wounding in the search for a 'health', that of Christ's 'self-crossing': the stigma of 'madness' is replaced by the stigmata of the Christian 'triple fool'.

Linguistic self-crossing, as I have described its operations in the Donnean paradoxical conceit, is not only linked to an *imitatio Christi*, but is also linked with another self-crossing in the search for health, in the activity of blessing oneself, making the Christian 'sign of the cross'. It should by now be clear that a great number of Donne's poems are, structurally, precisely the covert construction of such a 'sign' or 'crossing'. 'To bless' is derived from Old English *bloedsian, bledsian, bletsian*, and ultimately from *blod*, 'blood', means to mark with blood in an activity of consecrating (and sometimes even in an acitivity of nominating). To bless oneself implies its seeming opposite: it implies an activity of wounding oneself or 'cursing' oneself.

The praise of folly in Donne's circumlocutious writing is in some ways a counter to a primal curse: it is the attempt to exchange the primal Biblical curse for another version of that curse, for the 'self-crossing' constitutive of blessing. The Biblical curse is twofold: Eve (not yet named) is cursed with childbearing and sexual subservience (Genesis, 3:16); and Adam is cursed with death and the necessity of physical labour (Genesis, 3:19). Donne's 'mad' enterprise, is an attempt to 'cross' these bleedings and woundings, to 'cross' the *Authorized Version* with his own authorized tropes (and thus he challenges both church and state: hence the necessity for euphemism). The writing is an attempt to make the tragic bleeding into a comic blessing, and to convert labour into pleasure or play.

Donne's praise of folly, then, is instrumental in producing what he considers as theologically valid historical *action*, a mode of attaining health through the 'sickness' of folly in exegesis or understanding.

If there are such things as truth, health, divine blessing, then the way towards them, so this argument would run, is through acts of infidelity and betrayal (revelation), through a 'sickness unto death', and through the curse of human existence, a curse of secular history in the form of various woundings, or 'bleedings' (in birth and death: two forms of 'labour'), and thus through the curse of sexuality and sexual difference. Such, at least, is the Donnean theological 'praise of folly'. Lyly's intertwined hands at the close of *Euphues* are re-worked in Donne, in a version or trope which 'crosses' the hands or clasps them in prayer: a scene of commercial relation becomes a scene of theological relation. The intertwined hands and legs and eyes of Donne's 'profane' verse are 'sanitized' in their final realization as an ascetic theological relation, itself productive of instability and even 'insanity' or a wounding ill-health: 'Those are my best dayes, when I shake with feare'.[29]

Notes

1 Matthew Arnold, *Literature and Dogma*, London, Thomas Nelson & Sons, n.d., 15.
2 Terence Cave, *The Cornucopian Text*, Oxford, Clarendon Press, 1979, 85–6.
3 ibid., 47, 48.
4 Eugene Goodheart, *The Skeptic Disposition in Contemporary Criticism*, Princeton NJ, Princeton University Press, 1985, 57–8, makes a relevant comparison between Marx and Barthes in terms of the kind of 'demystificatory reading' which I am suggesting here. He writes: 'in the chapter on commodity fetishism, Marx could penetrate the false pretensions of commodities to an "existence as independent beings endowed with life, which entered into relations with one another and the human race," because he was confident that behind the illusion the real value of the product was ascertainable: the labor expended in its production. And it is not simply the truth or the conviction of truth that Marx possessed. The reality to which the truth corresponded was substantial and filled with promise, for the labor theory of value becomes the justification for the socialist revolution. Demystification may expose a corrupt reality – for example, the exploitation of the working class concealed in the exchange of commodities in the marketplace – but such a reality is substantial and, moreover, contains within it the dialectical possibility of progress to a condition that restores to the worker the product of his labor'. For Barthes demystification is a word which 'is beginning to show signs of wear' (Preface to *Mythologies*), and the reason for this, according to Goodheart, is that Barthes lends credence to the hypothesis that

'there is no reality behind illusion', and so, 'to "penetrate the object," is, as Barthes put it, not to liberate it but to destroy it. Demystification for Barthes shows signs of wear because, necessary as it may be, it cannot satisfy the appetite for wholeness, for substantiality, for presence as it did for Marx'. The implication of this distinction between Barthes and Marx seems to be that some kind of epistemological grounding is *necessary* as a justification for Marxian revolution; but this is not the case. The exposure of a *version*, the demystification of a transformation, even if it only reveals another version or trope, with no epistemological ground, can reveal the *fact* of transformation. This revelation can itself be instrumental in the demystification of a mode of production; and that is sufficient, in the Marxian analysis, to produce a critical consciousness. The distance between Barthes and Marx in this respect is not so enormous or fundamental. Demystification can be socially productive, even without a guaranteed epistemological verification of its object.

5 Desiderius Erasmus, *The Praise of Folly*, in John P. Dolan (ed.), *The Essential Erasmus*, New York, Mentor Books, 1964, 99.

6 Michel Foucault, *Folie et déraison*, Paris, Plon, 1961, 292.

7 ibid., 49.

8 The reference here is to G.W.F. Hegel, *Phenomenology of Spirit* (tr. A.V. Miller), Oxford, Oxford University Press, 1977, 493. In these closing comments Hegel writes of the trajectory of Spirit in terms which recall the tragic Christian myth: 'The *goal*, Absolute Knowing, or Spirit that knows itself as Spirit, has for its path the recollection of the Spirits as they are in themselves and as they accomplish the organization of their realm. Their preservation, regarded from the side of their free existence appearing in the form of contingency, is History; but regarded from the side of their [philosophically] comprehended organization, it is the Science of Knowing in the sphere of appearance: the two together, comprehended History, form alike the inwardizing and the Calvary of Absolute Spirit, the actuality, truth, and certainty of his throne, without which he would be lifeless and alone'. Cf. a telling comment in a footnote by Kenneth Burke, in his *Language as Symbolic Action*, Berkeley and Los Angeles, University of California Press, 1968, 20, note 2: 'In his *Parts of Animals*, Chapter X, Aristotle mentions the definition of man as the "laughing animal," but he does not consider it adequate. Though I would hasten to agree, I obviously have a big investment in it, owing to my conviction that mankind's only hope is a cult of comedy. (The cult of tragedy is too eager to help out with the holocaust . . .)'. The point of bringing these two together in this context is to indicate that it is in fact the cult of tragedy which is Optimistic: the apocalypse, religious or secular, is seen as some kind of purgatorial experience, which will leave or produce an ameliorated Edenic realm. In tragedy, the 'Calvary' leads to the 'throne'. The 'only hope' of which Burke writes, is actually a 'hope of no hope': comedy, according to my own theoretical position here, corrects the tendency to tragedy inherent in Optimistic schemes or organizations of history and is valuable for that reason. This approximates towards the mistrust of grand historical 'metanarratives', as outlined by Jean-François Lyotard in his *The Postmodern Condition* (trans. Geoff Bennington and Brian Massumi), Manchester, Manchester University Press, 1984. For a fuller

discussion of this philosophical opposition of tragedy and comedy, in terms of 'Optimistic' historical schemes or narratives, see my *On Modern Authority* (forthcoming).

9 Wilbur Samuel Howell, *Logic and Rhetoric in England 1500–1700* (Princeton University Press, New Jersey, 1956), 4; cf. Geoffrey Hartman, *Saving the Text*, Baltimore, Johns Hopkins University Press, 1981, 91, on Genet's reaction to Giacometti's sculpture: 'What is revealed by these appropriations is the *hand of a thief*, a particular, peculiar *main-tenant*, writing considered as a Discourse of Theft going back to Prometheus and Jason'; and cf. my suggestion in ch. 7 below that criticism as a mode of writing is intimately related to criminality.

10 Howell, op. cit., 4.

11 See Jacques Derrida, 'La mythologie blanche', in *Marges*, Paris, Minuit, 1972; and cf. Richard Rorty, 'Philosophy as a kind of writing', in *Consequences of Pragmatism*, Brighton, Harvester Press, 1982, and Berel Lang, *Philosophy and the Art of Writing*, Lewisburg, Bucknell University Press, 1983.

12 John Lyly, *Euphues*, in James Winny (ed.), *The Descent of Euphues*, Cambridge, Cambridge University Press, 1957, 14.

13 Strictly speaking, 'euphemism' and 'euphuism' are not etymologically the same: Euphues derives from *eu*=well, *physis*=nature; Euphemism from *eu*=well, *pheme*=speaking. The movement or slippage between them, brought about in Donne's writing, is a movement, then, from the body, from Euphues (well-endowed by nature, well-natured) to the voice, Euphemism (well-speaking).

14 Donne, 80–1

15 The most obvious instances in Shakespeare occur in *Hamlet*, IV, v, and in *The Winter's Tale*, IV, iv. There might indeed be a useful or suggestive argument in which Ophelia is construed as a textual or intertextual mother of sorts to Perdita, thus establishing some kind of matriarchal historical lineage in Shakespeare's plays. For a fuller exposition of this, see my *On Modern Authority* (forthcoming).

16 Frank Kermode, *The Genesis of Secrecy*, Cambridge, Mass., Harvard University Press, 1979, 3.

17 See, in this context, Paul de Man, *The Rhetoric of Romanticism*, New York, Columbia University Press, 1984, 262.

18 The link between legibility and legitimacy is an etymological one.

19 Donne, 132ff.

20 Donne, 21.

21 Cf. Geoffrey Hartman, *The Fate of Reading*, Chicago, University of Chicago Press, 1975, 255: 'The extinction . . . of the personal names of *both* author and reader shows what ideally happens in the act of reading: if there is a sacrifice to the exemplary, it involves the aggrandizement neither of author nor of reader but leads into the recognition that something worthy of perpetuation has occurred'.

22 Foucault, op. cit., 14; italics mine.

23 Paul M. Ochojski, 'Did John Donne repent his apostasy?', *American Benedictine Review*, 1 (1950), 535–48.

24 Donne, 136ff.

25 Hartman, *Saving the Text*, 79.

26 This, although like the notion of a 'community of interpreters' favoured by much reader-response critical theory, differs in the material means by which the

ecclesiastical or theological community is constructed; cf. ch. 7 below.
27 Erasmus, *Praise of Folly*, in ed. cit., 151–2; emphasis on 'sin' in 'insinuation' added.
28 Donne, 15–16.
29 Donne, 302.

Writing as therapy: a fishy tale and a diet of worms

KING: Now, Hamlet, where's Polonius?
HAMLET: At supper.
KING: At supper! Where?
HAMLET: Not where he eats, but where 'a is eaten; a certain convocation of politic worms are e'en at him. Your worm is your only emperor for diet; we fat all creatures else to fat us, and we fat ourselves for maggots; your fat king and your lean beggar is but variable service – two dishes, but to one table. That's the end.
KING: Alas, alas!
HAMLET: A man may fish with the worm that hath eat of a king, and eat of the fish that hath eat of that worm.
KING: What dost thou mean by this?
HAMLET: Nothing but to show you how a king may go a progress through the guts of a beggar.

(William Shakespeare, *Hamlet*, IV, iii, 17–31)

1

Wounds and illnesses seem oddly to have a major bearing on the production of writing. This is true at least all the way from Erasmus's *Praise of Folly*, written during an illness, through to Milton writing *Paradise Lost* and other poems 'On His Blindness', and on Swift, Pope, and in later centuries Keats, Flaubert, Baudelaire, Tennyson, Proust and many, many others. It is perhaps not so surprising, then, to learn that illness or wounds form a dominant factor in the structural organization of Donne's poetry as well. As was made clear in chapter 6, such 'wounding' can be construed either physically or, metaphorically, theologically. In this conclud-ing chapter I shall explain how a symbolic act of physical self-mutilation in Donne is seen as being therapeutic spiritually. Here it should become clear that the theology adopted by Donne consti-tutes a means whereby he seems to evade certain ethical and political pressures in his cultural moment; yet a 'symptomatic' reading of the poetry might reveal the nature of the 'dis-ease' which his stitched and woven texts hope to heal.

We should start near the end. Either during his illness in 1623 or, as Walton suggests, on his death-bed in 1631, Donne wrote the 'Hymne to God my God, in my sicknesse'. In this poem he described himself as an 'instrument' on which the music of God reveals or mediates itself and, typically, as the entire world or 'map' and the entire course of human history, between first and last Adams. The sickness seems to be optimistically welcomed, for it affords Donne a greater sight or vision:

> I joy, that in these straits, I see my West;
>> For, though theire currants yeeld returne to none,
> What shall my West hurt me?[1]

and it promises a new rising or reincarnation of the flat map, its re-embodiment:

>> As West and East
> In all flatt Maps (and I am one) are one,
> So death doth touch the Resurrection.

The precise dating of this poem is of interest if we want to identify the particular illness in question; but, perhaps more importantly, there is within the text an extrapolation from Donne's personal illness, as the text becomes a sermon, or proposes the matter for a sermon:

> And as to others soules I preach'd thy word,
>> Be this my Text, my Sermon to mine owne,
>> Therfore that he may raise the Lord throws down.

This is an address to Donne's own soul. But, since that soul has been characterized as an entire world and its history, it becomes a sermon on the illness and parlous state of that world. Donne had previously addressed this same topic, in 1611, where the body of

Elizabeth Drury became the catalyst or excuse for another sermon on the world's sickness. It was this larger illness, as a human condition, which was of interest for Donne:

> There is no health; Physitians say that wee,
> At best, enjoy but a neutralitie.
> And can there bee worse sicknesse, then to know
> That we are never well, nor can be so?[2]

In late Renaissance England the presence of plague was more or less continuous. The question of health was an important one socially, and politically; and this had repercussions aesthetically as well.[3] By this I do not mean that many poems were written 'about' disease, though that is true; rather I mean to suggest that the presence of a continuous threat of death from plague and related epidemic diseases affected the very grounds of poetry and delimited the kind of text which could be written. It became important, for instance, to strive towards an ethos of 'purity' or purification for the individual at this time and such 'purism' (even Puritanism) in the social sphere determined to some extent the cultural ideology of poetry. The desire for health is most obviously seen, aesthetically, in poems which vaunt their own perenniality or permanence. In the case of Donne, and some of his contemporaries, the desire for health becomes a desire for theological or ethical purity, most frequently mediated in terms of pure or healthy or good carnal, sexual relations.

Why might this be the case? After the Black Death, the fourteenth-century plague, had taken its incredible toll across Europe, another epidemic disease, syphilis, became more and more widespread. One of the first researchers into syphilis was Girolamo Fracastoro who was a colleague of Copernicus at the University of Padua, and whose treatise *Homocentrica sive de stellis liber* (1538) was instrumental in paving the way for Copernicus's own major work discussed earlier in this book. Fracastoro's major interests were medical, and he worked with a theory which was a forerunner of the work on microbic infection carried out by Koch and Pasteur in the nineteenth century. In his treatise on syphilis, *Syphilis sive Morbus Gallicus (Syphilis or the French Disease)*, he pondered both treatment and source of the disease. The treatment involved avoidance of sexual activity or of the flesh, a strict diet, and measured doses of mercury. Fracastoro made a hypothesis of the source of the disease through a narrative of the shepherd Syphilus, who tended the flocks of the mighty king Alcithous. In the midst of a summer drought, Syphilus cannot bear the sight of his flock suffering, claiming that his flock is no 'vulgar' flock but of special significance. As the drought continues, he blasphemes:

> This drought our Syphilus beheld with pain,
> Nor could the suff'rings of his flock sustain,
> But to the Noon-day Sun with up-cast Eyes,
> In rage threw these reproaching Blasphemies[4]

He threatens to transfer allegiances from Apollo (the sun-god) to the earthly king Alcithous; and it is this idolatry and blasphemy which is punished by the infliction of the disease. This original of the disease also has a specific spatial or geographical provenance: it derives from Atlantia, a place visited by exploratory sailors according to Fracastoro. But what is of importance in this is that the disease is characterized as 'foreign', an alien intrusion: hence, in England, its characterization as a 'French' disease, which sat easily with the cultural stereotype of the French as promiscuous in their sexual proclivities.

In Donne's time there was a similar cultural mediation of the disease. It is likely that syphilis was present in Europe for some considerable time before Donne wrote; 'leprosy' often exhibited symptoms consistent with the diagnosis of syphilis. But it was commonly thought that syphilis had been brought back from the 'new world', the world outside, by Columbus and his crew: it was a foreign, alien impurity which had been unwittingly imported into the very hearth of England, and even into the core of both the domestic family or household and the human body. Questions of theological or cosmic purity are now aligned more closely with more material concerns of pure sexuality or carnality: the health of the body. In Donne's case the ascription of a link, however tenuous in fact, between cosmic health and personal health is obvious in his 'anatomical' poems. Don Cameron Allen, pondering how much Donne knew of contemporary medicine, argues that Donne was more interested in the health of his own body than in that of the world:

> Donne, in many ways, was more interested in medicine than he was in those problems of cosmology and astronomy about which

scholars have been so agitated in their attempt to prove that Donne was well-read in the 'quantum theories' of his day. He was certainly interested in the extrinsic problems of the universe, but he was much more interested in the intrinsic agonies of his own viscera.[5]

But this concern with his own body was intimately related, in fact, to his other 'extrinsic' concerns. For Donne had some knowledge of Paracelsus, who had also written a tract on syphilis in 1530; and indeed at this time it was the Paracelsian notion of 'sympathies' between intrinsic and extrinsic, microcosmic and macrocosmic, which held some scientific sway and temporarily at least overshadowed Fracastoro in credibility.

Syphilis, as a foreign threat to the purity or hygiene of the body, calls into question the relations between self and other, and most specifically sexual relations. One result is an opposition established between the intrinsic purity of the individual, and her or his defence against extrinsic impurity. The incidence of the disease is also instrumental in the establishment of an ethics of 'privacy': the family unit or domestic unit has to become more and more 'private' or intrinsically pure and safe; and sexual relations have to be policed or regulated in some way in the attempt to arrest the spread of this alien threat. This is one contributory factor in the maintenance of a privatized nuclear family unit as the 'proper' or hygienic location of individual identity; and it becomes normative with regard to healthy human relations. The domestic family becomes a shelter from the storm of syphilitic invasion and dissolution of the body; and the growth of a kind of individualism, based on this ethics of privacy or the construction of a 'private' withdrawn inner Self, might be considered as something which was thought to be necessary for the self-protection of the species at this time.

However, the ethics of privacy is mediated as *normative*; and thus produces an ideology which prioritizes absolutely this 'intrinsic' or inner Self as if such prioritization were natural or logical. It is not the plague of syphilis as such which is responsible for this ethics of privacy and its concomitant prioritization of the inner Self; rather it is its mediation or understanding as a disease or impurity impinging from outside, from 'foreign parts' or 'foreign bodies' or, quite simply, from the social Other, construed as some kind of enemy.

People were driven more and more 'indoors', then, as a historical fact, by the advent of syphilis. Health laws were passed in an attempt to combat its spread; and significantly these laws concerned the regulation of brothels and female prostitution, contributing to the identification of women as the source and repository of the disease. This is made perfectly clear in the later years of the century, when Tate's translation of Fracastoro's *Syphilis* tract appeared. The translation was prefaced by a poem 'To His Friend, the Writer of the Ensuing Translation' which controverts Fracastoro's tale of the origins of the disease and offers a competing hypothesis that the source of syphilis is in the 'foreign' body of woman:

> Blame not the Stars; 'tis plain it neither fell
> From the distemper'd Heav'ns, nor rose from Hell.
> Nor need we to the distant *Indies* rome;
> The curst Originals are nearer home.
> Whence should that foul infectious Torment flow,
> But from the banefull source of all our wo?
> That wheedling, charming Sex, that draws us in
> To ev'ry punishment and ev'ry sin.[6]

Here syphilis becomes an alien, an enemy within, so to speak in Tate's paranoic mediation of woman as source and repository of the ailment. But such an equation of the disease with the woman is apparent in writing more exactly contemporaneous with Donne, as, for example, in Shakespeare's allusions to the sixteenth-century laws and regulations in *Measure for Measure*:

POMPEY: All houses in the suburbs of Vienna must be plucked down.

MISTRESS OVERDONE: And what shall become of those in the city?

POMPEY: They shall stand for seed: they had gone down too, but that a wise burgher put in for them.

MISTRESS OVERDONE: But shall all our houses of resort in the suburbs be pulled down?

POMPEY: To the ground, mistress.

MISTRESS OVERDONE: Why, here's a change indeed in the commonwealth! What shall become of me?[7]

Sex was to be no longer a matter for public houses or brothels, but was to become instituted in a form of privatization of civic, if not civil, urbane desire: a Renaissance 'courtly' love without its central element of adulterous promiscuity.

While all this prioritizes the intrinsic or private realm, especially in the domestication of female desire and the female body, there is a counterweight in the theological realm in a drive toward publicity. Syphilis effects an ethics of privacy. But the ritual of confession in theology depends upon publicity; at least, it drove people towards public confession or talk about the sexuality aligned with the disease (along with talk of other 'impurities' or sins, of course). Foucault indicates the increased attention paid to the confession of matters related to sexuality after the Council of Trent. Such confession was made in refined language, but with increased intensity:

> This scheme for transforming sex into discourse had been devised long before in an ascetic and monastic setting. The seventeenth century made it into a rule for everyone.[8]

Confession, which was one of the sacraments partially saved by Luther, is a kind of talking cure, an act which promises purification and health, at least of the soul if not of the material body. Yet since it involves a lacerating act of self-criticism, it can also be seen to be an act of self-wounding. The act of confessing, while bringing health, acknowledges the presence of sin or guilt in the individual, and thus carries a wounding element within its very articulation. The talking cure becomes talk-as-wound. One clear example of this occurs in *Othello*, when Cassio complains of his 'wounded name' or loss of reputation, a wound which Iago construes as, and tries to realize as, a physical wound. Cassio's confession on his drunkenness produces not a simple cure, but rather a greater degree of guilt to be exculpated, and hence the need for more confession:

> CASSIO: I will rather sue to be despised, than to deceive so good a commander with so slight, so drunken, and so indiscreet an officer. Drunk! And speak parrot! And squabble! Swagger! Swear! and discourse fustian with one's own shadow!.. O God, that men should put an enemy in their mouths to steal away their brains! that we should with joy, pleasance, revel, and applause transform ourselves into beasts!
>
> IAGO: Why, but you are now well enough. How came you thus recovered?
>
> CASSIO: It hath pleased the devil drunkenness to give place to the devil wrath. One unperfectness shows me another, to make me frankly despise myself.[9]

Here, confession of one transgression leads Cassio into the commission of another 'unperfectness'. The talking cure becomes the talk that wounds; and confession becomes an exercise in self-wounding.

It is within such a context of the search for health both physical and spiritual that Donne must be considered: the concern for social and theological health pervades the verse. As I have tried to suggest, however, the therapeutic exercise of self-exposure can bring about its own woundings or disease. Donne's most insistent self-exposures or 'confessions' concern the sexual realm of demonstrating his phallus and its related powers; it is time to attend to the means of self-wounding involved in these 'confessions'.

A general example of the exponential production of guilt and sin through confession can be seen in 'A Hymne to God the Father', where every admission of sin seems to breed 'more' sins, as in Shakespeare's Cassio. Quite apart from the possible sexual theme of guilt, in yet another extremely frank play on the names of Donne and More, there is a more general argument that Donne's guilt *increases* with the confession and absolution of sin:

> Wilt thou forgive that sinne where I begunne,
>> Which was my sin, though it were done before?
> Wilt thou forgive that sinne; through which I runne,
>> And do run still: though still I do deplore?
>> When thou hast done, thou hast not done,
>>> For, I have more.[10]

This 'sinne where I begunne' is not only an 'original' sin, committed by Eve and Adam; it is also the 'sin' of sexuality itself, a maculate conception or guilty conceit in which Donne was conceived and born, and which he repeats again with Ann More: 'I have more'. The poem becomes a confessional text which, in confessing to sins of the material flesh in fact admits more such sins, 'For, I have more'.

The more Donne confesses, the more he has to confess: but what exactly is this 'more', this dangerous supplement, so to speak, related to the world, flesh and devil which he overtly wishes to leave behind in order to acquire health? The very word 'more' has become charged with both sexual and theological guilt in Donne, and an ascetic exercise in pruning away such 'excess' becomes dominant in the search for health and sanitized salvation.

All those instances earlier attested to of Donne's 'self-crossing' poems provide further examples of texts where the search for health leads to greater suffering or disease (self-crossing as crucifixion); and the self-crossing, as an act of self-criticism, becomes, as I demonstrated, *hypocritical*, and hence necessitates a further cure. The health of body and soul in Donne depends upon the problematic relation between the movement inwards towards an ethics of privacy and a corresponding movement outwards towards publicity. Syphilitic entropy drives the culture to look within and develop an isolationist theology, which bears some close relation to Protestantism; and the 'rise of confession', so to speak, drives back outwards, towards a more socialized notion of *ecclesia*. This broad difference is that between a reformed and an unreformed church or 'body of Christ'; and this is the delicate area in and through which Donne writes. The Copernican 'revolution' which started to organize Donne's concern has become a matter of 'reform' in theological matters.

As in Fracastoro's tract, a healthy diet is prescribed in Donne. But it differs, as we shall see, from that proposed by the Fracastoro who wrote:

> Therefore from Fish in general I dissuade,
> All these are of a washy Substance made,
> Which though the luscious Palate they content,
> Convert to Humours more than Nourishment.[11]

In Donne the health of a specific part of the body is required. With the problematization of relations between inner and outer, there arises an attention to the 'middle' or median area *between* inside and outside, private and public.

Donne pays some attention to the material body as a medium of the environment; and, as such a medium, the body becomes precisely the locus of experience: here is his link to a burgeoning empirical philosophy. But one area of human experience dominates in Donne, and that is the experience of sexuality or, more broadly, love. In material sexuality, the important medium which is to be kept healthy, especially given the fact of syphilis and an ideology which locates the disease in the female body, is the hymen, a tissue-like medium between inside and outside. Despite his much-vaunted 'libertinism', Donne seems to favour, at least in some writings, the integrity or wholeness of the hymen; and this is for the precise reason, of course, that such female carnal health guarantees

the health of Donne's own body and the 'purity' of his relations
between inner and outer, the purity of his 'mediations' or meditative
experience. One sure way to maintain such health, in writing at
least, is to idealize the hymen, the 'Idea of a Woman', so to speak,
and this Donne does, imagining it as the locus of the 'angelic', a
'sprite' which occupies the median ground or pure air between God
and humanity. This, together with its effects on what I have
characterized as a phallogocentrism in Donne's writing, requires
further clarification and exemplification here.

2

Three things are important here: firstly, the problems raised by the
theological position of confession; secondly, what can be thought of
as the disappearance or dematerialization of woman; and thirdly,
the wounding or disappearance of the phallus in Donne's writing.

In 1215, at the fourth Lateran Council, Pope Innocent III
pronounced that confession should be performed at least once
annually. In 1521, Luther defended his own relative downgrading of
confession, questioning its status as a sacrament, at the Diet of
Worms. Here is a prime area of conflict, and one which shaped
discussion in some documents of the Council of Trent (1545–63).
This Council, at which Girolamo Fracastoro again played a large
part, ratified the decision of the Lateran Council, clarifying the
notion that confession must be full, public and detailed. In the
Canones et Decreta of Trent, it is recorded that:

> It is obvious that priests cannot pronounce judgment without
> knowing the cause, and that in fact they cannot preserve equity
> in the imposing of penalities, if the faithful declare their sins only
> in general, and not in detail, and one by one. It follows that the
> penitents must needs review in confession all their mortal sins,
> of which they have become conscious after diligently examining
> themselves.[12]

In short, what this demands in confession is the construction of a
mode of narrative, replete with detail and solidity of specification,
so to speak. This narrative lends a specific identity or individuality
to the narrating self or sinner. As I argued earlier, such narrative is
intimately involved with an act of self-nomination, a 'self-blessing'
which here brings with it the inevitable act of self-cursing or

self-damnation. In de Man's consideration of Rousseau's *Confessions*, he finds that confessed narrative involves excuses which 'will indeed exculpate the confessor, thus making the confession (and the confessional text) redundant as it originates'.[13] The narrated confession, in short, produces a linguistic excess, a 'more', in the name of excuse, and thus undoes itself, thus leaving a residue of 'wound' still to be healed. 'More', again, is part of the problem.

The paradox of confession comes clear in Donne's own Paradox, 'That Women ought to paint'. Here, Donne distinguishes the face, open to public gaze, from the 'secret parts' of the body which remain covered up. The paradoxical argument goes that, since foulness is loathsome, then any open foulness ought to be helped in some way and made to appear more beautiful; the private parts of the body, those not open to the gaze of the public, are frequently artificially beautified, but it is all the more important that the face be treated in this artificial way. Donne casts part of the argument in terms of confession and punishment:

> For as open confessing sinners are alwaies punished, but the wary and concealing offenders without witnesse doe it also without punishment; so the secret parts needs the lesse respect; but of the *Face*, discovered to all Examinations and survayes, there is not too nice a Jealousie.[14]

The face, then, if ugly, is like a confessing sinner and will accordingly attract punishment, vilification or blame of some kind. But this face, in making such a public self exposure or confession, finds itself in the paradox covered or veiled or, more precisely, painted. The impetus of the argument is that a guilt, taken for granted in the figure of the ugly face, confessed leads to a 're-covery'. The open, confessing face becomes, in the act of confessing to or revealing a guilt, paradoxically recovered; it becomes a veil of sorts, revealing and recovering in a single moment. This veil in turn becomes, for Donne, the median ground of artful representation, a *medium* of communication: it is the painted face which provokes the 'divinest touch of all', that of the kiss which is 'the strange and mysticall union of soules'.

Given the reversal of private and public within the paradox, in which the public face is veiled and the 'secret parts needs the lesse respect' and can be revealed, it is almost as if intrinsic and extrinsic have 'crossed' or exchanged places, 'kissing' on their way as they transgress the veil which separates and joins them, the face or figure. This hymeneal figure, according to the paradox, should 'confess' in order to be 're-covered' or in order to find health and beauty. The face is to be veiled in order to reveal its beauty, paradoxically. The face, or rather, the figure of the woman thus disappears from view, precisely at the moment when Donne is claiming that it most beautifully confesses, reveals or exculpates itself. Woman disappears behind the veiled confessing figure or face.

This dematerialization of the form and figure of the female body is an 'idealization' of woman which is reiterated in verse. 'Communitie' provides a good example of the manoeuvre, cast not in the form of paradoxical argument so much as in the language of the law and its sophisticated logic. The ostensible argument favours promiscuity and masculinist libertinism. Ethical questions about the bodies of women are removed from consideration in order to regard these bodies as so much 'meat' or flesh. But this materialist argument is entirely undone by a specific set of rhetorical flourishes, one of which 'dematerializes' this meaty body, and the other which theologizes the consumption of 'chang'd sorts of meat'.

Firstly, women are deprived of intrinsic qualities, of an inside, becoming instead the merest objects of a masculinist epistemology whose outlines were drawn in my discussion of 'The Flea'. Women, systematically denied specific 'properties' or qualities, become the merest media or empty vessels for 'our' male experimentation or empirical 'proving':

> Good wee must love, and must hate ill,
> For ill is ill, and good good still,
> But there are things indifferent,
> Which wee may neither hate, nor love,
> But one, and then another prove,
> As wee shall finde our fancy bent.[15]

Women fall into the median indeterminate category, neither good nor ill, but merely indifferent; that is, indistinct from each other and from the extrinsic environment. Their ontological status is reduced to that of the neutral 'thing'. There is then a progressive loss of more specific 'properties' or qualities:

> If they were good it would be seene,
> Good is as visible as greene,
>   And to all eyes it selfe betrayes:
> If they were bad, they could not last,
> Bad doth it selfe, and others wast,
>   So, they deserve nor blame, nor praise.

Here women lose the properties of being 'good', 'bad' and, most importantly, even 'visible'. If women are the properties of men, things for male use, it might be more precise to suggest that this male poet has, as it were, 'stolen' the property of women. One such property which he has clearly appropriated is that of 'indifference'. Not only does he advance himself as a typical male, speaking on behalf of a 'community' of indifferent or undistinguished men; he also vaunts the indifference, on behalf of that male community, which he has purloined from the other community in the poem, that of women.

This 'thinginess' of women, their status as even merest objects, is now called into question by the poem: if they are objects, they are both indistinct and invisible. The final stanza reanimates women once more, however, in the form of food and sustenance for this predatory male poet:

> But they are ours as fruits are ours,
> He that but tasts, he that devours,
>   And he that leaves all, doth as well:
> Chang'd loves are but chang'd sorts of meat,
> And when hee hath the kernel eate,
>   Who doth not fling away the shell?

This is a complicated stanza. Firstly, women become organically 'live' again, mediated as 'fruits'; but this fruit undergoes changes in the text. As fruit to be eaten, tasted or *proved* (a word stemming from *probus*, 'good'; and thus with the suggestion in 'proved' of a notion of being 'validated', rendered valid and well) by men, women become the very sustenance of male properties, and are vital to the continued existence of men who come to fruition through them, in every sense. Some men, however, diet and fail to prey on women in this way ('he that leaves all, doth as well'), and such discarding of the (seemingly female) flesh is important in making sense of the final lines of the poem.

Two important modifications or changes are effected in the last stanza. Firstly, the fruit mutates into 'meat' and, more importantly, it is a kind of meat which is itself open to change, transformation or crossing: 'Chang'd loves are but chang'd sorts of meat'. This echoes with theological reverberations concerning transubstantiation. The actual movement here is from an Edenic 'community' disrupted by preying on the fruit of the forbidden Tree of Knowledge (to which Adam and Eve should have remained 'indifferent'), towards the establishment of a community of ecclesiastic eucharist, in the consumption of a flesh of sorts (a consumption which, paradoxically, produces the body of Christ in the Christian church). Here, the second change dominates; for the meat which replaces the fruit is a meat characterized by its transubstantiation, the principle of changeability which defines it 'indifferently'. That is to say, this meat is not defined as any one essential thing, but is precisely the locus of a certain (theological) community of many 'indifferent' or indistinct fleshes in one flesh or meat.

This theological movement in the poem is further strengthened by the idea that when one partakes of the kernel of this meat, then one flings away 'the shell'. It is not out of line here to construe this shell as the corporeal rind or, in short, one's own fleshy qualities or body. Nor indeed is it inapposite to suggest that it refers to the material building of a church, the 'shell' enclosing a congregation. Existence for the material individual body is thus defined through its involvement in the 'kernel', in the ecclesiastic indifferent community. Here the 'idealization' of the female body (rendering it invisible and immaterial through predation by men) is the medium through which another idealization, of the body as fleshy entity, is carried out in the establishment of 'Communitie'.

'Indifference' forms one central orientation of this poem, in a specific sense. The poem seems to express some distaste at the mere fact of 'difference', of the fleshy difference which separates a community into its constituent elements: 'good', 'bad', 'female', 'male' and so on. It is the notion of a purity of identification, a purity of demarcated essence, which is the butt of the poem's attack: the text seems to vaunt and welcome the threat of messiness and impurity or contamination. It favours that which is neither good nor bad, but 'the indifferent' as such; and 'Communitie', as in 'The undertaking', sees a movement to 'forget the Hee and Shee'.[16] Here is the third 'change' which affects the poem, and this is its major 'crossing' of orientation. This masculinist text strives, in its first part, to validate masculinity at the expense of women: that is as much as to say that it renders the phallus healthy, as the fleshy 'thing' which distinguishes the male from a female who is characterized precisely as that which 'lacks' the flesh as such or as essence. The latter half of the poem, however, strives to forget this: which is as much as to say that, having 'confessed' or revealed this healthy phallus, it now strives to remove such a fleshy thing. The poem contrives the removal of the *male* flesh, the 'shell' which both contains and reveals the 'flesh' and, more pertinently, the fleshy kernel or seed. The poem, rather than being a simple celebration of the flesh, turns against the masculinist consciousness which is seemingly at its centre and symbolically castrates it: the poem then becomes 'crossed' or self-crossing in the usual way, bifurcated into a dialogical and bacchanalian 'carnival' or *carne-vale*, a text which tries to say farewell to the flesh (and with it, the world and devil). The legalistic argument, with its comic sophistications, works to castrate the male consciousness at its centre.

The text thus casts its speaker once more as a dialogical speaker with a forked tongue of sorts; but more pertinently here it frames the speaker as the male who 'diets', who 'leaves all' and 'doth as well'. It also indentifies the nature of this 'diet', for the now (sexually) indifferent body becomes itself the medium for community, an idealized eucharistic flesh which is to be eaten and, in that consumption, to construct the locus of a theologized 'crossing' place, an ecclesia around the crossed body of Christ. The health of the (male) organism seems to depend on a wounding of the flesh, the activity of symbolic self-castration. The 'shell' which is to be flung away, and which is usually construed as female genitals, for which it was common slang usage, turns out in fact to be the male genitals. The male in this poem has rendered the female shell 'invisible', has covered it and, most importantly, has assimilated or 'eaten' the properties of the female. Having 'incorporated' the female flesh, to cast off the shell is to cast off the excess of flesh which distinguished the speaker as male, that is, the phallus. Thus sexual difference as such is supposedly rendered 'indifferent', and human material and carnal relations are idealized in this theological formulation. There is a sense, then, in which the poem's ostensible distaste for women and for sexuality in general reveals a more fundamental self-disgust or *guilt* concerned with Donne's self-identification as phallic.

The dematerialized sexuality or love described here appears in 'Aire and Angels' as well. Part of the argument of this poem concerns the replacement of the sullied flesh with the purer angel who wears the airy nothing of the human body. One important part of this conceit depends on the fact that, if either character in the poem can be identified with the (unsexed) angelic, it is the male. The woman, as airy nothing, is realized only as she is elemented or as she appears in an assumed body, which acts thus again as a veil, concealing and revealing. The point is that the angelic male figure, descending to love the airy female, requires 'some fitter' vessel or shell for his love: 'For, nor in nothing, nor in things/Extreme, and scatt'ring bright, can love inhere'.[17] Love, as the 'child' of this angelic soul, cannot live in an airy nothing (another word sometimes used as slang for female genitals), nor in that other characterization of woman, the inconstant flame.

For the sustenance of this angel, and its child-love, another angel has to be sought, or the woman has herself to become angelic. That is to say, the female body has to be construed as a 'nothing', 'idealized' as the pure essence of an angel. The poem moves from validating the love of this 'airy nothing', which has to be elemented as the vessel or shell of the female body, towards love of something purer, less elemental or less material: that is, the idealized angelic medium, that pure medium whose integrity is healthily intact, never sullied into fleshy reality.

The idealization of the poet as angel is obvious in Divine Meditation 5, 'I am a little world made cunningly', which identifies the poet as the material or elemented body and flesh as well as 'an Angelike spright'. That poem further sheds light on the therapeutic diet, in which Donne asks for another kind of flame than the one the angel speaks through in 'Aire and Angels'. Near the close of Divine Meditation 5, he requests a purgative flame: 'And burne me ô Lord, with a fiery zeale/Of thee and thy house, which doth in eating heale'.[18]

The ambiguity here concerns who is eating what. The fire of the zeal consumes the poet certainly; but more importantly the poet also eats the Lord, and it is this eating which heals him. The 'incorporation' of this particular body, an angelic body or that of the Christian Lord, works to idealize, purify or de-realize the material fleshy body of the poet. As he eats, so he loses the airy elements and becomes purer angel: this meat does not flesh out the material body but rather heals by wounding it, by mortifying its flesh. The predator is preyed upon. Most importantly the flesh is revealed, admitted or 'confessed' here, in the opening lines, only so that it may be removed or wounded, supplanted by the angelic, and healed in that very movement which wounds it, eating and burning. An act of confession in these terms works not to excuse the self, but rather further to wound the self: the self-exposure of the male poet invites an act of healthy castration, removal of the flesh in this symbolic carnival.

There is then an equation to be made at some level in Donne's writings among three concepts: hymen, medium and angel. In a sense, Donne's symbolic self-castrations cast him in the figure of the female, and hence make of him a kind of hymeneal figure, mediating between confession or publicity and guilt or privacy. These terms coalesce in a major 'medical' poem, 'An Anatomie of the World', and, in that poem, in the figure of Elizabeth Drury. I mentioned earlier Ben Jonson's comment that the poem might have been more worthwhile had it been about the Virgin Mary, and Donne's response that 'he described the Idea of a Woman, and not as she was'. Donne's remark here indicates the admission of a guilt: the poem pretends to be about Elizabeth Drury, a commemoration of that person; but in fact it is about an idealized notion of woman and has worked to commemorate the name of Donne rather than that of Drury. This may not be entirely surprising, given the historical near certainty that Donne did not know or even ever see the girl in question, this 'invisible' woman.

Donne describes the various sicknesses of the world as if they are a direct corollary of the death of Elizabeth Drury, as if her death were not the model but the cause of the world's decay, its erring into blindness and lethargy, ignorant even of its own state of illness:

> And, as men thinke, that Agues physick are,
> And th'Ague being spent, give over care,
> So thou sicke World, mistak'st thy selfe to bee
> Well, when alas, thou'rt in a Lethargie.[19]

The healthier the world seems, the sicker it is; at the moment when it seems purged of disease, Donne finds its greatest need of therapy. One therapeutic device, according to the tenets of the poem, would be the 'return' of Elizabeth Drury in a state of health. It is for this reason that the poem, as poem, requires to be written at all; but the pretension of reinstating the name of Elizabeth Drury is undercut in the fact that the poem also tries to make a name for Donne as he curries favour with the family of the Drurys.

The poem's conceit is that Elizabeth Drury was a *genius loci*, a spirit of the place of the world and its informing intelligence or the pure angelic element that gave the world sense, direction, shape and meaning. With her dead, the world is in a state of decay, confusion and chaos. The poem is to work as an apotropaic talisman, restoring order with the 'return' of this ghostly genius, the name of Elizabeth Drury. The great issue is that no one, as yet, has striven to commemorate this name:

> Her death did wound and tame thee than, and than
> Thou might'st have better spar'd the Sunne, or Man.
> That wound was deep, but 'tis more misery,
> That thou hast lost thy sense and memory.
> 'Twas heavy then to heare thy voyce of mone,
> But this is worse, that thou art speechlesse growne.
> Thou hast forgot thy name, thou hadst; thou wast
> Nothing but shee, and her thou hast o'rpast.
> . . .
> Her name defin'd thee, gave thee forme, and frame,
> And thou forgett'st to celebrate thy name.

The world is 'speechless growne', silent; but this is also a description of Elizabeth Drury. Not only is she silent because she is dead; she died at the age of fourteen, as what would pass for an 'infant' (*infans* = speechless). She died at the moment when she could enter the social world and make a name for herself, through the acquisition of social, i.e. sexual, recognition (that is, by being married: at fourteen she is approximately the same age as Juliet in Shakespeare's *Romeo and Juliet*, or Maria Fairfax in Marvell's 'Upon Appleton House', both 'ripe' for marriage). It is not until the writing of this elegy, however, that she does begin to make such a name. The lethargy of the world turns out to be Donne's own lethargy, his belatedness in coming to 'recognize' or nominate Elizabeth Drury, his belatedness in writing this poem which is supposed to celebrate her name and set the world to rights.

This confession of Donne's failure to write the elegy becomes constitutive of some kind of success. Although the material body of Elizabeth Drury cannot be represented, even in an 'anatomy', still her spirit does achieve some kind of re-embodiment. It is towards her ghostly genius or spirit that Donne turns attention:

> For there's a kinde of World remaining still,
> Though shee which did inanimate and fill
> The world, be gone, yet in this last long night,
> Her Ghost doth walke; that is, a glimmering light,
> A faint weake love of vertue, and of good,
> Reflects from her, on them which understood
> Her worth

Though she is gone, there remains a trace or representation of her, a faded image or imagination available to those who understood her worth; that is, primarily to this elegist himself who comes to create her worth in the form of her reconstituted name. It is this ghostly representation, this ghost herself that Donne follows in his anatomy of the world; it is, in fact, this ghost which informs the speech or writing of the poem, this ghost which is embodied or articulated in *its* 'palace', the text of the poem itself. Elizabeth Drury and the poem as elegiac commemoration of her name, and even the world itself, now come to articulation, come into speech through the medium of this ghost. This comes very close to arguing that the poet is in fact none other than Elizabeth Drury: the ghostly spirit informing this world of the text with speech or language as such is not Donne but the young girl coming into adult womanhood.

This demands further explication. At the opening of the poem, we read that Elizabeth Drury made her progress up to heaven 'Where loath to make the Saints attend her long,/She's now a part both of the Quire, and Song'. She strove towards some kind of canonization or divine recognition then. But these lines suggest both that she is the singer (part of the choir) and the sung (the subject of this poem's or song's canonization). The poem itself becomes both the song of the angels about Elizabeth Drury, and also the song sung by her, as one of those angels. It is thus not only a canonization of her, but also the embodiment or articulation of her voice: her verbal reincarnation. This, given the fact that the poem is transcribed by Donne (even if 'really' informed by the spirit or ghostly voice of Elizabeth Drury) makes an angel of Donne as well: he too is one of the singers from the canonical choir as he sings these verses. The poem becomes Elizabeth Drury's own act of self-nomination, her canonization of herself and her name among that of the saints; and at the same time it becomes Donne's own act of self-recognition in the figure of the angel or in the figure of that hymeneal boundary on which Elizabeth Drury exists.

Two elements have coalesced then at this point. The poem sings of the virginal Elizabeth Drury and 'marries' her to John Donne in having the voice of the girl articulate or realize itself through Donne's material body and writing. This union of two, now angelic, souls is 'immediate' in the sense fantasized by Milton when he considered angelic intercourse in *Paradise Lost* (8: 620–9). Raphael there tells Adam:

> Let it suffice thee that thou knowst
> Us happie, and without Love no happiness.
> Whatever pure thou in the body enjoyst
> (And pure thou wert created) we enjoy
> In eminence, and obstacle find none
> Of membrane, joint or limb, exclusive barrs:
> Easier than Air with Air, if Spirits embrace,
> Total they mix, Union of Pure with Pure
> Desiring; nor restraind conveyance need
> As Flesh to mix with Flesh, or Soul with Soul.

This Miltonic fantasy is the 'dialogue of one' prefigured by Donne and is akin to the angelic union celebrated in the First Anniversary poem, between Donne as poet and Elizabeth Drury as informing spirit. Both are cast in the shape of angels or angelic *media*, singing the canonical verse which is the song and elaboration of their union and celebration of their joint 'immediate' names. In this mute epithalamion there is a 'pure' union which maintains the integrity of the symbolic hymeneal boundary, as a veil which both joins and separates: joined together as airy nothings or as the media between divinity and earth, Donne and Drury become precisely the veil-like medium or hymeneal realm of angels separating one world (heaven) from another (Earth). Donne resolves the enigma which separates Drury from the Earth and which thus wounds their identity (the 'name' which identifies both Drury and Earth), by coming to form and occupy the 'middle' ground, the medium itself, as the product of their relation. He construes himself in this hymeneal position of the angelic sprite, and the poem becomes a Kermodian 'fiction of complementarity'.[20] The biblical precept for this is to be found in Matthew, 18:20, for one instance, at the moment when Christ inaugurates confession and remarks that 'where two or three are gathered together in my name, there am I in the midst of them'. This text generates such a 'midst' as the location of the hymeneal tissue or text in which Donne and Drury meet.

The text, in a certain sense, embodies or gives birth to the Christian Word, making itself analogous to the Immaculate Conception of Mary, the real subject of the poem as Jonson was aware. In so far as the poet aligns himself with an imagined embodiment of the 'Immaculate Conception', the text becomes an articulation of a fantasized 'immaculate conceit'. Health and purity in this poem seem to depend on some 'unstained', 'immediate' form of communication, an immaculate communion; but this is itself determined by the poet's alignment of himself with some theological female principle, and his symbolic act of self-wounding, self-castration in the interests of the maintenance of the integrity and health of the (symbolic) hymen or medium. Donne's 'confessional' texts, his self-exposures, are therapeutic only in so far as they involve a further activity of self-wounding; he is purified and his language validated when it becomes the medium which allows an idealized discourse to elaborate, reveal or 'confess' itself in these 'immaculate conceits'.

3

There are two further dimensions to the therapy of confession as well: the legalistic practice of demanding confessions of guilt; and the question of the healthy 'diet'. The theological grounds for establishing and recommending confession at the Lateran and Trent Councils firmly linked the theological and the juridical. Biblical justification of confession rests on two main texts, Matthew, 18:18, and John, 20:23. Matthew is the more explicit: 'Verily I say unto you, Whatsoever ye shall bind on earth shall be bound in heaven: and whatsoever ye shall loose on earth shall be loosed in heaven'. 'Binding' and 'loosening' here are of utmost importance. The injunction from Christ to his disciples makes confession an activity which works to 'bind' and to legitimize certain actions and to invalidate others. Re*lig*ion and juridical ob*lig*ation are linked together, as they are etymologically through the root, *lig*, which demarcates notions of 'binding'. Donne's study of the law informs much of the ethical elements in his poetry of confession. The power to bind and to loosen, of course, is related to that of opening and closing the gates of heaven: the priest stands like the Sphinx at Thebes, a 'sphincter' opening, or more likely closing, the gates. There is an etymological link between 'sphinx' and 'sphincter': both derive from *sphiggo*, to bind tight; and regulation of the physical sphincters of the human body, that is, a healthy diet, was also of importance to Donne.

These two concerns, diet and the law, are not as far removed from one another as it may seem. There is clearly a great deal of stress laid on the pleasures of orality in the poetry. Lovers frequently 'suck' the souls of each other in acts of illicit kissing (itself a shadowy fantasized form of consumption or eating, of course); the famous 'Flea' eats the lovers in that poem which attempts to circumvent legal marriage; love 'swallows us' in 'The broken heart'; in 'The good-morrow' there is a consideration of whether we 'suck'd on countrey pleasures', and so on. This imagery of digestion and orality is more clearly bound up with matters of the law in the Satires. In Satire 5, 'Thou shalt not laugh in this leafe, Muse', there is a satirical commentary on the grandness of the officers at court who, while 'eating' or preying on the lesser suitors, are seen to be simply fattening themselves to become the proper diet of the levelling worm:

> All men are dust;
> How much worse are Suiters, who to mens lust
> Are made preys? O worse then dust, or wormes meat,
> For they do eate you now, whose selves wormes shall eate.[21]

But to remark that this is simply a reiteration of the truism that death is a great leveller is to miss an important ramification of that point. The 'diet' here is a predatory one, maintaining a hierarchy which only the digestion of a worm could hope to controvert. The poem constructs a relation of human to world as microcosm to macrocosm, arguing that:

> man is a world; in which, Officers
> Are the vast ravishing seas; and Suiters,
> Springs; now full, now shallow, now drye; which, to
> That which drownes them, run: These self reasons do
> Prove the world a man, in which, officers
> Are the devouring stomacke, and Suiters
> The excrements, which they voyd.

The way of the world, and the way of the body, according to this, is the way of the predator.

Despite its opening, 'Thou shalt not laugh in this leafe', an opening which denies comedy to the poem, the text itself is an elaborate joke or satirical attack not upon those in high office (the seeming predators) but rather upon the lowly suitors, caught out themselves and poisoned by their own suiting words in their activities of preying parasitically upon those in high office. They beg for favours, fawning on and preying on those with greater influence than themselves, trying to exert some influence on them. They are taken for a predatory ride by the higher officers at court:

> They are the mills which grinde you, yet you are
> The winde which drives them; and a wastfull warre
> Is fought against you, and you fight it; they
> Adulterate lawe, and you prepare their way
> Like wittals; th'issue your owne ruine is.

The cycle of predacity is outlined here: officers are cast as 'mills,' grinding suitors for food. But the suitors are their own worst enemy, cast as the wind which blows the mills around. Further, they are also the wind broken by the predatory officers after their daily 'diet' of suitors. Thus the circle is potentially endless; the more they prey, the more offal they become; in the production of bodily wind, the more they turn the mills and grind the offal to be eaten, and so on. The suitors here are the ones satirized as so much hot air or farts. The officers remain in control of the system, a control which is exercised over the 'possessions' of the suitors (wife, issue); and the suitors, like wittols or cuckolds, connive at their own victimization in the merest fact of suing to the officers, providing wind for the mills which grind them down.

The satire becomes more clearly an attack on a particular social institution of justice and the law, a law upheld by the dominant ideology of the predatory model of the human. This should, of course, have been questioned right from the outset of the poem, in lines which demonstrate that the greatest model of the human, according to this ideology, is the worm; a notion mocked by Hamlet in the epigraph to this chapter, and much later by Engels.[22] But the law itself becomes a 'diet of worms', so to speak, for the law devours those who turn to it in search of justice and reparation. This 'diet of the law' is of no real assistance:

> If Law be in the Judges heart, and hee
> Have no heart to resist letter, or fee,
> Where wilt thou appeale? powre of the Courts below
> Flow from the first maine head, and these can throw
> Thee, if they sucke thee in, to misery,
> To fetters, halters . . .

Here again is the image of the law as gaping mouth, preying on those who come to it in the hope of finding reparation or a juridical remedy for the predatory and iniquitous nature of society. The rule is 'only who have may have more', which is Donne's translation of Matthew, 13:12, 'For whosoever hath, to him shall be given, and he shall have more abundance: but whosoever hath not, from him shall be taken away even that he hath'. Donne's satiric version of Matthew, then, does not challenge the law of the parable of the predator. Rather the remedy proposed is another kind of 'diet' entirely, going without food or starving oneself entirely in the effort to purge oneself cathartically of the entire ideology in which the predator dominates. Hunger, a hunger after righteousness, is proposed:

> Why barest thou to yon Officer? Fool, Hath hee
> Got those goods, for which erst men bar'd to thee?
> Foole, twice, thrice, thou hast brought wrong, and now hungerly
> Beg'st right; But that dole comes not till these dye.

Patient hunger is suggested here; clearly not good advice from a satire which pretends to be pragmatically relevant to the material injustices at hand. But there has been a vital shift of emphasis in the poem leading up to this seemingly impractical suggestion that we 'diet' in this way. Before we can make the officers and judges die; before, that is, the judge can in his turn be eaten, the nature of the judge has to be changed metaphorically. This happens just after the clearest iteration of the corrupt ideology of the individualist self-seeking predator in the poem:

> All things follow their like, only who have may have more.
> Judges are Gods; he who made and said them so,
> Meant not that men should be forc'd to them to goe,
> By meanes of Angels; When supplications
> We send to God, to Dominations,
> Powers, Cherubins, and all heavens Courts, if wee
> Should pay fees as here, Daily bread would be
> Scarce to Kings; so 'tis . . .

Here, through another 'translation' from the *Authorized Version*, there is a slippage between earthly and divine judge, between legal judge and the judge who judges the judges. Psalm 82 is echoed here, especially its first and sixth verses: 'God standeth in the congregation of the mighty; he judgeth among the gods ... I have said, Ye are gods'. Judges are gods, then, in the poem; but this effects a slippage between earthly judge and God as judge of judges. It is this divine judge, in fact, who is to be eaten or who is to become the substance of the 'diet' in order to correct the wrongs of the secular system of justice and, indeed, of the human body politic and physical. The text, in short, uses a 'diet of worms' as bait in order to catch the real fish which becomes the model of the healthy diet, a theological diet of eucharist.

This, as they say, opens a whole new can of worms. The more or less explicit references to the 'Diet of Worms', both in Donne and in Hamlet's speech cited as epigraph here, brings the theology of the Reformation into play: Luther came to Worms to defend himself before the Emperor Charles V in 1521. But in so far as I have shown that Donne owes a great debt to the name of 'More' and all its close analogies with 'Rome', it becomes clear in his verse that there is some ambivalence regarding a theological position. The complication arises from Donne's covert praises of Rome through the name of More at a time when he is an Anglican preacher; and similar praises of woman, and by extension the Idea of a Woman, or the Virgin Mary, through the name of (Ann) More (as well as Elizabeth Drury and all other anonymous women in his verses). It might be the case that Donne is suggesting, covertly, that the way to a healthy 'diet' can be either through a diet of worms, so to speak, or equally through a more material poetry of sexual love in which the idealized healthy woman prevents any falling into sickness: a Mariolatrous verse.

I earlier cited Fracastoro on the question of a healthy diet in these times of epidemic syphilis, where he suggested the avoidance of fish: 'Therefore from fish in general I dissuade'. Such advice has a strange propriety in *Measure for Measure*, where the fish is used metaphorically. Claudio's 'offence' is described in fishy terms:

POMPEY: Yonder man is carried to prison.
MISTRESS OVERDONE: Well; what has he done?
POMPEY: A woman.

MISTRESS OVERDONE: But what's his offence?
POMPEY: Groping for trouts in a peculiar river. (I, ii)

Here it is the activity of 'fishing' and transgressing a private, 'peculiar' place which constitutes the offence. The fish seems, in these two different texts, to be somewhat problematic, either as real material food (in Fracastoro) or as metaphor of female genitals (in Shakespeare). Donne pursued his fish in theological streams of metaphors, closely related to Shakespeare's usage.

One context for this is, of course, 'The Baite'. Once again Donne's major 'anxiety of influence' here is Matthew. The initial stanza of the poem is a cliché, but one which turns out to have special significance for the rest of the poem:

> Come live with mee, and bee my love,
> And we will some new pleasures prove
> Of golden sands, and christall brookes,
> With silken lines, and silver hookes.[23]

The stanza is most overtly an invitation to come fishing in a special way; perhaps, as in *Measure for Measure*, a rather lewd way. But there is also a disturbing element here in the pun on the word 'christall', a fairly pervasive linguistic turn in the writing of this period, which should alert the reader to a submerged theological component in the text: 'Christ', even 'all' Christ, is here, at least linguistically, in this opening reference to 'christall brookes'. Rather than the reference to *Measure for Measure* then, it might be more apt to indicate the intertextual reference to Matthew, 4:18–20:

> And Jesus, walking by the sea of Galilee, saw two brethren, Simon called Peter, and Andrew his brother, casting a net into the sea: for they were fishers.
> And he saith unto them, Follow me, and I will make you fishers of men.
> And they straightway left their nets, and followed him.

The addressee of 'The Baite' looks as if she hears precisely the same kind of invitation and, as in the gospel, there is a casting away of 'windowie net'. Further, these fish in the poem seem only too willing to 'betray' themselves, which is a striking word for the apostate Donne to have chosen in the context:

> And there the'inamor'd fish will stay,
> Begging themselves they may betray.

These fish are suicidal, rather like that archetypal 'fish' in Christian iconography, the 'christall' Christ, characterized precisely as a model for suicide in *Biathanatos*. The argument of the poem, however, takes a slight turn, or crossing, in the third stanza when the woman, as fisher, becomes rather more like the fish to be caught, sought after by those fish already in the water. Seeker and sought after, hunter and hunted, change places:

> When thou wilt swimme in that live bath,
> Each fish, which every channell hath,
> Will amorously to thee swimme,
> Gladder to catch thee, then thou him.

The woman, in this transubstantiation, becomes a kind of female Christ figure herself: she is both bait and fish, attracting that other odd fish, the male speaker or reader of the poem, as a locus of truth and utter self-sufficiency:

> For thee, thou needst no such deceit,
> For thou thy selfe art thine owne bait;
> That fish, that is not catch'd thereby,
> Alas, is wiser farre then I.

The woman, in an odd sort of way, is both the fish itself, sought after by the others in the 'christall brookes', and, as bait for the fish, she constitutes the diet of worms. She is thus precisely a locus of exchange in all the ways suggested earlier in this study; but further that 'principle of exchangeability' which has played such a large role in these crossing-poems of Donne is now theologized. The woman, in 'The Baite', is precisely a locus of transubstantiation. At the very moment when Donne seems to be aligning himself with a reformed theology after Luther's legal 'diet' and the Diet of Worms, he is also precisely aligning himself with an unreformed theological position on the matter of the transubstantiation. Luther had of course denied transubstantiation; Donne seems here to be covertly reinstating it, in the figure of the iconographic fish/woman of the 'christall brookes'.

This is vital to Donne, for the act of eating the fish, the eucharistic sign of Christ in the ground bread, is important in effecting the transubstantiation not so much of Christ but rather of the recipient of the diet, whose condition is made healthy by becoming a locus of communion, and part of the ecclesia or body of Christ. But the fundamental transformation or transubstantiation which affects Donne here, in bringing this theological 'health', is that transformation which identifies him as this fisher caught by the woman in 'The Baite'. For, in being caught, he becomes not just the hunter but, like the woman, the hunted: that is to say, the 'crossed' and the wounded figure.

The metaphor of digestion, as well as the physical fact of digestion, makes the human body itself into a medium of sorts. But the medium of the body is an 'impure' one: it transforms the elements digested, the meat, into excrement, as the play on the 'diet of worms' demonstrates. This element of transformation is important when what is being digested is the eucharistic bread or meat.

In the first place, the 'diet of worms' metaphor no longer remains a purely material or social index of a possible revolutionary or political 'levelling'; for that levelling which the worms produce is now mediated in theological terms, as a purely spiritual 'democracy'.

Secondly, within this framework, the diet is thought of as one which demonstrates not so much the transformation or transubstantiation of Christ, but rather the transformation of the body which is doing the eating: this body, the body physical, not-so-political and theological, is purified, purged, and becomes its own bait, attractive to itself, healthy.

Thirdly, this purification of the body is one which makes it part, not of a political collective, but of a theological collective, an ecclesia, which formulates or constructs itself around the locus of exchange or of 'crossing', the transubstantial 'diet' or bread: it thus attacks the individual body but makes it 'healthy' as part of the 'Body of Christ' which is the ecclesia. In this way, the theologization of the legalistic diet of worms works to make the material historical body into an *imitatio Christi*, a repetition of the nonsecular but rather eternal 'Body of Christ'. More precisely it makes the human historical body into something more angelic: 'I am a little world made cunningly/Of Elements, and an Angelike spright'.[24] This is the genuine health for Donne: the human body becomes dematerialized, transformed into an angelic 'airy nothing'.

When that other Fish, the explorer of reading, Stanley Fish, chews on the text of Donne's sermons, he finds there an 'aesthetic of the good physician' in which Donne becomes a doctor of dialectic, producing self-consuming texts.[25] His wordy, trope-ridden sermons become examples of linguistic humility for Fish. But it has now to be added, in a great modification of this position, that this dialectic is neither material nor entirely spiritual: the entire point of the dialectic, in the poems at least, is to transform the material individual body into a spiritual organ of the ecclesiastic body of Christ, to counter the effects of the Copernican revolution through a series of self-crossing linguistic tropes which aim to 'substantiate' a fundamental theological crossing, that crossing which organized Donne's thought right the way through his writing career, the biathanatic crucifixion. This 'good physician' does not work at all on the material body, but is rather in a hurry to make it 'angelic'.

4

Given the condition of confession, that it undoes itself in the production of a narrativized linguistic excess ('excuse') or 'more' which undoes its founding intention, the act of confession is one which implies its own necessary repetition or rehearsal. The more the confessor confesses, the more she or he has to confess. This paradoxical condition of Donne's 'confessional' writing, the writing that confronts the opposition between the drive towards privacy and individuality (through a fear of syphilitic contamination) and the drive towards publicity and ecclesia (through the theological encouragement of confession), produces a text which is fundamentally 'comic'. If the repetition of confession is instrumental in producing a 'more', an excess in some way, and a 'more' which threatens to undo the confessor (as we have seen both Thomas More and Ann More, in varying ways, undo Donne both theologically and in legalistic secular terms), then it perhaps approaches the condition of *morias*, folly. The important point, however, is that Donne's comic writing attempts to avoid becoming a secular 'Comedy of Errors' and instead strives to become a kind of 'Divine Comedy'. This requires explanation.

I suggested earlier that a link should be drawn among three elements in Donne's writing: hymen, medium and angel. This can help explain how the verse becomes an 'angelic comedy', so to speak. Transforming the body into an 'airy nothing' through the 'dialectic' described above offers a means of exploring the very condition of Donne's linguistic medium. Such an 'airy nothing' is a description common in the period of the hymen of the woman's body. Cowley's 'Maidenhead' is a classic exposition of this:

> Slight, outward Curtain to the *Nuptial Bed*!
> Thou *Case* to buildings not yet finished!
> Who like the *Center* of the Earth,
> Does heaviest things attract to thee,
> Thou Thou a *point imaginary* be.[26]

Here, the hymen is a 'bait', but also an airy nothing, a point imaginary, a slight veil which, like confession, both reveals and conceals. The point in our consideration of Donne's poetry is that this particular airy nothing, understood as an angelic medium upon divinity or absolute, non-secular Truth, has to be kept whole, intact, healthy.

As might be expected with the epidemic of syphilis as a threat to sexual activity and the material body, there is a measure of supposed 'restraint' or 'moderation'. The 'healthiest' socio-sexual relations become those which practise a form of *coitus interruptus* which seems to preserve the integrity of the healthy, idealized female body, and which also maintains the ethics of privacy to some extent without entirely forgoing all 'public' sexual activity. The woman's body, or rather her idealized hymen, becomes a model of health; and this explains to some extent Donne's propensity for writing texts which threaten the male poet with a symbolic castration. The female body, as angelic medium, distinguishes itself by the 'airy nothing' or absence which, according to one rather sexist anatomy, constitutes her body as female.

Donne models himself on such an angelic body, in the interests of a purity and health both physical and spiritual. This female principle, so to speak, the hymen, becomes a focus for a number of related issues. Its integrity is, as mentioned earlier, important in the 'marriage-market': in material terms, the hymen is precisely the locus of the exchange of daughters and wives on the marriage-market and thus contributes to the sexual oppression of women. This is the 'angel' as both hymen and coin. Secondly, as a locus of exchange, it becomes also related to the very principle of a poetry of tropes, linguistic 'crossings' or punning exchanges and euphemisms which shape Donne's poetry. This is the hymen as linguistic medium. Thirdly, 'lacking' the flesh, the phallus, it aspires to the condition of spirituality and thus becomes a locus for the exchange of secular history for eternal stasis. This is the hymen as theological angel, mediating between humanity and divinity. Fourthly, and this embraces all these other effects, it is precisely the locus of 'crossing': Donne is 'crossed' in his attempts to reach the female hymen; 'crossed' or crucified, 'undone' and dying, when he does attain sexual activity; and he writes of these activities in a language which produces 'more', an excess in the form of puns, ambiguities and so on which partake in a principle of linguistic exchange or 'crossing', troping.

Donne is thus thoroughly 'undone' through the poetry and its writing. But in so far as this crossing takes place and finds its root in the angelic, that 'more' or angelic sprite which both constitutes and undoes Donne, it makes the mere comedy of linguistic errors into a comedy based entirely upon the angelic medium: this is, then, a comedy which aims to effect the move or transfer from a condition of paradise lost (secularity and material sexuality) to one of paradise regained (in 'immediate' communion with the body of the church, that of Christ who is, as I have suggested, frequently mediated in 'asexual' female terms.) At a more fundamental level, of course, coitus interruptus, the repeated attempt to 'publicize' the 'private', is a staple diet of comic farce: the frustrations and limitations of the material secular body *are* Donne's 'illness', and an angelic comedy, mediating that body as in communion with divinity, is his chosen therapy.

Repetition is also crucial to this comic formation. In Satire 4, 'Well; I may now receive, and die', the beggar whom the poet meets speaks many tongues in the attempt to prey on the poet and beg some money or food:

> This thing hath travail'd, and saith, speakes all tongues
> And only knoweth what to all States belongs.
> Made of th'Accents, and best phrase of all these,
> He speakes no language; If strange meats displease,
> Art can deceive, or hunger force my tast,
> But Pedants motley tongue, souldiers bombast,
> Mountebankes drugtongue, nor the termes of law
> Are strong enough preparatives, to draw
> Me to beare this: yet I must be content
> With his tongue . . .[27]

In listening to this beggar, a strange displacement occurs: the tongue of the beggar becomes that of the poet, now cast in the role of supplicant. The text and its poet now become the beggars, begging not only for an audience, but also for payment, feeding of some kind. The text itself becomes a kind of prayer, for it begs for a taste of the undivided tongue, for the Truth in a pre-babel discourse, a plain style or pure (puritanic) style. That is to say, it is a prayer which begs for the specific audience of God whose voice it aspires to hear.

The suspicion following on from this is that writing, or poetry itself, as a concealed offence (its linguistic duplicities or crossings) is in need of some cure. According to Satire 2, however, the cure for poetry becomes precisely the exercise of writing and/or reading poetry itself, a cure by repetition. This poem opens by elaborating the by now familiar notion of displacement:

> Sir; though (I thanke God for it) I do hate
> Perfectly all this towne, yet there's one state
> In all things so excellently best,
> That hate, toward them, breeds pitty towards the rest.[28]

In an emotion of hatred the hated object can become less hated, and even pitied instead, when placed alongside some other extremely 'ill' thing. That is, there is no value judgement of essential goodness or intrinsic evil as such, but all such judgements and their attendant emotions are relative, and the grounds of the judgement are constantly shifting, subject to change, displacement or eccentricity. Here, the primary object of hatred is poetry itself; but this becomes less hated when compared with the rhetoric of the law. The cure for poetry is outlined as another form of hunger, a cathartic purgation or starvation, like the cure for material disease such as the plague:

> Though Poëtry indeed be such a sinne
> As I thinke That brings dearths, and Spaniards in,
> Though like the Pestilence and old fashion'd love,
> Ridlingly it catch men; and doth remove
> Never, till it be sterv'd out; yet their state
> Is poore, disarm'd, like Papists, not worth hate.

Just as the body must be starved for its health, so likewise poetry has to be starved out. But this leads to a paradoxical relation of the acts of writing and reading. The cure for poetry, the starvation of the poet, is dependent, paradoxically, on the poetry being repeated, rehearsed or read. As others repeat the words of the poet, the poet is starved out and thus, it seems, cured:

> One, (like a wretch, which at Barre judg'd as dead,
> Yet prompts him which stands next, and cannot reade,
> And saves his life) gives ideot actors meanes
> (Starving himselfe) to live by his labor'd sceanes . . .

Here, the poet is judged through the activity of 'prompting' or bringing others into life and public speech or a kind of confession. Criminals at the bar could, in some cases, escape execution by giving some proof of literacy, which would align them with the educated clergy, able to speak in certain 'tongues'. They would usually be set to read the beginning of Psalm 51 in order to save themselves and it is to the prompting of this text that the cited lines refer here. But Psalm 51 opens as a mode of confession. It is not only a plea for mercy, but also an acknowledgement of transgression, and to that extent a confessional piece:

> Have mercy upon me, O God, according to thy loving kindness: according unto the multitude of thy tender mercies blot out my transgressions. Wash me thoroughly from mine iniquity, and cleanse me from my sin. For I acknowledge my transgressions: and my sin is ever before me. (Psalm 51: 1–3)

Here then is a confession which leads to salvation alongside the 'healthy' purgation or starvation of poetry and the poet, who is condemned at the bar while saving the lives of others through prompting them into confession or reading. This, of course, is a potentially extremely comic situation.

The argument, however, is even further displaced dialectically and turned on its antithetical head. The position thus far suggests that repetition or rehearsal, reading itself, performs the necessary purgation or comic catharsis. But this is then controverted in a counter-argument stressing the need for a therapeutic ordinary speech, for a return to authoritative origins in a plain style without any poetic mediation. This is a return to the notion from the Sermon on the Mount: 'let your communication be, Yea, yea; Nay,

nay: for whatsoever is more than these cometh of evil' (Matthew, 5: 37). This comes through fairly clearly in the implications of Donne's lines: 'And they who write to Lords, rewards to get,/Are they not like singers at doores for meat?,' for these lines establish an analogy between the kind of writing that this poem actually is and the activity of prayerful communication, 'writing to the lord', and asking for his 'meat', again a communion meat. This, in turn, produces an argument which presses the need or desire for an original writing, for the fundamentals of affirmation (Yea, yea) and negation (Nay, nay); and such a position is an inversion of the argument thus far:

> But hee is worst, who (beggarly) doth chaw
> Others wits fruits, and in his ravenous maw
> Rankly digested, doth those things out-spue,
> As his owne things; and they are his owne, 'tis true,
> For if one eate my meate, though it be knowne
> The meate was mine, th'excrement is his owne.

That is to say, then, in satirically catching the reader once more, that the reader ought to become an original writer, or poet. Thus it would seem that poetry does 'Ridlingly . . . catch men', as it aims to do in Herbert later too; for the reader is here entwined not only in this poem, but also finds herself argued into precisely the position of the diseased writer or poet whose 'illness' has caused the problem in the first place.

The reader is the one who is made sick here; for it is the reader who is now in the position of the pitiful poet. Starvation of poetry is prescribed and its replacement by some more 'original' discourse of affirmation or negation. The legal discourse of inappropriate rhetoric or of poetic tropes and judgement would be yet a further deviation away from these origins of affirmation and negation. Once again there is an implied or inferred discourse, to which the poem can refer but which it cannot of itself enact or articulate. This discourse looks, once again, remarkably like the movement of confession, involving the activity of bearing witness (affirming) and self-criticism (negation). One simple reason why the poem cannot enact such a discourse is that it belongs properly to the criminal/critical reader and depends on the particular 'sins' or 'illness' or indeed consciousness which the text arouses in the conscience of this sick reader.[29]

Some of Donne's contemporaries had comments to make on the nature of comedy which are relevant to this criminal reading or repetition. Comedy seems, at least in this period, to demand some justification. To this extent at least, it looks structurally akin to the notion of 'sin' which demands narrated confession or to Lutheran heresy which must be cross-examined at the Diet of Worms. Sidney, among others, justifies the 'right use of Comedy', a comedy which seems to be closely related to Error (itself, of course, another word for the theological concept of sin):

> Only thus much now is to be said, that the Comedy is an imitation of the common errors of our life, which he representeth in the most ridiculous and scornful sort that may be, so as it is impossible that any beholder can be content to be such a one.[30]

Comedy warns us of evil, and knowledge of this, argues Sidney, is vital if we are to understand goodness, its opposite – this, then, is an argument which prefigures Milton's Satan and another female medium, Eve, in *Paradise Lost*. The threat that people may learn how to be evil, rather than to spurn it, is dealt with by Sidney:

> And little reason hath any man to say that men learn evil by seeing it so set out; since, as I said before, there is no man living but, by the force truth hath in nature, no sooner seeth these men play their parts, but wisheth them in *pistrinum*; although perchance the sack of his own faults lie so behind his back that he seeth not himself dance the same measure; whereto yet nothing can more open his eyes than to find his own actions contemptibly set forth.
>
> So that the right use of Comedy will (I think) by nobody be blamed, and much less of the high and excellent Tragedy, that openeth the greatest wounds, and showeth forth the ulcers that are covered with tissue . . .[31]

According to this, tragedy is simply a different form of comedy, differing in the degree to which the 'tissue' or (hymeneal) medium is to be rent in tragedy in order to produce self-knowledge and health, while in comedy no such violent action is required to perceive the same 'ulcers' and 'wounds' from which the human individual suffers: in comedy this tissue both reveals and conceals, like a mystifying veil.

Sidney recommends a comedy which provokes more than

laughter: 'I speak to this purpose, that all the end of the comical part be not upon such scornful matters as stirreth laughter only, but, mixed with it, that delightful teaching which is the end of Poesy',[32] and, most importantly, laughter at sinful things is to be discouraged, according to Sidney who follows Aristotle here. Comedy, then, like tragedy, has its own form of therapeutic catharsis or purgative function: in Donne it produces texts which are a kind of mediating *purgatorio*. The aim, fundamentally, is some theological therapy rather than any historical, material modes of producing social health. Vital to the comic paradoxicality of this writing is the notion of repetition: the errors to be confessed must, in fact be rehearsed or reiterated in order that they can be 're-cognized' and thus corrected, exculpated and confessed.

These texts then do not aim to save their reader, but in fact work to damn that reader, by making her or him repeat the texts' errors, crossings or 'sinful' posture. In Donne's poems there is the production of self-criticism, a comic self-laceration or self-satirization produced through the activity of writing/reading or rehearsing the texts. It is important to note, however, that this 'Fishy' process of digesting the texts in this way is not in any way productive of a materialist dialectic; rather the whole process aims to re-theologize the material or the historical. Theology turns out to be Donne's only mode of escaping the struggle against history that I outlined in the first part of this study. There are, of course, other ways of struggling, not against history, but within it. I will close this study with the opening of another text, *The Eighteenth Brumaire of Louis Bonaparte*.

There Marx offers a hint of a theory of comedy in terms of the farcical nature of historical repetition, and in a language which prefigures studies on 'anxieties of influence' in an uncanny way. The text begins:

Hegel remarks somewhere that all the events and personalities of great importance in world history occur, as it were, twice. He forgot to add: the first time as tragedy, the second as farce ... Men make their own history, but they do not make it just as they please; they do not make it under circumstances chosen by themselves, but under given circumstances directly encountered and inherited from the past. The tradition of all the generations of the dead weighs like a nightmare on the brain of the living.

And just when they seem involved in revolutionizing themselves and things, in creating something that has never before existed, it is precisely in such periods of revolutionary crisis that they anxiously conjure up the spirits of the past to their service and borrow names, battle cries and costumes from them in order to act out the new scene of world history in this time-honoured disguise and this borrowed language.[33]

Donne, writing his 'farcical' poetry, works, as here suggested, under the anxious influence of an inherited past, his familial Roman Catholicism. Just when he seems to be writing the most revolutionary forms of poetry in the midst of cultural and epistemological crises, he anxiously conjures up 'spirits' from that past. Donne does not merely remember his links with Thomas More, but in a sense goes for an even 'purer' source or spirit of the past: confronted with the age of a truly secular history, he attempts to go beyond mere history to a theological source, in the realm of the eternal or some theological divinity itself. The anxiety of influence becomes, quite clearly, the Word of God, understood, in Christian theology, both as a mode of language and as a figure, Christ himself. He borrows, as I have shown, the names of various evangelical figures, especially Matthew, More and Maria (Mary), and even the subdued name of Christ himself, dressing himself in their borrowed language. Through his symbolic self-wounding, a crossing or symbolic castration, he dresses himself, or disguises himself, comically, in the form of a woman. But this woman is the figure who 'labours' to bring forth the purer Word of divinity, whose labour transforms that 'pure' Word into an ambiguous punning, but material or historical 'embodiment', the figure of an angelic medium, Mary whose hymen remains intact. His costume finally is that of the Immaculate Conception which allows him to write or contrive his 'maculate conceits'.

Notes

1 Donne, 336
2 Donne, 210
3 Christopher Ricks, '*Doctor Faustus* and Hell on earth', *Essays in Criticism*, 35(1985), 101–20
4 Girolamo Fracastoro, *Syphilis: or a Poetical History of the French Disease* (trans. N. Tate), London, Jacob Tonson, 1686, 76. See the French translation (Paris,

Lucet, 1796), note 3, pp. 140–1, for the element of nationalism involved in tracing the source of the disease.

5 Don Cameron Allen, 'John Donne's knowledge of Renaissance medicine', *Journal of English and Germanic Philology*, 42(1943), 322.

6 Fracastoro, op. cit., unpaginated prefatory material.

7 William Shakespeare, *Measure for Measure*, I, ii.

8 Michel Foucault, *History of Sexuality* (1976) (trans. Robert Hurley), Harmondsworth, Penguin, 1981, vol. 1, 20.

9 William Shakespeare, *Othello*, II, iii.

10 Donne, 337.

11 Fracastoro, op. cit., 41.

12 Quoted by Pierre Janelle, *The Catholic Reformation*, Milwaukee, Bruce, 1963, 75–6.

13 Paul de Man, *Allegories of Reading*, New Haven, Conn., Yale University Press, 1979, 280.

14 Donne, *Selected Prose*, ed. Helen Gardner and Timothy Healy, Oxford, Clarendon Press, 1967, 7.

15 Donne, 29.

16 Donne, 10.

17 Donne, 21.

18 Donne, 295.

19 Donne, 208ff.

20 See Frank Kermode, *The Sense of an Ending*, Oxford, Oxford University Press, 1967, reprinted, 1977, *passim*.

21 Donne, 149ff.

22 See Shakespeare, *Hamlet*, IV, iii; and cf. Friedrich Engels, *The Origin of the Family, Private Property and the State* (introduction and notes by Eleanor Burke Leacock; from trans. Alec[sic]West, 1942), London, Lawrence & Wishart, 1972, 98.

23 Donne, 41–2.

24 Donne, 295,

25 See Stanley E. Fish, *Self-Consuming Artifacts*, Berkeley and Los Angeles, University of California Press, 1972, especially ch.1.

26. Abraham Cowley, 'Maidenhead', in A.R. Waller, ed., *English Writings of Abraham Cowley*, Cambridge, Cambridge University Press, 1905.

27 Donne, 142; some editions give 'one language' for 'no language' here.

28 Donne, 132ff.

29 The link here between 'crime' and 'criticism' is fundamentally an etymological one.

30 Philip Sidney, 'Apology for Poetry', reprinted in Edmund D. Jones (ed.), *English Critical Essays XVI–XVIII Centuries*, Oxford, Oxford University Press, 1975, 26.

31 ibid.

32 ibid., 47–8.

33 Karl Marx, *The Eighteenth Brumaire of Louis Bonaparte*, Peking, Foreign Languages Press, 1978, 9–10.

Index

Entries in bold type indicate a substantial discussion of the topic. Donne's poems are listed under the entry for 'Donne, John'.